Praise for this Book

'*Sex at the Margins* rips apart distinctions between migrants, service work and sexual labour and reveals the utter complexity of the contemporary sex industry. This book is set to be a trailblazer in the study of sexuality.' – Lisa Adkins, Professor of Sociology, Goldsmiths, University of London

'*Sex at the Margins* elegantly demonstrates that what happens to poor immigrant working women from the Global South when they "leave home for sex" is neither a tragedy nor the panacea of finding the promised land. Above all, Agustín shows that the moralising bent of most government and NGO programmes has little to do with these women's experiences and wishes. This book questions some of our most cherished modern assumptions, and shows that a different ethics of concern is possible.' – Arturo Escobar, Kenan Distinguished Professor of Anthropology and Director, Institute of Latin American Studies, University of North Carolina

'In restoring those living on the fringes of western societies to their full humanity, this invigorating book undermines our stereotypes and provides a challenging but unforgettable picture.' – Jeffrey Weeks, London South Bank University

About the Author

Laura María Agustín studies cultural and postcolonial issues linking commercial sex, migration, informal economies and feminist theory. She currently lives in London, researching the situation of migrant workers in the sex industry.

SEX AT THE MARGINS

Migration, Labour Markets and the Rescue Industry

Laura María Agustín

Zed Books
LONDON & NEW YORK

Sex at the Margins: Migration, Labour Markets and the Rescue Industry
was first published by Zed Books Ltd, 7 Cynthia Street, London N1 9JF, UK,
and Room 400, 175 Fifth Avenue, New York, NY 10010, USA
www.zedbooks.co.uk

Designed and typeset in Perpetua and Eurostile
by Long House Publishing Services, Cumbria, UK
Cover designed by Andrew Corbett
Printed and bound in the UK by Biddles Ltd, Kings Lynn
www.biddles.co.uk

Distributed in the USA exclusively by Palgrave Macmillan, a division of
St Martin's Press, LLC, 175 Fifth Avenue, New York, NY 10010

A catalogue record for this book is available from the British Library
Library of Congress Cataloging-in-Publication Data available

ISBN 978 1 84277 859 3 Hb
ISBN 978 1 84277 860 9 Pb

CONTENTS

ACKNOWLEDGEMENTS

Thanks to everyone whose conversations and writings have given me pleasure and sparked my thinking over the years and to those who welcomed me into a social movement. Special thanks to Arturo Escobar, Pat Crain, Julie Graham, Tony Bennett, Pam Beach, Félix Tremiño, Priscilla Alexander, Wendy Harcourt, Carol Leigh and Pocho.

Laura María Agustín
Granada, Spain, and Leicester, UK

To those who leave home

1

SEXUAL COMMOTION

Some years ago, on a trip to Australia and Thailand, I met five Latin American women connected to the sex industry: the owner of a legal brothel and two migrants working for her in Sydney, and two women in a detention centre for illegal immigrants in Bangkok. These five women were from Perú, Colombia and Venezuela; they were from different strata of society; they were different ages. They also had very different stories to tell.

The brothel owner was a permanent resident in Australia. Her migrant workers came to Australia on visas to study English, which gave them the right to work, but getting the visa required paying for the entire eight-month course in advance, which meant acquiring large debts. The madam was very affectionate with them but also very controlling; they lived in her house and travelled with her to work, where she was teaching them the business. The outreach workers from a local health project did not speak Spanish.

Of the two women detained in Bangkok, one had been stopped at a Tokyo airport with a forged visa for Japan. She had been invited by her sister, who once worked illegally selling sex and now was an illegal vendor within commercial sex *milieux*. This traveller was deported back to Bangkok, the last stage of her journey, where she was imprisoned for a year before being sent to the detention centre. The second traveller was caught on camera in a robbery carried out by her boyfriend and others in Bangkok, after she had travelled around with them in other parts of Asia; she completed a three-year prison sentence before being sent to the centre. Her papers were completely false, including a change of both name and nationality.

Both detained women were waiting for someone to pay their plane fare home, but there were no offers. The women's complicity in events leading to their detention disqualified them from aid to victims of 'trafficking'; not all Latin American countries maintain embassies in Thailand, and only one person from local organisations visiting the detention centre spoke Spanish. While the two new migrants in Sydney seemed to accept the work they had just begun doing, I sensed ambiguity and ambivalence about the language course on which their visas were based, and the size of their debts did not leave them any real choice about what jobs to take. Both appeared to be recent graduates of secondary schools. The migrant to Japan believed she had not been destined to sell sex, but her own upper-middle-class family had been involved in getting her the fake papers, and she was suffering considerable guilt about letting them down. The woman caught in the robbery, who was in her mid-thirties and from a working-class background, gave the impression that she had sold sex, but she did not appear to give much importance to it. Her eyes shone when she told me about the thrill of seeing places like Hong Kong and Singapore.

Numerous characters had participated in fixing up these women's journeys, including Pakistanis, Turks, Australians and Mexicans. On the surface, the stories have all the ingredients of exotic melodrama. But people who desire to travel, see the world, make money and accept whatever jobs are available along the way do not fall into neat categories: 'victims of trafficking', 'migrant sex workers', 'forced migrants', 'prostituted women'. Their lives are far more complex – and interesting – than such labels imply.[1]

Media Panic

An open space near a highway, at night. Cars continuously drive up, headlights shining on figures standing about who are scantily dressed, in high heels, thick makeup, wigs. Brief snatches of conversation, raucous laughter, taunts.

Scene from Pedro Almodóvar's *Todo sobre mi madre*[2]

Within seconds, most viewers guess what's happening in such a scene, which is depicted in the media most days of the week. This is what people call 'prostitution', buyers of sex approaching vendors who make themselves available in marginal urban spaces. The following treatment is not unusual:

French working girls lose their privileged role
Paris's sex trade is threatened by a new conservatism and a wave of East European prostitutes.

Casual visitors to the Bois de Boulogne at night find they have wandered into a surreal enchanted wood. Among the trees gleam exposed flesh, bottoms and breasts are displayed in bizarre leather arrangements, thighs spring from high boots – here almost all the prostitutes are men. Some have been operated on but most are pumped full of hormones and silicone.

Behind this carnivalesque scene is a rigid organisation. Each section of each alley relates to a geographical area – Colombian, Brazilian, Peruvian, North African, Spanish, and so on.[3]

References to carnival, risqué clothing, distinct nationalities, sex change and – not least – some 'loss' Europeans are suffering because of migrants: these are the standard ingredients of stories about Europe's sex industry. Another typical treatment invokes slavery:

Once they were girls. Now they are slaves
Frightened and penniless children from Eastern Europe are trapped in prostitution in London.

'I start work at six most evenings and sometimes don't finish till eight the next morning. I must see up to 30 men a night if all the bills are to be paid. I owe a lot of money to the men who brought me here.' It is hard to hear Aura's quiet voice over the noises in the Soho street below. She is sitting on the edge of a small double bed. The sheets are soiled, the floor covered with a stained carpet. Her dark features and highly made-up face belie her age. She is only 17 . . .[4]

Here the focus is on the age of a victim, her helplessness, and the barbaric conditions she is forced to endure. Repeated continually with little variation, these treatments keep the gaze squarely on the non-European Others who have moved onto the sex scene. Statistics are tossed out without sources and the focus stays on miserable tales of a few individuals. On the way to football's 2006 World Cup, media coverage intensified, giving unsubstantiated figures concerning the millions of men expected to converge on Germany:

Angela Merkel's World Cup trafficking silence
. . . German officials are in denial about what the rest of the world sees: There is a human-rights disaster in the making in the coming months. In short: Where are all the women needed for this increased demand for prostitution going to come from? And under what conditions will they 'work'?
   For the most part, they won't be German women. Over three quarters of the women in prostitution in Germany are foreign nationals, the majority of them from poorer Central and Eastern European countries. The German Women's Council estimates that 40,000 women will be brought into Germany to service the fans. Experts estimate that most of them are trafficked, meaning they are in prostitution as a result of force, fraud, or coercion. In most cases, they are literally controlled and in many cases effectively enslaved by criminals and organized crime groups.[5]

Sensationalism is common enough in the media's attention to all migrants – and it should be noted that both Right-leaning and Left-leaning media are implicated, as in the above examples. But where sex is involved, not only the media (where it is unsurprising) but many sober authority figures take the same tone, decrying migrations that involve working in the sex industry and setting up projects to prevent them. The urge is to help or even save migrant women, and it has spawned a veritable Rescue Industry.

   Sex at the Margins examines the intersection of two groups of people: those who migrate to Europe and engage in domestic, caring and sexual labour, and those working in the social sector with these migrants. By social sector I mean people whose jobs, whether paid or voluntary, are dedicated to improving the condition of society in a wide range of ways. Many social agents identify themselves as doing work dedicated to helping others, providing them with services to improve their lives, and for this reason they consciously spend time thinking about how people ought to live and how to achieve that vision. The social sector takes in projects that are broadly aimed to affect a large population, and projects that are narrowly aimed at particular problems. Social agents include social workers, policy makers, individuals in charge of funding, religious personnel, counsellors, academics and non-governmental organisation (NGO)[6] employees and volunteers: anyone who, in their work, consciously attempts to better other people's lives.

Increasingly, people who work in home and personal services in Europe are migrants who enjoy few rights. Some discussions of commercial sex are just beginning to reflect this sea-change, an acknowledgement that the traditional debate about whether 'prostitution' is violence or work does not address the hundreds of thousands of illegal migrants earning money in this sector. Overwhelmingly, however, media, academic, government and most NGO voices either infantilise these migrants or ignore their existence.

Sex at the Margins examines current ideas about this phenomenon of travel and work, demonstrating the discursive gaps and silences through which poorer and undocumented people slip, especially women who sell sex. Usually, these slippages are blamed on abstractions – society, the state – but this book argues that those declaring themselves to be helpers actively reproduce the marginalisation they condemn. I aim to connect domains usually treated separately – studies of migrations and service work, the sex industry, feminism, philanthropy and social projects – to show that these separations cannot be justified once all the cards are on the table.

I began to brood about this topic fifteen years ago while working in Latin America and the Caribbean as an educator with adults, including women and men who sold sex. Many were thinking of travelling to work in Europe or had already returned from there, or they had friends and family working abroad. Trips were a common topic of conversation everywhere: trying one's luck abroad, making money, seeing the world, meeting new people, learning new things. As part of my NGO job, I talked with families of daughters selling domestic and sex services abroad. I wrote a proposal for education for travellers, an interesting project we framed as 'capacity-building', aimed at averting the most drastic kind of problems confronted by poorer people who travel to Europe. However, the European funder's desire to discourage migration forced us to reduce the proposal to a single aspect: psychological

support for traumatised returnees. Similarly, when a funder com-
missioned a film on the experiences of migrant women in Holland, the
result was a nightmare vision of police raids, client violence, economic
desperation and social shame.[7] The film was shown widely to poor
women, who were invariably sceptical about the melodrama. All of them
knew people who were successful in their working travels to Europe,
whether they sold sex or not. In an attempt to understand why funders
viewed the situation as they did, I spent a year in several European
capitals, talking with people in a number of NGOs and with migrants
themselves. Later, I enrolled for a Master's degree and carried out
ethnographic field work in Madrid among outreach projects and
migrants selling sex in the street.[8]

Taken together, these experiences showed me that how people on the
southwestern side of the Atlantic talked about their own trips had little
in common with European ways of talking, and this is still mainly true.
The crux of the difference concerns autonomy: whether travellers are
perceived to have quite a lot versus little or none at all. I decided to try
to find out how this difference comes about and what it is made of, but
where I expected to find theory to enlighten me, I found little: either
the whole problematic was reduced to a few simplistic concepts, or they
were ignored. Thus when I looked at work in the fields of migration and
diaspora studies people selling sex were not there (until extremely
recently), migrant women from poor countries being figured as
domestic workers and migrant men as engaged in construction and
agriculture. Studies of services, the concept usually invoked to describe
migrant women's work, omitted sex. There was a new area,
'trafficking', which dealt with the criminal aspects of the worst kind of
migration and could not be imposed on all migrants. People selling sex
were dealt with and normalised in AIDS research, but there the interest
was reduced to condom use and other aspects of 'risk behaviour'.
Nowhere did I find these migrants treated as having a range of interests,
occupations and desires – as being people who read newspapers, cook,
go to church, films and parties or who count themselves as activists in
any political or social cause. At the beginning, then, I was dealing with
absences and silences, except in one area.

Within feminist theory, a hyper-production of writings existed on the concept of 'prostitution', repetitively arguing about whether or not it is always and intrinsically violent and exploitative. In this literature, it was common for each side to do little more than criticise the other. There were also scores of research studies about women who sell sex in the street, tending always to try to explain *why* in the world they did it, the assumption being that it was uniquely perverse and devastating. With few exceptions, this large literature, including epidemiological and health-promotion research, time and again arrived at the same conclusions. Descriptive studies seemed more open-minded but often concentrated on a specific locale or epoch ('female sex work in Calcutta', 'prostitution in *belle époque* New Orleans'), and this specificity could not be extrapolated to current migrant subjects.

I wanted to know about the abundant social programming aimed at helping these migrants. Given the lack of information, the incoherence of so much social action was not surprising. But why had social agents not come up with their own theories, based on their experiences? Are they so caught up in their projects that they do not stop to measure the effects on the people they want to help? By and large, they accept the 'prostitution' discourse – and the 'prostitute' as victim – as fact, not as social construction. From there, they position themselves as benevolent helpers, in what seems to them to be a natural move. Through historical research, I found that this self-positioning began at a time in European history when interest was awakened in the art of government and the welfare of the governed. Those who were concerned, the growing middle class, saw *themselves* as peculiarly suited to help, control, advise and discipline the unruly poor, including their sexual conduct. I speculated that examination of this impulse to control during the period when the modern sense of 'prostitution' was produced would help explain what goes on today, and my historical research did prove that early, proto-feminist concepts relied on notions of helping and saving that go some way to explain social programming today.

In my field work, I found that the theorising, with its silences and fixations, can be understood as the desire first to *know* and then to *control* people whose activities are considered deviant. The focus I bring to this study belongs to a postcolonial framework that questions missions to help non-Europeans, particularly the maternalistic tradition

— even when it is called feminist — to rescue non-European and poorer
women.

This book argues that social helpers consistently deny the agency of
large numbers of working-class migrants, in a range of theoretical and
practical moves whose object is management and control: the exercise
of governmentality. The journeys of women who work in the sex
industry are treated as involuntary in a victimising discourse known as
'trafficking', while the experiences of men and transgenders who sell
sex are ignored. The work of migrant women in Europe, not only in sex
but in housework and caring, is mostly excluded from government
regulation and accounts, leaving these workers socially invisible.
Migrants working in the informal sector are treated as passive subjects
rather than as normal people looking for conventional opportunities,
conditions and pleasures, who may prefer to sell sex to their other
options. The victim identity imposed on so many in the name of helping
them makes helpers themselves disturbingly important figures.
Historical research demonstrates how this victimising and the
concomitant assumption of importance by middle-class women, which
began two centuries ago, was closely linked to their carving out of a new
employment sphere for themselves through the naming of a project to
rescue and control working-class women.

Sex at the Margins portrays social agents' current practices in services,
education, outreach, publications, conferences and policy-making, and
shows how they perpetuate a constructed class — 'prostitute' — which
justifies their actions and serves an isolationist immigration policy.
When possible, I let the words of those who sell sex describe their own
experiences; the translations of testimonies not originally in English are
mostly my own.

I hope that this book will be of interest to both non-academic and
academic readers. For the former, I have taken out the insistent citation
behaviour required by the latter; for the latter, I have preserved the
references in notes at the end of each chapter.

I have found the concept of discourse extremely helpful. The discourse on a subject refers to a language or way of talking that develops,
through use, a series of conventions and becomes institutionalised

through use. The discourse defines the socially accepted, mainstream or apparently official version, the version that seems obvious or natural. At the same time, this discourse always leaves out experiences and points of view that do not fit, silencing difference and producing unease in those who do not see themselves included. To understand the concept of discourse is to remember that what we say about any given subject is always constructed, and there are only partial truths.

NOTES

1 This argument is developed in Agustín 2002a.
2 Almodóvar 1999
3 Hannah Godfrey, *The Observer* (UK),19 January 2003
4 Kate Holt, *The Observer* (UK), 3 February 2002
5 Donna Hughes, *National Review Online,* 1 May 2006
6 NGO is the general term for an array of projects large and small, also known as charities, non-profit organisations, foundations, etc. They may provide direct services, do research, publish and/or fund other projects.
7 Krom 1993
8 Agustín 1999a

2

WORKING TO TRAVEL,
TRAVELLING TO WORK

The story begins with ideas about migration, because social helping projects classify people according to labels, such as 'migrant domestic worker' or 'migrant prostitute'. I begin with notions of travel in general, because so much stigmatising and bad publicity derives from wrong impressions about what people are doing when they leave home to work.

Migrancy is at best a temporary identity, referring to a stage of life when people are in transit. Migrants are often assumed to have moved from their country with the intention of settling down in another, but research shows that some who think they are leaving for good actually return, others never consider their journey to be other than temporary no matter how long it lasts, and some who settle abroad still feel permanently uprooted, meaning that physical location and even legal status are not good indicators of affiliation to a migrant identity. Societies on the receiving end want newcomers to 'integrate', which depends on migrants' desires and abilities to adapt, assimilate and *lose* an identification with migrancy. Yet receivers make this difficult by constantly finding migrants lacking in necessary skills and culture and making legality and security hard to acquire.

So it seems to me that these travellers have in common a process, not an identity: they have all left their countries and they have to earn money to live. When a particular group of them is treated sensationally in the press or defined as needing to be rescued, the difference is not in the people themselves but in how they are supposed to have arrived and how they are making a living. Jobs selling sex form part of a vast, unregulated, unprotected, informal economic sector. Migrants engage in many other commercial activities, such as selling leather goods, silk scarves and sunglasses on the street, that are also unrecognised and uncontrolled, but these provoke neither the passionate desire to help nor a scandalised media gaze. The association with sex overwhelmingly affects how migrants are treated, excluding them from migration studies and stories, disqualifying them as travellers and workers, and constructing them as passive objects forced to work and travel in ways they never wanted.

Theories of tourism and migration are changing, in part because of this kind of ambiguous situation. Rather than surveying them exhaustively, I expose odd silences in the theories to reveal a story common to all, in which migrants are considered separate, uncreative and unsophisticated. In this metanarrative, leisure is considered an aspect of western modernity that facilitates tourism, which is character-ised by the absence of work, while migration is undertaken by less modern people impelled by identifiable causes to leave home. The tourism and pleasure seeking of people from 'developing' societies rarely figures, as though migration and tourism (and working and tourism) were mutually exclusive. Why should the travels to work of people from less wealthy countries be supposed to differ fundamentally from those of Europeans? To answer this, I examine concepts of labour migration and the so-called feminisation of migration, as well as theories of global flows and transnationalism.

The particular travel I'm looking at involves women, men and trans-genders who work in personal and home services in Europe. Since many people do more than one of these jobs, I don't attempt to keep them separate and later show that the boundaries between them cannot be maintained. I also blur the line between men's and women's migra-tions, since migrant men from the third world are often presented as feminised, vulnerable and victimised and because they work in service jobs, too. On the other hand, I pay more attention to women, not because there are *not* many transgenders and men in the situations discussed, but because women provoke the scandal. For this reason, I closely examine concepts of 'trafficking', an account of women's travel that ties it up with the sale of sex.

I have carried out several kinds of field work during my nearly fifteen years of study. In the area of the México–US border known as The Valley, near Brownsville and Matamoros, I did participatory action research with a group of migrants from Central America, Cuba and México who were applying for political asylum in the US. At the suggestion of one of them, residents in a Roman Catholic refuge taped the stories of their journeys, beginning with the complex and sometimes desperate situations they were living in before they left.[1] In the Dominican Republic, I interviewed people living on remittances from women working in Europe. I did research among migrant women selling sex in Spain.[2] Apart from these more formal situations, I have been making friends with people trying to travel to work for decades, all over Latin America and the Caribbean, and talking with migrants all over Europe, not only from Latin America but also from West Africa, Eastern Europe and countries of the former Soviet Union. Some of these felt they were victims and were living in shelters.

Travel and Travellers to Europe

On the European continent, the desire to make a European Union places emphasis on what defines a member, a European, as opposed to a non-member, outsider, non-European. In matters of culture, there is considerable tension between a project to mark out Europe as an entity and efforts to conserve and protect particular national identities from outside influence. The current drive toward pan-European policies means members would like to agree on a single immigration policy, but all have complicated migration histories, and several had or have colonial dependencies. Members perceived to have inadequate border controls (like Spain) or to be too liberal towards migrants (like Holland) are under pressure to 'close up' their borders better. These divergences of policy do not apply when the outsiders are called tourists.

Tourism

For several decades now, tourism has been a major source of income for some European countries, and others consider it to be their future economic salvation. Tourists are generally defined as people who have time and money to spend on leisure and who journey somewhere to do it: they travel for pleasure. Many scholars define tourism through the absence of work. For Erik Cohen, 'tourism only remains functional so long as it does not become central to the individual's biography, his life-plan and aspirations'.[3] So tourists are believed to leave their regular jobs behind to indulge consciously in *not* working, the word *vacation* referring to vacant time.

Despite these ideas, European tourism advertises itself as not only pleasurable but educational, and some tourists are said to be doing hard work, arriving with long lists of items to be seen and appreciated, in pressed and crowded conditions, at a high cost and without necessarily having a very good time. But though seeing the world may be educational, it is not a necessity, so tourists are not considered to be on the brink of making important life decisions, acting under duress or intending to stay, characteristics associated with refugees, exiles and migrants.

Most of the concepts developed in the sociology of tourism are masculine. Since women have been theorised as experiencing space and time differently from men, much of what defines tourism may change as more information on women's tourism comes in. Many women have different ideas about work, too, so the positioning of tourism as Other to work may change. I believe the dichotomy work/no work is misleading and that there are multiple forms of travel that have aspects of both. Deconstruction of this taken-for-granted duo allows me to make postcolonial and class analyses of various themes involved.

Returning the gaze

John Urry gives us the concept of the tourist gaze,[4] which, like other gazes, has been called peculiarly male. Some claim that *flâneurs*, wandering urban observers in the nineteenth century, could only have been men.[5] Laura Mulvey theorises the male gaze as a visual power held by male spectators, particularly in relation to female objects: 'pleasure in looking [as] split between active/male and passive/female' in patriarchal society (in reference to the idea of scopophilia, the pleasure of looking at other people's bodies).[6] While work guiding film, photography and other visual arts suggests the gaze's inherent masculinity, there is no evidence that disempowered or oppressed women and men do not also gaze, or gaze back, at the eyes that make them objects. For Malek Alloula, writing of French postcard photos of undressed Algerian women:

> These veiled women are not only an embarrassing enigma to the photographer but an outright attack upon him. It must be believed that the feminine gaze ... is a little like ... the photographic lens that takes aim at everything ... Thrust in the presence of a veiled woman, the photographer feels photographed; having himself become an object-to-be-seen, he loses initiative: he is dispossessed of his own gaze.[7]

Leonore Davidoff, writing of the long-lasting love between a nineteenth-century English gentleman, Arthur Munby, and a domestic servant, Hannah Cullwick, shows the essential equality of their desires and how Hannah changed her social destiny even while exaggerating her role of grimy cleaner.[8] Katherine Frank notes that 'men's interactions in strip clubs are with women who look back at them, from the stages ("Remember to make eye contact!" managers urged)'.[9] These are all examples of how people in disempowered and overtly sexist situations assert agency, take action, resist.

The modern tourist gaze is usually associated with Europeans, but travellers like Flora Tristán (1840, Perú) and Domingo Sarmiento (1849, Argentina) wrote extensive counter-accounts of the peculiar habits of Europeans. Sarmiento describes how he caused Paris crowds to form by staring, *flâneur*-like, at cracks in walls and wonders how these French could possibly be the same people that made the revolutions of 1780 and 1830:

> What Humboldt saw in the jungles and pampas, Sarmiento sees in the shops of the Rue Vivienne, the collections of the Jardin des Plantes, the museums, galleries, bookstores, and restaurants ...[10]

Being less modern, in the European sense, does not impede travellers from gazing, questioning and joking about aspects of modernity, nor does it exclude them from engaging in tourism.

Hybrid Categories: Tourists that Work
and Working Travellers

Travellers are sometimes said to seek exotic, intellectualised or esoteric trips untypical of tourists.[11] Some travellers say their trips are unplanned, open-ended and longer than tourists', and that they work along the way. They are proud of not travelling in groups, of spending little money, of trying to speak local languages, of meeting local people and appreciating 'real culture' more than tourists supposedly do:

> [W]e experienced the country in a totally different way than a Tourist. A Tourist wants to observe and experience only the best of the culture. A Traveler travels with humility and respect of the culture . . . While working with the people we made friendships with them. By doing that we are immediately connected . . . and always will be.[12]

Many travellers who position their experiences as more authentic than tourists' and want to 'interact with the culture' get jobs. Unless they are wealthy, they need to make money if their travels continue long enough, whether they call themselves vagabond, beach bum, drifter or travel writer. Combining travel and work is perhaps a hybrid form of tourism, indicating that the supposed contradiction between leisure and work is not true.

Business travellers engage in tourism while travelling, their expense accounts increasingly important to European city economies as they entertain themselves and clients in theatres, cabarets, restaurants, bars, sports arenas and sex clubs. Sports professionals, entertainers, musicians and theatre companies work while touring and do tourism when not working. Sailors, soldiers, airline and train personnel, commercial fishermen, farm workers, long-distance truck drivers and a variety of others travel as part of their jobs. Academics, consultants, missionaries, 'development' workers, diplomats and social-sector personnel attend conferences, do field work and provide expertise while also seeing the sights. Explorers search for oil, minerals, endangered species and archaeological artefacts. Many of these people spend long periods away from home, their work lives punctuated by leisure and tourist activities. Religious pilgrims may work and engage in tourism on their way. And then there are the people called Roma, gypsies, and Travellers, whose itinerant way of life includes working while on the road.

Many theorists distinguish between all these people and migrants on the grounds that the latter settle: for example, 'If the nomad can be called the Deterritorialized *par excellence*, it is precisely because there is no reterritorialization afterwards as with the migrant.'[13] People from wealthier countries who decide to settle abroad are often called expatriates, not migrants, or émigrés, which may imply politically motivated self-exile.[14] In comparison with postmodern, first-world, innovative individuals, migrants are made to seem earthbound and barely modern.

What and Who Is a Migrant?

In 2005, the UN estimated that only 3 per cent of the world's population were migrants (191 million) and that 30–40 million might be unauthorised (undocumented). They also estimated unauthorised migrants in Europe in 1998 to be around 3 million, but the Migration Policy Institute's estimate is 7–8 million. Some figures also state that 'illegals' are 10–15 per cent of migrants already present in Europe and 20–30 per cent of those entering it.[15]

The combination *Europe migration* until fairly recently referred to Europeans who left to colonise other parts of the world, either as immigrants or during inter-European wars and ethnic conflicts. Since World War Two, this situation has reversed, with European countries receiving ever more migrants. Since the 1980s, economic booms in Europe and the disarticulation of 'iron curtain' countries have promoted mobility.[16]

Most governments publish statistics not on immigrants *per se* but only on different statuses related to immigration, such as visas, work permits and municipal registrations; official countings of 'migrant workers' inevitably include only people with legal status. Statistics depend on how calculations are done, and results can vary widely. The attempt to distinguish legal from illegal or unauthorised is, furthermore, too crude to be useful. The figures cited above illustrate the muddle.

Categories of unrecorded, or inadequately recorded, labour migrants include EU nationals such as posted workers, transit migrants of all nationalities, suitcase traders from different countries of origin, the self-employed, 'forced' migrants and hidden migration including clandestine movements. Additional statistical definitional problems arise from the equation of unrecorded as illegal, and with the many outstanding areas of unharmonised legislation on migration across Europe. 'Category switching', the movement of an individual over time between different administrative categories and legal statuses, further complicates the question of obtaining up-to-date data on recorded migration.[17]

Statistics in general must be understood as constructions, not truth, deriving as they do from labels and methods that reflect subjective visions.[18] Statistics coming from countries left behind are also skewed:

> [The usual data] refer to legal labor migration and only to that part which is officially recorded as overseas employment migration. They do not cover women who leave a country for reasons other than work (most commonly tourism and education) but in fact end up working at the destination nor women who leave or enter a country illegally, not going through border check points, also to work as migrants. When undocumented or illegal flows are also considered, both the numbers and proportions of women are likely to be much higher.[19]

These various confusions in terms cause misunderstandings. Theories of migration have tended to concentrate on why people move to new countries, some focusing on international structural conditions such as recomposition of capital (for example, in export trading zones) or globalisation of markets, others on the national policy level or on household units, and still others on wage differentials between countries. Migration is described as caused by the desire to make better money, by loss of land, by recruitment by employers abroad, by flight from violence, persecution and war, by the need to reunite with family, and by the 'feminisation of poverty'. None of these causes is exclusive, and no single condition guarantees that someone will migrate. Nevertheless, migrations are commonly discussed in terms of 'push–pull factors'. Armed conflict and loss of farms may push people away from home, while labour shortage and favourable immigration policy may pull them elsewhere: the basic concept is unarguable, but it also envisions migrants as acted upon, leaving little room for desire, aspiration, anxiety or other states of the soul. In contrast, first-world travellers are imagined to be modern individuals searching for ways to realise themselves.

One sign of changing discourses is the gradual abandonment of the distinction between *emi*grate and *immi*grate, which depends on two easily separable standpoints deriving from distinct events: the definitive leaving of a country (emigration), and the arrival in another with the intention of staying (immigration). Immigration was traditionally viewed as a masculine project, according to a generation of scholars trying to inject gender into research and analysis.

Commentators also try to distinguish migrants from refugees, who are imagined to have no *desire* to leave but to be abruptly forced to go by disasters, fighting, persecution. The United Nations High Commission for Refugees grants refugee status to people fleeing from selected situations, failing to recognise many similar situations (for example, armed conflicts not considered 'war' because rebels are not acknowledged by governments).

The arbitrary nature of these categories and the assigning of people to nation states constitutes a form of international biopolitics, a means of controlling populations.[20] According to nations' statuses (first-world, poor, at war, non-European), governments decide whether to label people migrants, refugees, guest workers, tourists, students or business travellers; according to which label is assigned, the traveller is subject to more or fewer rights and obligations.

Against the determinism that produces poor people as shunted about by purely external factors, Saskia Sassen writes:

> If it were true ... that the flow of immigrants and refugees was simply a matter of individuals in search of better opportunities in a richer country, then the growing population and poverty in much of the world would have created truly massive numbers of poor invading highly developed countries, a great indiscriminate flow of human beings from misery to wealth. This has not been the case. Migrations are highly selective processes; only certain people leave, and they travel on highly structured routes to their destinations, rather than gravitate blindly toward any rich country they can enter.[21]

'Only certain people leave' applies in places of violence and crop failure as well as in urban ghettos. The question of who becomes a migrant is deeper than traditional theorising suggests and can even be viewed as 'individual resistance by way of physical relocation'.[22] But the predominant discourse concentrates on economic factors, especially work, and, as such, is gendered:

> The underlying assumption in studies of migration has been the male pauper – a single or married male who looks forward to amassing capital with which to return to his native country. Thus, the corollary assumption has been that it is males who typically make the decision to migrate and that females follow.[23]

Women do, of course, migrate for family reasons, as men do, but statistics estimating that women constitute more than half of migrants in the past few decades cannot be explained by the desire of family members to join each other. Men's decisions to travel are generally (and seriously) understood to evolve over time, the product of their normal masculine ambition to get ahead through work. But when women decide to travel, commentators search for reasons. The desire to be more independent, see the world, make money and travel is not gendered. A recent UN report found that women who accept the challenge of migration worldwide are increasingly motivated by the desire for personal betterment as well as, or even rather than, by family responsibilities – yet also send a large proportion of their salaries home and become the principal sources of family income.[24]

Although statistics show that in many areas of Europe other *European* migrants still predominate, the word *migrant* is generally used to signify non-Europeans. Ambiguity arises also because migrants now 'assimilated', or who have become European citizens, are sometimes included and sometimes not in both popular definitions and official censuses.

The Concept of Labour Migrations

In formal discussions of labour markets, classic economic and demographic concepts and dichotomies prevail: legal and illegal workers, formal and informal sectors, the real market and the black market, and, in Europe, Community and non-Community states. These constructed concepts[25] fail to describe large numbers of job searches, jobs and workers. If the divisions between tourism and working travel are fuzzy, those that attempt to classify labour migrations are even less clear.

Governments may organise labour migrations, conceiving them as *temporary*. In Europe, examples include Algerian migrations to French factory work and Turkish migrations through the German guestworker system. In such programmes, states actively recruit workers and control their stays with permits that may prohibit changing jobs.[26] But formal programmes describe only a small portion of labour migrations, omitting even the movements of individuals to take up legal jobs when they undertake them independently. And, of course, many or most people actually called migrants arrive without a concrete job offer, although someone may have told them a job is available. State discourses on immigration, social services and social integration describe migrants as always seeking legality, but job seekers often expect to work in informal or illegal jobs, even though they know they can never regularise their status this way. Migrants are excluded when their professional qualifications are not recognised across country borders, with the result that trained and experienced dentists or teachers end up driving taxis and doing manicures. Some countries impose quotas on how many professional licences may go to non-natives, and many countries simply do not allow even experienced migrants to apply for many posts, keeping these for their own citizens, who continually worry that migrants will steal good jobs.

For jobs to be considered legal, employment must be recognised by official government accounting as part of the formal economy. Legal migrant workers possess work permits and corresponding visas. Quasi-regular situations arise when migrants work in the formal sector *without* a work permit or work in jobs for which no work permit exists. Large numbers of migrants who intend to look for jobs arrive in Europe on tourist visas, which by definition prohibit them from earning money.[27]

The informal economy is also called underground, hidden, cash, black, grey, shadow, irregular, subterranean and twilight, and encompasses all areas not included in government accounts, which does not mean that the regular economy of capitalism is 'wholly formal'.[28] The artificial dichotomy formal/informal obscures more than it reveals, and the range of income-generating occupations excluded from accounting is too wide to be coherent: do-it-yourself work, selling without a licence, guarding parking spaces, bet running, providing bed-and-breakfast, begging, selling home-grown produce or cooked food, drug dealing and supplying places to use drugs, unlicensed taxi services, loans, pawn and check-cashing services, carpentry and construction services, selling sex, 'pimping' and other protection services, sports coaching, card-sharking, running dice or shell games or neighbourhood card and chess games, cleaning windshields, dog walking, childcare, street and party entertainment, car repair, home computer help, messenger services, manufacture of pirated products, language teaching and homework tutoring: the list is long and ranges from small-time infractions to more important ones, which also include smuggling, embezzlement, robbery, burglary and fabricating false documents.[29]

Some of these occupations resemble formal-sector activities but do not fulfil local regulations; some are forms of tax evasion or money laundering; some are crimes that require a victim; others fit definitions of alternative or solidarity economies (mutual aid, community projects, voluntary work, self-help) and household economies where women and children are expected to go unpaid. Legal citizens also perform these jobs. When the informal sector is criticised, blame goes to those selling, but those who buy are equal participants. Informal work often comes about as the only available way to earn a living:

> Anna ... worked in a hairdressing salon until it was taken over by a Spanish man, who told her he would have to hire Spanish people. Now she works informally as a hair stylist, visiting customers in their homes. All her customers are British and pay her with cash. These women have not chosen informal work within their own ethnic niche as a preference, or as a means of avoiding integration. It is merely a way of earning an income where formal employment is not an option.[30]

Thinking about a first-world character is instructive. Somehow, Anna has travelled from Britain to Spain, where she needs to make money. Because of the bureaucratic requirements surrounding work in the formal sector, she must work informally. To describe Anna as doing something wrong, all travel outside one's country of passport would have to be limited to tourism or business, which would require hundreds of thousands of people to abandon their second homes in other countries.

Technically, when Anna works for cash she is doing wrong, but how many people would blame her? And if Anna is excused, why should a Moroccan or Romanian not be?

The popular prejudice that informal activities are criminal and *caused* by migrants is mistaken. Sassen sees the informal economy as 'a necessary outgrowth of advanced capitalism',[31] and Ruggiero shows how the entrepreneurial activities of many people, including illegal migrants, are interlaced in informal economies; he asks whether 'the official rhetoric is part of what organizational theory would term as *manifest goals*, ... destined to be ignored because they are inoperative'.[32]

Many legal citizens spend their lives in the social margins, engaging in activities not considered crimes. Both Prince Charles and Prime Minister Thatcher, for example, claimed that the existence of an irregular economy proved that 'the British are not work shy'.[33] Bureaucratic processes involved in becoming legal can be overwhelming and trigger investigations inconvenient to numerous people. And then, some people prefer a more marginal life, avoiding taxes, enjoying independence or taking pleasure in the company and lifestyles found away from the centre.

European policies promote the idea that migrants can be easily divided into legal and illegal, in terms of how they travelled and got their jobs, but a German example shows otherwise:

> There is more than anecdotal evidence that the different ways in which people from the East can legally obtain employment in Germany constitute bridges for undocumented workers ... both employers and employees often benefit from overstaying. In addition, the more people there are coming and going, the greater the opportunity to spread information in sending regions about the destination country in general and about the structure of job opportunities.[34]

Travelling and working people who have correct documents mix with others who do not, often with the help, collusion, tolerance and for the convenience of regular citizens in states with restrictive policies.

Women are disproportionately represented in informal economies worldwide, predominating in domestic service, sweatshop labour, home piecework, export processing zones, caring jobs and commercial sex.

Globalisation theorists link the growth of production, commerce and finance with the increase in women's participation on the production side, and note that migration is often the only way for women to get jobs.[35] Although there have been complaints of a lack of interest in working women within migration studies,[36] migrant domestic and caring workers are currently the subject of considerable research. Migrants working in the sex industry, however, are usually ignored, as in the generalisation 'the domestic sector is the only economic sector that employs a large number of female immigrants from developing countries'.[37] Alternatively, those selling sex are minimised, as in the statement 'quantitatively this sector is far less important then the migration of domestic workers',[38] though no reliable numbers are available for people who sell sex. Scholars of the sex industry estimate migrant workers there to be equal to numbers of migrant domestics. Again, statistics may not be used to prove these points.

'Feminisation' and Gender in Migration

References to the feminisation of migration are now routine, but although migrant women are believed to outnumber migrant men in Europe, proof is impossible, since so many of the people involved are undocumented. For the process-word *feminisation* to make sense, one must believe that previous to recent history, women did not migrate in great numbers. It has been said that 'histories of travel make it clear that women have never had the same access to the road as men',[39] but several kinds of research disprove this idea.[40] One study of European migration examined 7,000 English life-histories covering 1660 to 1730, finding that more than three-quarters of country women left their villages, in greater numbers than men. All types of migrations were included, from inter-parish to long-distance.[41] A very different kind of study, carried out in Africa to determine the geographic range of sex-related DNA, revealed that male chromosomes tend to be more localised. This points to a rate of female migration eight times higher than male, owing to traditional practices of patrilocality, under which brides move to their husbands' houses: patrilocality is a common practice worldwide, and in countries with enormous populations.[42] Two sets of data from the UN

show that women and girls have constituted a large proportion of all
international migrants for many decades: in 1960 at least 47 of every
100, in 1998, 48, in 2000, 49. Talk of a significant change in recent years
is not substantiated.[43]

Industrialised countries' shift to a service economy while moving
manufacturing to 'developing' countries contributes to an increase of
jobs for the 'type of worker represented by immigrant women ... gender
cannot be considered in isolation of these structural arrangements ...
whether within their countries of origin or outside'. [44] In addition, the
International Monetary Fund (IMF) has, since the late 1970s, imposed
policies of 'structural adjustment' on third-world countries that seek
loans or want to refinance debts. Structural adjustment policies mandate
severe cuts in government spending, and social programming is always
cut first. Women, who predominate in the social sector, lose jobs – as
teachers, hospital workers and social workers, as well as support
personnel such as cleaners and secretaries. Structural adjustment
policies are also often blamed for the disintegration of families and the
migration of women looking for incomes far from home. In the case of
the Philippines and Sri Lanka, official government programmes facilitate
women's going abroad on contracts to do domestic work, while the bulk
of their earnings are sent back home.

Migrants describe how economic factors influence their decisions to
leave home:

> The alternative would have been working for one of your Italian firms
> that have come to Albania to exploit our work. Two years ago, when I
> left home, a worker in one of your shoe factories made 150,000 lire a
> month [€77]. A woman, half that amount. I don't understand why
> Italy is amazed if young Albanians come here to try to make money
> the fastest way possible. Girls like me in one evening earn 800,000
> lire [€413] and sometimes more than a million. Should we be making
> shoes for 150,000 lire a month? (Albanian woman in Italy)[45]

> You work, work, work and then they don't pay you, because there's
> no money. For example, I worked in an ashtray factory, and when
> there was no money to pay me they said 'take ashtrays', 100 ashtrays.
> So? Can you eat ashtrays? (Ukrainian woman in Spain)[46]

Giving economic need as the 'reason' for selling sell sex can also be a performance of 'poverty' that listeners will accept as an excuse for immoral activity.[47] However, migrants' reasons cannot be reduced to economics only:

> I worked in a company, but they were letting people go. I had problems with my children's father, he mistreated me, he threatened me, they were going to fire me. I have a sister who's a resident here ... I came with the money they gave me when they threw me out of work. (Ecuadorian woman in Spain)[48]

> I separated [from my husband] and then began to work in my city in a [sex] club ... Since the work was hard, I said to myself, I'm going to go far away ... to Spain, because I had a friend here and my mother came years ago and stayed five years ... My friend helped me come and my mother helped with the money for the ticket. (Brazilian woman in Spain)[49]

> Before, I just want to stay in my province, but then I found out there was something else in life ... I did not even know there was such a thing as a lamp ... then I had experience with a light you could simply plug in ... now that I have lived in the city, I do not think I could live in the province any more. (Filipina migrant in Manila)[50]

Pleasure and desire for travel enter into the migration project:

> Sometimes I enjoy working, I can travel and see beautiful places. I can go to nice restaurants. I enjoy that the Turkish men view us as desirable. (Ukrainian woman in Turkey)[51]

> When you work a lot in one place then you ... get tired of the clients ... Even though it will be the same, you imagine another place with other people, and then you come to life inside ... I go to another country, another city. Lately I live between Mallorca and Barcelona ... In summer I always go to Mallorca to spend a little time with my son. (Latin American woman in Spain)[52]

Women are widely considered the least demanding workforce

> for all the stereotypical reasons: lower labor costs; manual dexterity; greater tolerance of and better performance in repetitive and monotonous tasks; reliability; patience; low expectations and lack of employment alternatives; a willingness to put up with dead-end jobs; higher voluntary quitting rates; and so on.[53]

So the fact that women predominate overwhelmingly in poorly paid or unprotected labour is usually treated as unremarkable.

> What we see at work here is a series of processes that valorize and over-valorize certain types of outputs, workers, firms and sectors, and devalorize others. Does the fact of gendering, for example, the devaluing of female-typed jobs, facilitate these processes of devalorization? We cannot take devalorization as a given: devalorization is a produced outcome.[54]

Mirjana Morokvasíc considers that the general lack of surprise at women's undemanding ways and concentration in unprestigious sectors comes about because no one considers their paid employment their primary role – neither themselves nor their employers; their wages are considered complementary.[55] Although more and more information exists on female migrants as protagonists of their own lives and family heads, policy and discourse are mostly stuck in the past, perpetuating the dichotomy of 'males producing and females reproducing'.[56]

Within migration studies, therefore, a specialisation has arisen concerned with examining issues of gender: not only to pay attention to women but to compare women with men and to investigate why ideas about their travels to work do not enter mainstream discourse. Of course, we know that women do not form a homogeneous group: their experiences are mediated by class, colour, nationality, age and so on, and what happens to a migrant in one place might not happen to her or him in another. Pierette Hondagneu-Sotelo writes that feminist concerns with gender used to focus on the domestic arena, while a more integrated gender perspective looks at everything from 'ethnic enclave businesses' to 'hometown associations'.[57] Maintaining that gender is still not given its due in mainstream migration circles, Sarah Mahler and Patricia Pessar propose a framework called 'gendered geographies of power', to study gendered identities and relations across borders, along 'multiple axes of difference' and across 'sociospatial scales – from the body to the globe'.[58] Nicola Piper suggests that the gender-and-migration concept needs to be 'integrated into a larger socio-economic and cultural context of men–women relations and women-to-women.'[59] This is a field in flux.

Ways of Leaving and Arriving

Until recently, there was little concern with *how* individuals migrate. Now, however, as wealthy countries increasingly aim to tighten border controls and keep out irregular travellers, research is proliferating. This material reveals the abundant, creative methods that migrants and intermediaries use to evade official checks; it does not validate stereotypes of large-scale gangs as major actors in the 'smuggling' of humans (defined as helping people get into countries illegally). Many of these studies have centred on women who sell sex, but they demonstrate that all informal migrations share basic characteristics; researchers mostly view people who facilitate these travels as service providers.[60]

To come to Europe, people have two basic choices: to enter as a tourist or temporary traveller, with an appropriate visa, or to enter with a job offer and official working papers in hand. The latter being difficult, many people get in with a tourist visa whose term they are prepared to violate by simply staying on. However, even obtaining a tourist visa can be next to impossible for citizens of many countries, or may require years of waiting. Or the potential tourist-migrant may be able to get a visa but not have the money to buy tickets and survive while looking for work. So would-be travellers commonly seek help from intermediaries (known as travel agents, coyotes, snakeheads, *prestamistas*) who sell information, services and documents. When travellers cannot afford to buy these outright, they go into debt. Those who sell these services are often family members, old friends, tourist acquaintances, independent entrepreneurs or any combination of these, and they may play a minimal part or offer a whole travel package linking them closely to the migrant at every step of the way. Marriage may be part of the deal.

Services offered for money include the provision of passports, visas, changes of identity and work permits, as well as advice on how to look and act in interviews with immigration officials, police and other authorities (at the border, at airports, on trains and buses, in the street), the loan of money to show upon entry to a country as a tourist, pick-up services at airports, transportation to other countries or to pre-arranged lodgings and contact with potential employers. These services are not difficult to find in countries where out-travel has become normal; in many countries, formal-sector travel agents offer these informal services.

> In Trujillo there are international travel agencies, and some of the people who work there know the ways out of Perú ... he says 'Look, I'll take you to Spain in a roundabout way' ... then you give him the money ... but if you can't get in, and the police deport you, you can't get your money back ... Then you go to an EU country, you take a tour, then they pass you to some smugglers who bring you by land to Spain. (Peruvian domestic worker in Spain)[61]

> They lent me for the ticket ... My mother signed, and if I don't pay they'll take things from her house, the television, the refrigerator. There are people who live by lending money, people leave their car, motorcycle as collateral. (Colombian domestic worker in Spain)[62]

> Hari-prar arranged my illegal documents. It took him months, many trips to Chandigarh and Delhi, and cost me everything Prakash had saved. My passport name, officially, was Jyoti Vijh. My date of birth made me safely nineteen years old. 'Otherwise, problems.' Said the travel advisers. All over Punjab 'travel agents' are willing to advise. The longest line between two points is the least detected. (Indian nanny in New York)[63]

> Our research indicates that the market for human smuggling services is in most cases not dominated by overarching mafia-like criminal structures that have monopolised all smuggling activities from the source to the destination country. Rather, in many regions there exists a complex market for highly differentiated smuggling services offered by a multitude of providers from which potential migrants can choose.[64]

Travellers need these services before, during and after their journeys; to get a safe job with decent pay and without severe labour abuses, workers need advice, names, addresses, transport, translations, technical and cultural information, medical references and so on. Being involved in selling sex does not change this process.

> Once I was talking with a friend and she asked if I wanted to go to Spain. I knew why, so I said: 'Ah, do you want to?' ... and I don't know where she met this guy, he got the papers for us, ... the money

and we left ... This guy went to look for work, where are the best
places to work, where there are men ... Because one place has a lot
of men, another doesn't ... I worked in Logroño a month or so, ...
then back to Málaga ... then I came here ... He talked first with the
boss of this place, ... said he was looking for work for us. (Ukrainian
woman in Spain)[65]

Far from being the most desperate poor, migrants need social capital –
networks and reliable information, as well as the ability to judge character, to compare offers and to bargain.

My brother lives in Germany. I had to negotiate quite some time with
the smugglers until I knew about the safest route to get there. The
safest route proved to be the most expensive one. But for me arriving
safely was the only thing that really counted. (Turkish migrant in
Germany)[66]

Travellers in countries that many are trying to leave often find
themselves being sized up. Once, in a Caribbean town near beaches full
of holidaymakers, a young waiter asked me if I could help him travel to
Europe, in exchange for any kind of services I liked. My sympathy could
have led me to help with money, ideas or contacts, so becoming a link in
the chain of informal networks assisting migrations. Help may come in
many forms and unexpectedly:

In the train, one of us had to sleep with the conductor. He had
collected all our passports together – we all came illegally via Paris.
There were five of us and we'd had no border inspections. But then
the next morning one of us slept with the conductor ... and that's
how we came to be here. (Latin American woman in Germany)[67]

The entry of intermediaries into migration networks can be thought
of as a way to redress the imbalance between the number of people
seeking entry and the limited visas available:

This imbalance, and the barriers that core countries erect to keep
people out, create a lucrative economic niche for entrepreneurs and
institutions dedicated to promoting international movement for
profit, yielding a black market in migration. As this underground
market creates conditions conducive to exploitation and
victimization, voluntary humanitarian organizations also arise in

developed countries to enforce the rights and improve the treatment of legal and undocumented migrants.[68]

Considering *all* outsiders who insert themselves into migration networks downplays the significance of profit-making versus charitable intentions and the possibility that some participants may have criminal intentions. These networks have always existed, but only with heightened anxiety about the sex industry has the entrepreneurial side been attacked *en masse*. According to the myth, travel to sell sex is different from all other travel.

Trips to Work in the Sex Industry

In Europe, as in the rest of the world, itinerancy has long been associated with selling sex. A myriad of vendors accompanied pilgrims and campaigning soldiers,[69] and people have always sold or bartered sex when moving from the countryside to cities or from richer countries to poorer (including Europeans who travelled to Argentina in the nineteenth century and contemporary young Japanese women known as 'yellow cabs' who travel with foreigners).[70] In recent times, migrants selling sex are found travelling in every possible direction to, from and within Europe, and networks have arisen all over the world to facilitate finding jobs. Newcomers need to meet insiders with connections to the sex industry, whether they charge money for information and services or not.

Research shows that most migrants who work in the sex industry knew from early on that their work in Europe would have a sexual component.[71] But 'knowing beforehand' is a poor measure of exploitation and unhappiness, since no one can know what working conditions will feel like in any future occupation. The sex jobs migrants might have done or seen at home may be unlike some in Europe, such as standing nude in a window or performing blowjobs day after day with no other social contact with clients. Furthermore, assertions like 'the majority of female migrant workers finding themselves in sex-related work migrated for work of a different nature'[72] fail to understand that interviewees may not reply truthfully to questions that require them to admit 'immorality'. Besides, an honest reply can disqualify them from the 'victim' status that receives help from social agents and police; as one research team says,

> The apprehended smuggled migrants that we interview usually have a vested interest in describing themselves as hapless naïve people who have been betrayed and cheated by powerful gangsters.[73]

Some intermediaries deceive migrants egregiously, as when the package includes signing a contract whose language and foreign currencies they cannot comprehend. Some overeager travellers do not investigate what they are promised, and some permit false documents to be prepared which render them vulnerable in ways they cannot imagine.

> A friend proposed that I come, she knew a girl who could bring me … You sign a note for seven million pesos [= 4,207] and they tell you that you can pay it back working for a month. You know what you're going to be doing. Anyone who says she didn't know, it's a lie – a married lady with children, how can she not know what she's going to be doing here? When you arrive, you crash, because the work is bad and it's a lie that the debt can be paid in a month. You talk with the other girls and see that the debt is more than it cost the girl to bring you. [But] I want to pay her, because she takes a risk, too, to bring you over … (Colombian woman selling sex in Spain)[74]

> Many people say that you go to Spain, you earn a thousand dollars, you pay back your debt in one year – and finally you get here, and it's not like that. It takes you six months to find work, your debt is increasing because of interest. You don't earn a thousand dollars … and you spend rent, food and all this and your stay, which was going to be one year, becomes two, three, and you are still here. (Dominican domestic worker in Spain)[75]

> Often we work for a month or longer and don't see any money. I had worked for a month, then the woman there said to me: 'You are illegal. I don't pay you.' And me, with the fear of deportation … and her: 'I'll call the police this instant.' (Latin American woman in Germany)[76]

Some entrepreneurs take tremendous advantage of these situations, withhold personal documents and threaten migrants and their families at home. Others rely on the dependency that recently arrived and disoriented travellers inevitably feel or simply follow a policy of secrecy. Migrants from any context and working in any kind of job may encounter these abuses.

> To come to Spain, my brother-in-law lent me the money. My cousin encouraged me to come, saying that I could work as a waitress in the bar her husband had opened. When I arrived in Pamplona, I found that he wanted me to work in the bar, but without getting paid; he said the bar didn't make enough to be able to pay me. (Colombian woman in Spain)[77]

> [He] told me what would happen three days before departure. He was going to get a passport and he would hold the passport and the ticket, I should remain behind him and follow. But he did not tell me where I was going. (Ethiopian asylum seeker in the UK)[78]

In some cases, deceit is total: a traveller who never thought of doing *anything* sexual when accepting a trip to Europe is forced into selling sex.

> As soon as I was brought to Turin I understood that I had ended up in a blind alley: I found myself with a 'madam' who ordered me onto the sidewalk and wanted 50 million [lire] [€25,800]. It was a real nightmare ... (Nigerian woman in Italy)[79]

> I was deceived. On arriving I began to rebel and the problems began. The first few days they made me come down and I sat there in a chair and wanted to throw stones at the drunks that came near me. Then the guy told me: look, things can't go on like this, you owe me 300,000 pesetas [€1,800] that you have to pay me with your work here. Everyone owes me that money and all work to pay me it. When you pay me, you can leave. (Colombian woman in Spain)[80]

Some commentators hold that *all* these travellers were forced, but the concept of force must also be dismantled. Some people feel forced who could physically escape; others start out doing other work but feel obligated to sell sex because they will make so much more money if they do. Women in Nairobi who were asked if they realised that sex jobs could be dangerous, answered that they were not selling sex in order to live safely but to earn money and be independent.[81] Migrants widely understand that *any* migratory project carries with it risks and dangers; leaving home represents a momentous life change.

> To return to the provinces and to live as poorly as your parents would be like dying. So there is no choice! You have to pay for your right to live in the capital, to have a good job and a flat with what you have got. With your body ... today thousands of girls are calmly and calculatedly selling themselves. The stupider ones do it just for money, those with more brains and bigger plans do it for a prestigious job and a place to live. (Russian commentator on 'sugar daddies' in Moscow)[82]

> In the beginning you have no money, nothing to eat, so you have to do things, make some money here and there ... There was a café on the Martelaarsgracht where all the illegals came. You could always make some money there, hustling, dealing. (Algerian in the Netherlands)[83]

Obviously, an infinite array of relationships is possible between migrant and entrepreneur, boyfriend, sugar daddy and madam, and there is no doubt that some of these figures talk in disagreeable ways. 'The cargo changes every 10–15 days' demonstrates how people-movers may commodify their clients.[84] This kind of talk is not, however, evidence that the speakers *behave* violently or exploitatively. Many researchers approach this field with the preconceived (and sorrowful) notion that migrants have been abused, which can cause interviewees to tell them what they expect to hear: 'sad stories'.[85] The opportunism and willingness of some migrants to steal, cheat and manipulate others is usually ignored.

Many assume that women who live inside sex establishments have lost all freedom, but sometimes workers prefer less free situations, for a variety of reasons:

> When you live in the club it's cheaper, because it's a daily rate that you pay for food and lodging, while if you live outside you have to pay the expenses of flat, food, transport ... Most of the time you're in the bar, you save more. My sister and I finished working, went to bed and slept as much of the day as we could to avoid expenses and to feel that the time was passing faster. (Colombian woman in Spain)[86]

No one mistreats you, except if you leave to go outside and something could happen to you, but inside nothing can happen ... you end up feeling protected. (Ecuadorian woman in Spain)[87]

When we lived in the club we had the owner on top of us taking care of us: 'don't go with this one', 'don't go with the other one'. He was like our father. (Colombian woman in Spain)[88]

Migrants without permission to work may feel safer if someone else takes charge of finding new venues and arranging jobs. The media, police and helping projects, on the other hand, only hear about the most tragic situations precisely because something has gone wrong.

The debt that migrants contract is often referred to as bondage or slavery, but all debts are not alike and not all require working in a specific place or in oppressive conditions.

People come here that have a debt, for example one girl I have right now. They've all come on their own feet, they have a debt they have to pay ... The last girl had to pay a million [pesetas] [€6,010] ... After five months she was finished. (Dominican woman running a sex business in Spain)[89]

You ask the bank for a loan, giving collateral or guarantees, they give you the money and you pay interest every month. I did it with a friend's guarantee. (Ecuadorian domestic worker in Spain)[90]

The woman who brought me told me that they gave us everything in the club, food, a place to sleep ... I didn't know how the debt worked ... After twenty days the woman came to get the money I had made ... She told me what I owed ... it seemed too much to me ... The owner said: I give you your money and you fix it with her. He was different from the woman who brought me ... I had trouble with the woman and finally stopped paying her ... The deceit is in the debt and the payback, not in the work. We pay the debt and we are free. (Colombian working in Spain)[91]

I never considered it to be a debt. For me it was like a favour that they did for me. (Colombian working in Spain)[92]

Even when migrants feel deceived, they usually complain of working conditions, not the fact that the work is sexual,[93] and they often prefer to remain in the industry. Many migrants' primary goal is paying off debts in the shortest possible time, so they focus on the future and play down unpleasant stages already behind them.

Yet migrants who sell sex are routinely treated as victims. Altink notes that the word transmits shades of meaning insinuating that *these* victims are chaste and ignorant, which

> ignores the sense of responsibility which leads women to migrate in search of work ... 'It hurts, but don't call me a poor thing,' one woman ... said. Victims can also be very tough who will do anything to avenge the damage done to them and make a better life for themselves. Some victims don't go to the police but start trafficking for themselves, or side with the traffickers to avoid reprisals.[94]

When someone is shanghaied and forced to work, everyone agrees that it is a crime. But 'rescue' raids by police and NGOs often fail because arrested workers refuse to denounce anyone.[95] Critics conclude that workers are afraid of reprisals, but it could be that they have nothing to denounce.[96] Nonetheless, *doubt* is always planted about the condition of the sex worker's state of mind, if not of her soul. Nickie Roberts describes working as a stripper in London's Soho in the 1960s:

> A lot of the girls were Northerners who, like me, had hitched down to London with lots of high hopes, big dreams and fuck-all else. One or two had escaped from children's homes and crazy fathers who beat or raped them. These were the ones the media and all the 'experts' call 'sick victims'. They were nothing of the sort – they were kids who had the guts to do something about their bad 'home' situation: they ran away, and found sanctuary in the sex industry. That may sound absurd, but it isn't. Those young runaways, some as young as 14, 15, were independent; they had control over their lives, whereas back where they came from they had none.[97]

None of this nuancing of deceit and coercion lessens the multiple abuses sometimes committed by those facilitating travel, whether against migrants who end up working in sex or against migrants in any other job. What needs examining is why so many people insist that this is criminal *by definition*, the crime being called 'trafficking'.

'Trafficking': A New Keyword

The enormous interest and concern for trafficking and human smuggling in governmental, inter-governmental and non-governmental organizations, in the media and popular opinion, is running ahead of theoretical understanding and factual evidence.[98]

The identification of activities called 'trafficking' began to take off in the mid-1990s, carving out new areas of research such as 'modern forms of slavery', or expanding older ones, such as transnational crime. Some activists speculate that large-scale criminal organisations are dedicated to enslaving migrants, but research does not prove this, including a study from the UN Crime Commission itself.[99] Rather, opportunist and many-branched networks develop in situations where people see travel to work as the solution to their problems.

All attempts to quantify cases of 'trafficking' are questionable. An Italian study estimated 18,000–25,000 'foreign prostitutes' in Italy through interviews with 50 women identified as 'trafficked', extrapolating to estimate 2,000 such women in Italy.[100] However, there was no consensus among sources on the definition of 'trafficking' or other terms that attempt to pin down enigmatic issues of will, consent and choice: whether people travelling with false papers 'chose' what awaited them, whether they 'really' understood their contracts, whether they felt in love with an intermediary, how their parents' participation affected their judgement or if they understood how being in debt would affect their mobility. If such epistemological questions are difficult for people secure in their homes, they are more so for those who have left home to face cultural disorientation on a grand scale and who might be best thought of as giving their 'resentful consent' to those helping them.[101]

Some projects attempting to quantify victims count all migrants who sell sex, others consider anyone who agrees to denounce a 'trafficker' according to local law, others count everyone who gives money to a boy-friend, and yet others include all illegal sex workers. Victims may be tallied only in countries of origin or only in destinations or in both; studies may include transit countries or not.[102] Attempts at quantification are made more unreliable, moreover, because most segments of the sex sector are not recognised by governments, which means there can be no proper counting of 'sex workers', as a category, either. In 1999, a European AIDS prevention project, Tampep, estimated migrants selling sex as percentages of all sex workers by country. The numbers were entirely schematic, coming from a limited number of projects that did not use the same method for counting, that did not all have the same type of contact with the industry (for example, some only met street workers, others only people using health services), that were not conducted in all languages necessary to communicate with all migrants, or that operated only in big cities.

Other complications to counting victims include irregular migrants' reluctance to give correct information, and their use of forged documents and nationalities, which means that tallies by country of origin are unreliable. Migrants who do not pay taxes may prefer to avoid being counted. Some studies count transgender workers as women and some do not, while most counts omit men. Some health projects count 'attended persons' or 'medical attentions', meaning that a person who visits a mobile unit every week, for example, could be counted 52 times a year.[103] For 2003–4, Tampep's figures describe migrant percentages of member projects' contacts with sex workers. Such countings cannot be considered definitive or dependable.

Outside the Tampep network, projects count migrants who sell sex using a range of criteria. For example, one cannot compare the statistic '23% (412) and 14% (117) of women with visas to work as dancers in Switzerland were from the Dominican Republic and Brazil' with '75% of foreign prostitutes in Germany are from Latin America and the Caribbean'.[104] Moreover, projects that refer to 'prostitutes' do not count migrants working for erotic telephone services, or as dancers, or in other sex jobs. Given the impossibility of counting not only undocumented migrants but all workers in informal economies, there can be no trustworthy numbers, so the published statistics are mostly fantasies. Even those who admit this propagate estimates obtained by entities such as the US Central Intelligence Agency:

> Because sex trafficking is so far underground, the number of victims in the United States and worldwide is not known, and the statistics

vary wildly. The most often cited numbers come from the US State Department, which estimates that 600,000 to 800,000 people are trafficked for forced labor and sex worldwide each year – and that 80 percent are women and girls. Most trafficked females, the department says, are exploited in commercial sex outlets ... 'The number will always be an estimate, because trafficking victims don't stand in line and raise their hands to be counted, but it's the best estimate we have,' said Ambassador John Miller, director of the State Department's Office to Monitor and Combat Trafficking in Persons. The CIA won't divulge its research methods, but based its figures on 1,500 sources, including law enforcement data, government data, academic research, international reports and newspaper stories.[105]

Many of the sources referred to, when investigated, are simply small local NGOs, local police and embassy officials, extrapolating from their own experience and from reports in the media. Most of the writing and activism on this issue does not seem to be based on empirical research, even when produced by academics. Many authors lean heavily on media reports and statistics published with little explanation of methodology or clarity about definitions.[106] The 'evidence' is often circular, as officials cite news reports which cite officials ... Sweeping generalisations often feature in such writing:

> [W]omen are *never* made aware of the extent to which they will be indebted, intimidated, exploited and controlled. They believe ... that they can travel to a richer country and earn large amounts of money in a short space of time, which they can then use to move themselves and their families out of poverty and despair. *In reality,* they are told they owe a huge debt which must be repaid through providing sexual services, and they are able to exercise virtually *no control at all* over their hours of work, the number of customers they serve, and the kinds of sex they have to provide.[107]

Such passages erase diverse experiences and claim reality for only the worst. The many research projects referred to in Note 60 of this chapter show that many women *do* achieve the goal of earning a large amount of money in a short time and are glad of it. The Coalition Against Trafficking in Women (CATW), an international NGO, agitates for a discursive change that would make 'prostitution' *by definition* a form of violence against women, eliminating any notion that women who sell sex can consent. CATW also proposes that the word 'prostitution' be made to mean the same thing as the word 'trafficking', so that

> all children and the majority of women in the sex trade would be considered victims of trafficking ... Unless compelled by poverty, past trauma, or substance addictions, few women will voluntarily engage in prostitution. Where the demand for prostitution is high, insufficient numbers of local women can be recruited. Therefore, brothel owners and pimps place orders with traffickers for the number of women and children they need.[108]

The movement against 'trafficking' (and 'prostitution') uses the theory of violence against women, conceived as a 'manifestation of historically unequal power relations between men and women, which have led to domination over and discrimination against women by men and to the prevention of the full advancement of women'.[109] The feminist project to reveal the routine nature of violence against women has led to widespread understanding of the insidious workings of patriarchy; the problem comes about when the roles of 'perpetrator' and 'victim' are treated as *identities* rather than temporary conditions.[110] But services that want victims to become 'survivors' sometimes reinforce passivity, particularly in therapeutic contexts, diagnosing syndromes and disorders and emphasising damage over coping.[111] Ratna Kapur explains that in the legal context

> it is invariably the abject victim subject who seeks rights, primarily because she is the one who has had the worst happen to her. The victim subject has allowed women to speak out about abuses that have remained hidden or invisible in human rights discourse.[112]

Victims become passive receptacles and mute sufferers who must be saved, and helpers become saviours, a colonialist operation warned against in discussions of western feminism's treatment of third-world women[113] and now common in discussions of migrant women who sell sex.[114]

The 'trafficking' discourse relies on the notion that poorer women are better off staying at home than leaving and possibly getting into trouble; men are routinely expected to encounter and overcome trouble, but women may be irreparably damaged by it. The lack of a coherent definition of the term 'trafficking' has inspired an avalanche of meetings, conferences and reports all over the world. In multiple sessions between 1998 and 2000, the UN Commission for the Prevention of Crime and Penal Justice listened to the arguments of two groups lobbying in different directions, especially over words describing consent (obligation, force, coercion, deceit).[115] Agreement was reached on two protocols appended to a UN Convention against Transnational Organised Crime, and entire documents of footnotes and explanations have been published to reveal the conflicts behind the final words.[116] The protocols produced two separate concepts: 'trafficking' and smuggling. The 'trafficking' protocol expresses women's presumed greater disposition (along with children) to be deceived, above all into 'prostitution', and their lesser disposition to migrate;[117] the consent of the woman victim is sidelined. The smuggling protocol positions men as capable of deciding to migrate but also of being handled like contraband, and 'prostitution' is not mentioned. The conflation of the 'trafficking' discourse with migrations to work in the sex industry has caused enormous confusion:

> Does not this trend towards 'criminalisation' of individual movements of migrants have the paradoxical consequence of promoting the development of organised trafficking in persons?[118]

Unfortunately, efforts to prevent 'trafficking' often try to prevent migration itself, and, when researchers find women and girls absent from a village, they tend to list them as 'missing persons'.[119] But despite attempts to distinguish between 'trafficking' and 'sex-work migrations',[120] public debates focus on criminal abuse, and matters are not helped by some campaigners' virulent attacks on those who don't agree with them:

> There is an international movement to legitimize, legalize and regulate prostitution, which is referred to as 'sex work' ... At every opportunity, they interpret law and policy to support this point of view ... They advocate for the acceptance and legalization of prostitution, and fail to assist victims of trafficking, even when they come in contact with them.[121]

Everyone wants to prevent abuse, so the waste of energy in such assaults is deplorable. But women who cross borders have long been viewed as deviant,[122] so perhaps the present-day panic about the sexuality of travelling women is not surprising. To migrate is to make risky decisions, and only one link in the chain needs to be weak for things to go wrong. But is that a good reason not to treat the people who act within it as real and whole?

> [A]utonomous migration means more than unauthorized ('illegal') border crossings: it means a community strategy implemented, developed, and sustained with the support of institutions, including formal ones, at the migrants' points of origin and ... points of destination. Precisely because core institutions (legal, religious, local governmental, etc) support this migratory strategy, undocumented migrants do not perceive its moral significance as deviant. Migrants may see their autonomous migration as extralegal, but not necessarily as criminal.[123]

The core institutions of many countries accept that people travel in quasi-legal if not outright illegal conditions, and embassies and consulates often grant spurious visas.[124] Furthermore, the money that migrants send home not only contributes to individual families but now represents a large proportion of many countries' Gross Domestic Product.[125] So migrants may be forgiven for paying scant attention to the bureaucratic 'illegality' that may be involved.

To grant agency to migrating individuals does not mean denying structural conditions, nor does it make them over-responsible for their fate, but it does consider their own perceptions and desires to be crucial. Moments occur during migrations when travellers must choose between doing things legally and doing them so that they might turn out well. The Colombian woman in Bangkok I mentioned in the Introduction felt guilty because she had knowingly bought fake papers. She was a victim, but she had made choices and felt responsible, and I would not want to take this ethical capacity away from her. She was caught in global forces, but she also wanted to be.

Autonomy in a Space of Flows

Manuel Castells's term a 'space of flows' attempts to represent all kinds of movements – not only human but financial and informational.[126]

According to tradition, migrants 'settle', but very many don't, either because they never mentally or physically relinquish a house, village, city or culture, or because they set themselves up to do business between the old and new country or because they find it unavoidable or impossible *not* to go back. The last by no means signifies failure of the migration project, which may end up taking the shape of repeated use of tourist visas or repeated attempts to cross borders without getting caught. Many such people come to feel they have more than one home and that they live in both of them.

The concept of flows may seem to mask inequalities that determine their direction. Some see the flow of culture as asymmetrical, stronger from centre to periphery than the other way round.[127] But we don't know *how* to measure cultural impacts deriving from the periphery and affecting the centre, which may be less concrete and visible than cultural or social. Some authors emphasise mobility's power relations, with some people initiating movement, others organising it, others receiving it and some apparently imprisoned by it.[128] The migration project is mixed up in a vast complex of circumstances, from the national and global to the most local, personal and serendipitous (a meeting in a café, the detection of a false visa). How people move, how necessary knowledge moves toward them, how they move their money, how its value moves them and how they encourage other people to make similar moves: all form part of these flows. Castells describes how the current downsizing of large corporations depends on plans to subcontract work out to individuals afterwards without offering them job security or benefits; he refers to the replacement of 'the organisation man' with 'the flexible woman'.[129] Many migrants are flexible women *par excellence*:

> I had a three-month visa, I came for tourism, to see if I could find work; I began in a restaurant, cooking, on the coast; there were many women from different countries. After the season, the restaurant closed and I began domestic work, and now I pick fruit. (Moroccan woman in Spain)[130]

> I arrived in Almería through a friend's mediation. I began to work as a domestic, I was badly paid and mistreated. Sundays I came to the edge of the sea and cried. One Sunday a Moroccan man saw me crying, I

explained my situation to him, he took me to his house. I was a virgin, he promised he was going to marry me ... he got me a residence card ... He found me work in a restaurant and let me stay in his studio, he told me I had to pay rent. I began to sleep with some clients from the restaurant ... Now, I would like to go to France, I want to get married ... My sister who lives in Bézier says she's going to find me a Frenchman, to get a residence card. (Moroccan woman in Spain)[131]

What employers call flexibility (closing up shop in one country, moving to another, relying on subcontracting or homework) often translates into oppressive conditions for workers. Flexibility can be reduced to regimes in which workers are passive objects:

Transferability, ephemerality, servitude, diffusion. Transferability: to be transferred across places or labour procedures, according to market necessities; ephemerality: to be involved with projects of short duration, fragmented, and directly consumed; servitude: to be involved with tasks that necessitate the further decentring of identity and work and to be used as an auxiliary to the main economic activity; diffusion: not to hold any attachments or loyalties that may impede the completion of the labour process.[132]

Such classifications do not recognise how workers use grassroots networking to their own advantage. As the story of the domestic worker in Almería shows, everyone becomes an opportunist, women as well as men. Everyone looks for chinks to exploit for their personal benefit: places to live, jobs, husbands. Ownership of high-technology or expensive items such as laptop computers is not necessary, as migrants use cybercafés, phonecall shops and mobile phones like anyone else. Networked social relations are everywhere.

Living in More than One Place

Since a real link is often imagined between culture and place, migrants are often envisioned as ripped up by their roots. But many studies suggest that migrants come to feel equally at home in multiple places. Research describes Dominicans who live in both Santo Domingo and New York or live 'between' them.[133] These stories are about how people move, make homes and get jobs, as well as return to other homes and jobs, in series of trips that last indefinitely, involve extended and multiple families, and often branch into migrations to other countries.

> Although having more than one household in two different countries might be a source of emotional stress and economic hardship, it also arms family members with special skills to deal with uncertainty and adversity. They become more sophisticated than nonmigrant people in dealing with a rapidly globalising world.[134]

This way of living is sometimes described as transnationalism, its protagonists people with 'dual lives', gaining their living through continuous contact across national borders.[135] I remember one day in a rural Caribbean town when everyone turned out to greet a returned migrant known to sell sex in Germany. Festooned with gold jewellery and extremely pregnant, she had arrived to give birth to and leave her child with its grandmother, as well as to sell items of clothing brought in her suitcase. The grandmother's house was, not suprisingly, the best in a town both poor and cosmopolitan.

A lively debate currently questions whether working-class migrants can be cosmopolitan or whether that term must be reserved for elite, urbane globetrotters. Some fix migrant identity in a reluctant leave-taking and wariness toward the new, seeing their lives as a series of dry, instrumental decisions.[136] Belittling treatments of migrants abound. Arjun Appadurai says Mira Nair's *India Cabaret* is about the 'tragedies of displacement' of women from Kerala who go to Bombay 'to seek their fortunes as cabaret dancers and prostitutes'. Characterising men who frequent these cabarets as migrants returned from the Middle East whose 'diasporic lives away from women distort their very sense of what the relations between men and women might be', Appadurai falls into moralistic universalising about sex and relationships.[137]

Other thinkers, and I am one, see no reason for poorer travellers to be disqualified from cosmopolitanism. Bruce Robbins argues this for the protagonists of two novels, third-world nannies in the west whose discoveries about the metropole and ability to reflect on culture are as astute as anyone's.[138] A raft of terms attempt to describe such phenomena.[139] And if working-class people can be cosmopolitan, then some who sell sex also can. In many commercial-sex sites, migrants from Brazil are found working alongside others from Russia, Thailand and Nigeria. These are workplaces where employees in erotic uniforms spend their time socialising, talking and drinking with each other and the clientele, as well as with cooks, waiters, cashiers and bouncers. The experience of spending most of their time in such ambiences, if people adapt to them at all, can help produce cosmopolitan subjects.

Anyway, at what point does a person stop being a migrant and become something else? At the beginning newcomers may feel reluctant and wary, but most do not remain in this stage for long. James Clifford's travel theory seems to have a place for ordinary working people, whether they sell or consume sex or not. Taking in popular notions like New York City as part of the Caribbean and Los Angeles and Miami as Latin American capitals, Clifford focuses on encounters between the local and the global.[140] bell hooks, noting that the concept of home is different for those who have been conquered, occupied or forced into slavery, is sceptical,[141] but I think an emphasis on flexibility and mobility, rather than identity and fixed location, allows people in low-prestige jobs to figure as something other than victims. Finally, Akhil Gupta and James Ferguson, considering today's deterritorialisation of identity, suggest that 'refugees, migrants, displaced and stateless peoples ... are perhaps the first to live out these realities in their most complete form'.[142]

These ideas take us away from the traditional focus on migrants' losses, which tends to sentimentalise 'home' with warm images of close families, simple household objects, rituals, songs and foods. Religious and national holidays reify concepts of home and family as part of a folkoric past. In this context, migration is constructed as a last-ditch or desperate move, in which migrants are *deprived* of the place they 'belong to'. Yet for millions of people all over the world, the birth and childhood place is not a feasible or desirable one in which to undertake adult or ambitious projects, and moving to another place is a conventional – not traumatic – solution.

In the sentimentalising that occurs around 'uprooting', the myriad possibilities for being miserable at home are forgotten. Many people are fleeing from small-town prejudices, dead-end jobs, dangerous streets and suffocating families. And some poorer people *like* the idea of being found beautiful or exotic abroad, exciting desire in others. Valerie Walkerdine criticises middle-class abhorrence of children's talent contests popular with the working class:

> Girls form ambitions and desires around aspects of femininity which are presented to them. In fact ... the lure of 'fame', particularly of singing and dancing, offers working-class girls the possibility of a talent from which they have not automatically been excluded by virtue of their supposed lack of intelligence or culture.[143]

The same can be said of many who end up selling sex. Whether or not they are misled or mislead themselves about the meaning of an offer to work, they have their own desires.

> I wanted to be independent. I have a big family, but I didn't get along with them. I wanted to be on my own. I saw the neighbours who are doing OK, who have money because there's someone in Italy. (Nigerian woman in Italy)[144]

> I left my job in the Ukraine because it was boring there. I wanted to go abroad and experience the world. After my experience in Italy I came to Turkey two years ago because I was looking for a chance . . . When I came to Turkey I didn't know about the opportunity to work as a sex worker. I first worked as a translator in Karakoy. (Ukrainian woman in Turkey)[145]

Many travellers and migrants believe they have the right, after enduring conquest, looting and colonisation, to 'reconquer' Europe. Consider Stuart Hall's wry account of ex-colonial citizens of the British Empire:

> [The British] had ruled the world for 300 years and, at last, when they had made up their minds to climb out of the role, at least the others ought to have stayed out there in the rim, behaved themselves, gone somewhere else, or found some other client state. But no, they had always said that this was really home, the streets were paved with gold, and bloody hell, we just came to check out whether that was so or not.[146]

Few people would deny that historical colonial relations are involved in migration, especially where migrants move to their former 'mother countries'. But Abdelmalek Sayad considers a more serious proposition, that migrations are a structural element of colonial power relationships that have never ended. His case study, the Algerian migration to France in the second half of the twentieth century, shows how the economic and social life of a rural colony was subordinated to another country's industrialism, peasants became 'workers', and immigration was turned into a social problem. With this move, the dominant member of the migration relationship firmly maintains control over knowledge and management of the 'problem', according to which immigrants are always lacking necessary skills and culture.[147]

Many argue that national borders should not exist at all:

I don't come from the sun or moon, I'm from earth just like everybody else and the earth belongs to all of us. (Kurdish migrant in Holland)[148]

In this chapter I have described concepts that for one reason or another disqualify the experiences of a large number of people travelling today. These concepts rely on opposites: work/leisure, worker/tourist, gazer/object, home/abroad, work/pleasure, legal/illegal, formal/informal, backward/modern, victim/criminal. Direct opposites rarely exist in pure forms, and the label *migrant* does not adequately describe the travels and work of millions of people. Specifically, the field of migration studies is guilty of ignoring women who sell sex and consigning them to the miserable field of 'victims of trafficking'.[149]

Despite being largely excluded from normal discourses of pleasure-seeking, work and travel, migrants who work in low-prestige jobs fit into – and prove – interesting contemporary ideas of flows, transnationalism and cosmopolitanism. To look at them in these ways, we have to grant the possibility that less empowered, or simply poorer people, are not by definition passive victims. We have to realise that there is more than one form of autonomy, the western one, which can only occur within western 'progress' and modernity. Considered as people in flux and flexible labourers, rather than people with identities attached to the jobs they carry out, these travellers become ordinary human beings working to overcome specific problems.

I want to emphasise the *quantity* of empirical studies carried out in many parts of the world, and which use reputable, ethical, social-science methodologies, on which I am able to draw information about (and direct quotations from) migrants stigmatised by sex.[150] When I began to collect these in 1998, I found fewer than ten; eight years later I am able to cite 55. Since there must be many more, the total refutes accusations that migrants who talk this way are an insignificant minority. The words of these migrants tell us not that there are no abuses or problems but that 'trafficking' is a woefully inadequate way to conceptualise them.

NOTES

1   Proyecto Libertad 1994
2   Agustín 1995, 1996b
3   Cohen 1979: 181
4   Urry 1990
5   Wolff 1985. In Chapter 4 I argue that this idea does not hold up to a class analysis, and that European city streets were also populated by women.
6   Mulvey 1975: 11
7   Alloula 1986: 14
8   Davidoff 1979
9   Frank 2002: 89
10 Pratt 1992: 192
11 Munt 1994
12 Global Perspectives 2001
13 Deleuze and Guattari 1986: 52
14 Bailey and Hane 1995
15 'UN Trends in Total Migrant Stock 2005', Migration Policy Institute 2006; Committee on Migration, Refugees and Demography conference on the situation of illegal migrants in Council of Europe member states, Paris 2001
16 Held et al 1999: 304
17 Singleton and Barbesino 1999: 20
18 See Hacking 1991; Black 2003
19 Lim and Oishi 1996: 87
20 Dean 1999: 100, after Foucault 1979b
21 Sassen 1999: 2
22 Ruggiero 1997: 234
23 Pedraza 1991: 306
24 UN Department of Economic and Social Affairs 2005
25 See Sassen 1996 and 1998; Bauman 2000
26 Rudolph 1996: 288

27   A contradiction occurs when local authorities decide to permit work by tourists, as happened in Groeningen, Holland, a few years ago, for women who sold sex.

28   Henry 1987: 139

29   What I deliberately mix together has been schematised by Enzo Mingione into seven categories: Formal, Mixed Formal/Informal, Pure Informal, Illegal, Work Not Exchanged for Income, Extraordinary Work for Self-Consumption, and Normal Domestic Work (Mingione 1985: 20).

30   O'Reilly 2000: 237

31   Sassen 1998: 155

32   Ruggiero 1997: 231-2

33   Henry 1987: 147

34   Rudolph 1996: 299

35   Sassen 1998; Pyle and Ward 2003

36   For example, Morokvasíc 1984 and 1991; Lutz, Phoenix and Yuval-Davis 1995

37   Mendoza 2001: 51

38   King and Zontini 2000: 47

39   Wolff 1993: 229

40   Agustín 2004c

41   Moch 1992

42   Stoneking 1998; Davin 2005a

43   Zlotnik 2003. Wolff's positioning of women as lacking 'access' to travel may apply better to the nineteenth-century middle class, with its new ideas about women's place in the home.

44   Sassen-Koob 1984: 1161

45   Corriere della Sera, quoted in Danna 2004: 85

46   Agustín 2001a

47   Ratliff 2004

48   Oso 2003: 30

49   Bueno 1999

50   Ratliff 2004: 42

51   Gülçür and İlkkaracan 2002: 419

52   Cuanter 1998: 93

53   Tolentino 1996: 54, on a 1985 ILO report, Women Workers in Multinational Enterprises in Developing Countries

54   Sassen 1998: 87

55   Morokvasíc 1984: 888

56   Kofman 1999: 272; also Boyd and Grieco 2003

57   Hondagneu-Sotelo 2000: 117

58   Mahler and Pessar 2006: 42; Pessar and Mahler 2003

59   Piper 2003: 25

60   Among those that confirm information on informal migrations, love and sexual relations, commercial sex and 'trafficking', through empirical research and critical analysis, are Tabet 1989; COIN 1992; ALAI 1994; Kelsky 1994; Altink 1995; Murray 1991; Skrobanek et al 1997; Law 1997; Pickup 1998; Polanía and Claasen 1998; Anarfi

1998; Bueno 1999; Kennedy and Nicotri 1999; Cabezas 1999; Campani 1999; Ratliff 1999; Brussa 2000; Casal 2001; de Paula Medeiros 2000; Carchedi et al 2000; Agustín 2001a; Mai 2001; Brennan 2001; Signorelli and Treppete 2001; Gibson et al 2001; Ruíz 2001; Gülçür and İlkkaracan 2002; Cheng 2002; Andrijasevic 2003; Corso and Trifirò 2003; Likiniano 2003; Constable 2003; Oso 2003; Emerton and Petersen 2003; Monteros 2003; Lenz 2003; Danna 2004; Oliveira 2004; Cabiria 2004; Piscitelli 2004; Riopedre 2004; Schaeffer-Graebiel 2004; Yea 2004; Rodríguez and Lahbabi 2004; Janssen 2005; Unal 2005; Ribeiro and Sacramento 2005; Kastner 2006; Lu 2005; Solana 2005; Díaz Barrero 2005; CATS 2006; Davies 2006; Vogel 2006. In addition, several articles on the 'smuggling' of migrants to particular European countries support the more specialised research listed above: Neske 2006; Bilger et al 2006; Pastore et al 2006.

61 Anderson 2000: 33
62 Oso 2000
63 Mukherjee 1988: 98–9
64 Bilger et al 2006: 64
65 Agustín 2001a
66 Bilger et al 2006: 82
67 frauenlesbenfilmkollectif 2002: 1
68 Massey et al 1993: 450
69 Roberts 1992
70 These cases are mentioned in Jaget 1975, Guy 1991 and Kelsky 1994.
71 See list in Note 60.
72 Richards 2004: 155.
73 Pastore et al 2006: 98
74 Oso 2003: 34
75 Anderson 2000: 29
76 frauenlesbenfilmkollectif 2002: 2
77 Oso 2003: 32
78 Gilbert and Koser 2006
79 Kennedy and Nicotri 1999: 36
80 Oso 2000
81 Pheterson 1996: 18
82 Bogdanova quoted in Pickup 1998:1000
83 Herman 2006: 212
84 Lazaridis 2001: 85
85 Negre i Rigol 1988. See also Pastore et al 2006.
86 Bonelli et al 2001: 81
87 Bueno 1999: 380
88 Bonelli et al 2001: 81
89 Agustín 2001a
90 Oso 2000
91 Oso 2000
92 Riopedre 2004: 25

93   See note 60.

94   Altink 1995: 2

95   For example, Dirección General de la Policía de Córdoba 1999

96   In the worst situations, sex workers denounce rescuers; see, for example, Ashok 2002, Empower Chiang Mai 2003 and Thomas 2006.

97   Roberts 1986: 57

98   Salt 2000: 32; years later this is still true.

99   Bilger, Hofmann and Jandl 2006; Neske 2006; Pastore et al 2006; CICP 2003

100   Carchedi et al 2000

101   Comment by Jacqueline Bhabha, 3 October 2004 at the Gendered Borders conference, Amsterdam.

102   Kangaspunta 2003

103   Tampep's statistics on the percentage of migrants among sex worker populations were estimated in 1999 at: 90% in Italy, 25% in Sweden and Norway, 85% in Austria, 62% in the north of Germany and 32% in the south, 68% in Holland and 45% in Belgium. The Spanish figure, 50%, covers only street prostitution in Madrid (Tampep 1999). Since 1997, when the previous study of this kind was done, the percentage of migrants in the sex industry increased in all European countries.

104   The first comes from the International Office on Migrations and the second from AGISRA (Arbeitsgemeinschaft Gegen Internationale Sexuelle und Rassistische Ausbeutung), both quoted in Azize-Vargas et al 1996.

105   May, *San Francisco Chronicle*, 6 October 2006

106   For example, Johnson 1999

107   Kelly and Regan 2000: 5, *my emphasis*

108   Hughes 2002

109   Declaration on the Elimination of Violence against Women, United Nations General Assembly Resolution 48/104: 20 December 1993

110   Agustín 2003a

111   Kelly, Burton and Regan 1996

112   Kapur 2002: 5

113   See, for example, Mani 1990; Kapur 2002: 6 and Pupavac 2002. In the last, social agents trying to help refugees from Kosovo defined them as not resilient, 'dysfunctional' and incapable of recovery, rendering them politically illegitimate.

114   Goodey more reasonably advocates a 'victim-centred' policy on 'trafficking' without falling into essentialising migrants as victims (2004: 40).

115   Ditmore 2002

116   CATW 2003; IHRLG 2002

117   Cynthia Enloe characterises the situating of women with children as 'womenand-children', a concept suiting the propagandistic ends of patriarchy (1991).

118   Marie 1994: 19. For other critiques, see Irwin 1996; Doezema 2000; Campani 2001; Pickup 1998; Kapur 2005.

119   Kapur 2005: 118

120   Alexander 1996; Carchedi et al 2000; Skrobanek 2000; Mai 2001; Agustín 2002b, 2003b, 2003c

121 Hughes 2002

122 Stallybrass and White 1986; Ong and Peletz 1995: 6

123 Rodríguez 1996: 23

124 Ruggiero 1997 discusses the difficulty of distinguishing between services provided by officials and criminals.

125 Stalker 2006; Acosta 2002

126 Castells 1997

127 Hannerz 1996: 60

128 Massey 1994: 149

129 Castells 1997: 10

130 Rodríguez and Lahbabi 2004

131 Rodríguez and Lahbabi 2002: 217

132 Psimmenos 2000: 84

133 *Between Two Islands*, Grasmuck and Pessar 1991; and *One Country in Two*, Guarnizo 1992; see also Georges 1990

134 Guarnizo 1994:77

135 Portes et al 1999: 217-8; see also Smith and Guarnizo 1998; Kapur calls people who cross borders and occupy an inferior status 'transnational migrant subjects' (2005: 109).

136 Hannerz 1990: 243

137 Appadurai 1996: 38-9

138 Robbins 1994; Kincaid 1990; Mukherjee 1988

139 Werbner 2006

140 Clifford 1997: 24

141 hooks 1992

142 Gupta and Ferguson 1992: 9

143 Walkerdine 1997: 50

144 Danna 2004: 84

145 Gülçür and İlkkaracan 2002: 415

146 Hall 1989: 24

147 Sayad 2004

148 Herman 2006: 214

149 Agustín 2006

150 See list in note 60.

3

A WORLD OF SERVICES

In employment market terms, European demand is strong for migrant women in three areas: cleaning, cooking and housekeeping inside private houses; caring for sick, disabled, elderly and young people inside private houses; and providing sex in a wide variety of locales.[1] The great majority of these jobs, casually referred to as *services*, are not regulated or formalised, in part because of the enduring exclusion of traditional female labour from definitions of economic productivity. In cultures where one's waged occupation is considered crucial to one's identity, there is scarcely a lower-prestige job than 'maid', yet cleaning and caring are said to be 'dignified' work (in comparison to selling sex). The result of these contradictions is rampant exploitation for employees. How can one understand societies that first encourage the migration and employment of people to do particular jobs and then refuse to recognise or value them? Though all migrants are affected by these contradictions, those employed in the sex industry – widely assumed to make up half of the whole – are most consistently ignored.

Undefined Sectors, Undefinable Jobs

Service jobs in what economists call the formal sector are varied, one government website listing beautician, cashier, embalmer, florist, hairdresser, nail technician, newsagent, pharmacy assistant, salesperson, service station attendant, ticket writer. In all these, one person pays another to help get what the consumer needs. Some relationships are dry; others involve emotions or physical contact. Service jobs *not* formally recognised and counted by governments are not included in such lists: these are the ones available to migrants.

Behind this incoherency lie distinctions between the perceived usefulness and agency of persons, and the 'productive' or 'unproductive' nature of their labour. In ancient Athens, men who maintained households were granted the status of citizen, while women and slaves who performed household work were not. In the eighteenth century, the Physiocrats deemed only agriculture to be economically productive; later, Adam Smith called services unproductive because they do not contribute to the accumulation of physical wealth. John Stuart Mill began to argue that some services do contribute to economic growth, but analysts then shifted their attention to another pair of concepts, market versus nonmarket labour, disqualifying unpaid work. By the twentieth century, economists agreed that all *paid* services are productive, leaving housewives to languish as unproductive, 'unoccupied' and 'dependent',[2] a 'prejudice bred by Western capitalism and its interest in industrial labor markets'.[3]

Economic philosophising and political ideologies translate into government policies, census-taking and calculations of growth. In the late nineteenth century there were British proposals to include housework in government accounting in order to present a picture of Britain 'as a community of workers and a strong nation', while Australia divided its population into 'breadwinners and dependents ... to provide an image of a country where everyone did not need to work, and thus to appear to be a good place for British investment'.[4] But what do the jobs actually have in common, and what makes them come to be considered work?

> If [another] person could be paid to do the unpaid activity of a household member, then it is 'work'; so clearly cooking, child care, laundry, cleaning and gardening are all work, as a household servant could be hired to perform these activities. On the other hand, it would not be sensible to hire someone to watch a movie, play tennis, read a book, or eat a meal for you, as the benefits of the activity would accrue to the servant, the third person, not the hirer.[5]

Some call housework reproductive labour, because it replicates social life by maintaining families and the houses they live in. But this brings up questions of what is 'necessary' to human life.

> Nobody has to have stripped pine floorboards, handwash-only silk shirts, ornaments that gather dust. All these things create domestic work, but they also affirm the status of the household, its class, its access to resources of finance and personnel, and the adequacy of its manager, almost invariably a woman.[6]

> Employers here have a disease, it's a disease of cleanliness ... There are employers that look for something to clean even when the house is already clean. (Filipina in Italy)[7]

Necessity is a subjective term, and some tasks may have a priceless symbolic value to employers. Consider the sales pitch of an employment agent who offers domestic servants on the market:

> Imagine coming home at the end of a workday, and all the stress is off. The kids are happy, the laundry is washed and folded, you can smell the chicken cooking in the oven. The girls don't want to stick around with you and your husband at the end of their work day, so you have all the time alone you want ... they leave to their room and you are home with your kids. It gives you peace of mind and it gives you your equilibrium.[8]

This vision conveniently ignores the unjust issues inherent in the idea of adult employees 'going to their room'. Employers widely expect maids to be available continuously, even when they are in their bedrooms. With timetables rarely fixed, many maids work twelve-to-eighteen-hour days; to be free of demands, they have to leave the house, but many are given only Sunday off. Domestic servants are routinely expected to carry out a seemingly unlimited range of tasks — walking dogs, helping at neighbours' parties — that many people consider excessive. This amorphous, never-ending labour is excluded when governments assess productivity; even housewives are omitted from counts of both employed and unemployed.[9] In 1997, the Office of National Statistics published estimates about unpaid work in Britain, finding that

> If a monetary value were put on such work, at 1995 values it would have been at least equivalent to £341 billion, or more than the whole

UK manufacturing sector, and perhaps as much as £739 billion, 120% of gross domestic product ... Yet ... the dominant public and social-scientific understanding of 'work' remains paid work. Since the ONS figures confirmed that women do much more unpaid work than men, and that although men do more paid work, they also have more leisure, men's work is more acknowledged, as well as more highly rewarded, than women's work.[10]

The performance of housework ensures that the labour force is cared for and also contributes to the economy through the consumption of vast amounts of manufactured products,[11] so the non-recognition of house-keepers is blatantly illogical.

Caring labour cannot ultimately be separated from other kinds of housework, usually referring to personally helping people live their daily lives in their own homes – meals, exercise, health, cleanliness and sleep (sex is never mentioned). The increase in paid caring jobs happens as 'the personal and emotional content of home life is becoming more and more concentrated in a relatively small number of activities, such as sharing meals or telling bedtime stories, for which substitutes cannot be purchased.'[12]

Definitions of caring vary, some saying it requires face-to-face inter-action, or that the person in need must be incapable of taking care of him- or herself.[13] Some distinguish between care of the body and care of the mind,[14] or between moral, emotional and material care.[15] There are employers who stipulate that people working in their houses must be 'affectionate, like old people or be good with children'.[16] The whole area is fraught with subjective and cultural norms. Consider how, in the present-day west, washing and dressing are assumed to be tasks people do for themselves, when they could be delegated to servants. On the other hand, westerners routinely pay others to cut and fix their hair, when they could do it themselves. Are these activities work, needs or leisure pursuits?[17] For many of those employed as carers, employers' expecta-tions of emotional labour are excessive.

> I'm telling you, on top of what they are paying you for, the physical work, there is also psychological work ... Sometimes, when they say to me for example, that I should give her lots of love, I feel like saying, well, for my family I give love free, and I'm not discriminating, but if it's a job you'll have to pay me. (Dominican woman in Spain)[18]

And why should women, particularly, fulfil these roles? A man presenting himself as a candidate for live-in work nowadays seems like an anomaly, although boarding a Filipino couple remains an elite status symbol and men were once commonly employed as domestics. Psycho-analytic feminism, the sociology of emotions and the ethics of care all argue that differing treatments of boy and girl children result in differing capacities for intimacy, but are women *innately* better at caring?[19] Certainly societies widely believe that they are, across cultures: women are thought to 'know how' to care. One theory suggests that to develop an ethic of care 'people must experience caring for and being cared for by others; women do and men don't, with the result that men are morally deprived'.[20] The painful contradiction here is that those considered morally superior are expected to work in a feudal, exploitative employ-ment sector. Productivity is positioned as masculine; reproductivity and nonproductivity as feminine.[21]

Arlie Hochschild considers one moral consequence of the employ-ment of migrant women as carers:

> Are first-world countries importing maternal love as they have imported copper, zinc and gold from third-world countries in the past? Love is not simply a 'resource' that can be taken from one person and given to another, but nor is it entirely unlike a resource. Is time spent with the first-world child 'taken from' a child further down the care chain? Is the Beverly Hills toddler getting 'surplus' love just as the mine owner gets surplus value from the worker digging for gold?[22]

Many migrant domestic workers describe the pain of leaving children behind, but some start new families abroad, some hire women at home to take care of children left behind, and some find that sending money to support families back home compensates for feelings of guilt, inade-quacy or rage at being separated from them.[23]

Introducing Sex into the Equation

Economic growth is judged on very partial statistics, deriving (in a UK example) from 'tax returns, VAT records, payroll data and company records'. Cash transactions not reported to tax and customs entities were excluded in the UK sample but were valued at £700 million for stolen goods, £800 million for gambling, £9.9 billion for drug dealing and £1.2 billion for 'prostitution'.[24] Which sex businesses were included in the last category is not known.

Most commentators view carers and domestics in the same light, and a few include people who sell sex,[25] but many refuse strenuously on the grounds that selling sex can never be work. These arguments begin with a presumption as to what sex is supposed to be: the expression of love for a particular partner.[26]

> It certainly signifies the nadir of human dignity if a woman surrenders her most intimate and most personal quality, which should be offered only on the basis of a genuine personal impulse and also only with equal personal devotion on the part of the male . . . [27]

> Sexual services, that is to say, sex and sexuality, are constitutive of the body . . . sexuality and the body are, further, integrally connected to conceptions of femininity and masculinity, and all these are constitutive of our individuality, our sense of self-identity.[28]

> 'Prostitution is disgusting because what you're doing is so intimate. It's different . . . it just is.'[29]

For these critics, sexuality and the body are at the core of individuality, a given, needing no explanation. Karl Marx believed that 'prostitution' was only the specific expression of the wage-labourer's general condition in capitalism, and Friedrich Engels found that 'prostitution' and marriage were the same except that the one involves 'piecework' and the other permanent slavery.[30]

Debates usually exclude the arguments of buyers of sex, some of whom are precisely *not* looking for the kind of intimacy assumed most desirable and valuable.

> This is good value. It's neat and tidy. You walk out the door and you're free. Physically, emotionally, in every way.[31]

> I've got three children of my own and grandchildren, and I spend a lot of time with them and enjoy it. I'm just not interested in any sort of permanent or even semi-permanent arrangement.[32]

In order to get a woman to have free sex with you, you have to find someone who is attracted to you and wants to have sex with you. For most of us, this takes a lot of work. If you go after a one night stand, then you're having sex with a stranger, just as you would with an escort . . . If you want to keep fucking her, then you're going to have to develop some kind of relationship with her. If you start a relationship, you run into one of the biggest problems with free sex: you both have to want it at the same time. You can't just get it when you want it.[33]

These subtleties rarely surface in the battle over how to define 'prostitution', a key field in the development of different kinds of feminism. In just the past twenty years, hundreds of academic and other research articles and books have centred on a single issue: whether selling sex can ever be acceptable, a job freely chosen, or must be conceived as violence and exploitation. Most publications can be read in terms of 'anti' and 'pro' stances. A number of recent works deliberately eschew a simplistic stance, but the nature of this conflict means that a stance seen as nonmoralistic by one side is demonised as immoral by the other side.[34]

Research is often used as a weapon against those whose ideology differs, as researchers insist that their local results can be generalised to enormously diverse contexts. Research done on a small scale but in different countries may be titled 'prostitution in four countries', or five, or nine. Research done with people who do not consider themselves victims, any argument that an individual may prefer to sell sex, and any absence of moral indignation are all interpreted as 'promoting' the sex industry. Methodologies are frequently not described, including ethical questions such as how interviewers got to talk to people who sell sex, and many researchers do not appear to realise how stigmatised individuals may react to being questioned. The prestige of sponsoring institutions is used to assert the definitive 'truth' of research. These problems are endemic to social research in this field.[35]

Traditional analyses of 'prostitution' also do not address the involvement of large numbers of migrants without civil rights in the place where they are working, which substantially complicates ideological discussions.

Beyond Ideology

Debates assume that an object of study exists. To perpetuate the 'prostitution' debate, participants must ignore a wide variety of activities constituting the sex industry, which occur in different cultural, economic, geographic and social contexts. Services include manual, oral and penetrative stimulation of genitals, anus and other body parts; massage; erotic conversation in person, by telephone or via the Internet; dance on stages, tables, between viewers' legs, watched on websites or in 'peep shows' (and variously called striptease, lapdancing, poledancing, tabledancing, exotic dance); bondage and domination that may include spanking, whipping, crossdressing and other fetishes (with clients either dominant or submissive); sexual healing and therapy; attentive company at dinners and events; nude services like table waiting and telegram delivery; and acting in sexual cinema and videos. The industry also includes the sale of sex toys, clothes and gear, erotic literature, videos and DVDs.

Despite some commentators' confidence that normality and abnormality can be defined, it is impossible to draw a line between all the above-mentioned commercial services and those that provide spaces for partner swapping, swinging and polyamoury, or those devoted to health and well-being, where sex may be opportunistically sold. Moreover, the sale of sex aids has a long history (virility potions, aphrodisiacs, contraceptive devices) even before the modern medical industry began to define dysfunctions and to prescribe therapies that may involve paid surrogate sexual partners.[36]

Queer theory questions the idea that one kind of sex or sexuality is more natural than others. Those who oppose 'prostitution' believe that a good, healthy, full sexual relationship must proceed along a prescribed route and that financial payment ruins everything, making true intimacy out of the question.[37] Research on sexual desire shows, however, that

> For some people, it is important that sex be embedded in contexts resonant with meaning, narrative, and connectedness with other aspects of their life; for other people, it is important that they not be; to others, it doesn't occur that they might be.[38]

Many commentators believe that diverse services encouraging 'the

fantasy of sensuous reciprocity' are replacing traditional street 'prostitution'.[39] Such a change can be called the commercialisation or commodification of intimacy and posed as wholly negative, or it can be
viewed as more normal.

> The retailing of intimacy is a common feature of modern life and of
> other paid work like therapy and massage ... [where] equality and
> reciprocity are not usually features of the professional relationship.[40]

> The variable among [the] 'listening occupations' is the degree to
> which a client may assume that the service provider is genuinely
> concerned about the client or the intimate revelations the client has
> unilaterally offered ... the psychotherapist – explicitly seen as a
> 'caregiver' – is assumed to care the most while the barber, bartender,
> and nonsexual masseuse are expected to care the least; expectations
> about the call girl's caring probably lie in the middle ground.[41]

This normalising logic offends those who deplore all sexual acts that are
paid for. The two perceptions – that sex is *in*comparable to anything else
and that it *is* comparable – are so fundamental and so opposed that alone
they explain why the traditional debate has lasted so long.

But those who sell sex themselves reveal that their jobs are far from
being 'just sex':

> I only went upstairs with three or four, I couldn't do more, it was hard
> for me, not like for other women who did ten ... The truth is I worked
> more with drinks, because I like talking with people and there a lot of
> people go to talk with you ... you become a bit of a psychologist for
> them. For me it worked well to talk with people, I like that a lot.[42]

> When we go out and eat, the customer tries to pretend he's a man of
> the world ... They try to make interesting conversation ... but they
> can't manage, they're incredibly boring. My role is to cast a glow over
> them, so the older men look like they're out with an attractive
> woman, who looks expensive.[43]

> When you're *simpático*, it's not because you want to be, it's to earn
> money. There's always a lie. You have to maintain the lie, maintain the
> illusion ... It's like a game of cat and mouse. You have to provoke
> illusions.[44]

What I try to do is get the client to invite me to his table, get into conversation in order to make friends and so he doesn't feel he is paying and I don't feel he is paying me. I have regular clients who are rich who buy me champagne that costs €250 or €300 a bottle. You try to make it last ... and then you don't have to be with so many people.[45]

Men who sell to women also sell more than sex:

The street guides present themselves as friends, as someone who wants to help. As street guides told me over and over again, their foremost aim is to make tourists *senang* – happy. If the tourist is happy, then he or she is in the mood of spending.[46]

As do men who sell to men:

Yes, of course, I give a boy money or buy him clothes or something like that. But that doesn't mean he's a prostitute ... There is just no affection like there is in Prague, where the boy really wants to be with you and where you can have much more than just a one-night stand.[47]

Sex-service discourse is not so different from discourses on housework and caring, all trying to define tasks that can be bought and sold *as well as* assert a special human touch. Paid activities may include the production of feelings of intimacy and reciprocity, whether the individuals involved intend them or not, and despite the fact that overall structures are patriarchal and unjust.

The ability to maintain emotional distance is an aspect of the work that some workers master and some do not.[48] Hochschild explains the concept of emotional labour in her study of flight attendants, arguing that their ability to handle the job is determined by 'control over the conditions and terms of the exploitation of [their] emotional resources'.[49] Sex workers often perform their own sexual arousal and orgasms for clients who feel more excited and gratified if they believe that workers are;[50] they also act out flirting, counselling and diplomacy.[51] But there is no reason to limit such faking to those selling sex: babysitters and carers of grannies may also pretend to care, by smiling on demand, listening to boring stories, or doling out caresses without feeling affection.

These kinds of practices can be viewed as conventional professional efforts to control the job, reduce risk, guard against annoyance, and maximise profits, all 'considered admirable demonstrations of sound work ethic in any other regular profession' but read as 'signs of greed and laziness' when associated with sex.[52] Research on the management of sex businesses also reveals conventional practices.[53]

Perceptions of service are subjective, too. How can we define 'good sex' or pleasure? Clients are not satisfied by orgasms alone. What makes them feel fulfilled? How are sensuality, lust, sexual acceptance and caring performed? The success of every commercial sex interaction is open to individual judgements, and few clients limit definitions of satisfaction to the purely physical.[54] Moreover, not only buyers but at least some vendors want to feel satisfied by their work, as do some shoeshine boys and street sweepers, likewise tasks viewed as low-skill and low-prestige. Some find selling sex more enjoyable than other jobs:

> I know I should get out of this business, but I don't know if I would like any other job as much. In the bar, I spend my time dancing, drinking and talking.[55]

> The stuff I did in minimum wage service industry work – this is where I can draw the most comparisons, and this is where I can see why sex work is so much more preferable. The things I like least about clients you can see in bosses who don't respect you in the service sector. At least in sex work, you're there for only an hour and you're being paid as much as you'd make in a week at McDonalds.[56]

> For me, this is not really work, like in a factory or store. I like living here in Makati and working in the bar ... sometimes the customer will take me to a nice restaurant or disco; I also go on vacation with customers sometimes ... and we stay in nice hotels.[57]

> I work in a bar and actually it's not really sex work. Partly it is, partly it isn't ... because you only get with a man if you want to, if not then not. There in the bar you are mainly paid for talking to the men and drinking with them.[58]

> I can satisfy my [sexual] need at work! Earning money and earning pleasure at the same time. Ha ha ha![59]

Although much discourse treats those who sell sex as damaged, drugged or incapable of handling emotional relationships, the flexible schedules and independence of the work are attractive to and empower many.

One day I met a friend of mine while I was walking in the town centre
... I learned that she was a prostitute so her children could live in a
decent way. This work has the advantage of financial ease and freedom
to work schedules that allow spending more time with the children.
(French woman of Algerian parents in France)[60]

At the beginning he was giving me a lot of money but later on he
started to perceive me as his living partner ... His family and his
friends know me and accept me but I don't want to marry him
although I love him. I'm afraid that if I marry him our love will dis-
appear, he won't value me any more, he will try to restrict my
freedom. So I started to go into the suitcase industry and also to work
as a sex worker. (Kazakh woman in Turkey)[61]

In a way, you can't say you like it a hundred per cent, but you can't say
you don't like it, either. Because it's interesting. Also you meet a lot of
people. Whether you like it or not, [clients] are ... of all kinds.
(migrant in Murcia, Spain)[62]

For many, it is obvious that selling sex is a job – not like any other, but
still, a feasible occupation.

About the sex itself, many say they don't feel anything when they are
with clients, while others feel disgust, fear, loneliness, sadness, or a
sense of sin.

We go to mass at least once a week. But we can't take communion
because we do this work. We can't because we are committing
adultery; because we do it with married men.[63]

But people also mention feeling disgust and sadness in their jobs
cleaning bathrooms or bodies, and they experience emotional dangers
when living in houses and taking care of children not their own. At the
same time, there are those who enjoy the sex in sex work at least some of
the time. Finally, there are emotional pitfalls for those who buy services,
as well: clients fall in love with professionals, whether sex workers or
carers.

Once we replace the concept 'prostitution' with *commercial sex*,
debates about whether 'it' can ever be a job seem irrelevant. As for
whether these activities are services or not: if they are not, what are
they? To give them *no* name means erasing them and all the people doing

them, whether to survive, get ahead, become wealthy or support other people, as well as eliminating all the nonsexual support and management services implicated in the industry. In the end, it is *only* possible to isolate sexual services from other services if sexual communication and touching are accepted as utterly different from all other contact. This isolation also requires us to accept that the *only* thing that happens in a sexual service is 'sex', reducing the relationship to physical contact between specific points of the body and pretending that nothing else happens. And this is patently not true.

The Sex Industry

The term *sex industry* attempts to convey the large scale of sex markets in general, their capacity to generate income, their interrelationships with other large industries and infrastructures and also the diversity of the businesses involved. Growth follows conventional patterns of diversification and proliferation under contemporary globalised capitalism. Incomes cannot be known where businesses are not regulated or included in government accounting. In Europe, Holland and Germany regulate some operations, but others remain outside the system. Governments may recognise businesses on the basis of their providing other, nonsexual products and activities, such as alcohol. The sex industry is estimated to generate enormous sums; in Germany alone €5 billion a year.[64]

The International Labour Organisation (ILO), in its report *The Sex Sector,* published statistics on Thailand indicating that, of a total of 104,262 employees in 7,759 establishments where sexual services could be bought, 64,886 people sold sex while 39,376 were support personnel, owners, managers, intermediaries and 'procurers'. This means that more than one third of the employees did not sell sex but gained their livelihood from the industry.[65] Supporting employees include parking attendants, waiters, guards, drivers, cashiers, cleaners, cooks, barmen and laundry workers.

However, a host of other people participate: investors in property, entertainment and tourism; business owners and entrepreneurs; lawyers; accountants; airlines, limousine and taxi services; telecommunications businesses (land and mobile telephones, lines and equipment, phonecall shops, phonecards). Internet services are essential for virtual sex, peeping, escort services, freelance workers, the rental and sale of explicit sexual materials, catalogues of possible girlfriends and wives as well as clients' information exchanges. Newspapers and others that publish announcements and advertisements make the crucial link between consumers and those offering sex for sale. Businesses that manage money are central (bank and commercial electronic transfers, money orders). Many kinds of vendor specialise in selling costumes, makeup, hair products and wigs, drinks, food, cigarettes and condoms at sex venues, and behind these are specialist manufacturers.

The industry can also be viewed as an array of sites: brothels, bars, clubs, discotheques, cabarets, sex shops, peep shows, massage parlours, saunas, hotels, fetish clubs, flats, barber shops, beauty salons, restaurants, karaoke bars, dungeons, bachelor and hen parties and, in fact, anywhere that occurs to anyone, including boats, airplanes, automobiles, parks and the street. In many activities, consumer and vendor are located in different places, interacting via online cameras, chat or videos or via telephones. In the case of magazines and films, time as well as space separates the moment of sexual production and the moment of consumption.

Theoretically, there are many ways the industry might be measured: the number of consumers of services, the number of services consumed, the incomes of owners of businesses, the number of employees of all kinds, business profits, tax payments, prices charged for products and services. Such measurements require that businesses be included in government accounting procedures, meaning that conventional data become available for them. Data on Malaysia, for example, relate the location of the worker (freelance, with 'pimps', in brothels, at home and so on) with hourly rates and averages and weekly transactions and averages.[66]

Although different countries offer local forms or traditions, businesses have more in common across borders than not, as the following four settings from Spain illustrate:

- Lavish, multi-storeyed clubs paved in marble and offering videos, live shows and jacuzzis, sites of conspicuous consumption where customers pay as much as ten times the ordinary price for drinks. Long-distance truck drivers mix with businessmen, young men in groups, lovelorn bachelors and widowers amidst a kaleidoscope of workers representing many nationalities and languages. Customers may spend hours drinking, talking and watching without purchasing any sex at all, and if they do, it typically occupies no more than 15–20 minutes. Workers pay daily rates to live and work for three-week periods. €5,000 a month is a conventional income.

- Whereas many clubs specialise in ostentation and publicity, private flats offer discretion, in respectable-looking buildings and neighbour-hoods. Clients ring up to make an appointment, managers arrange for clients not to run into each other, and interiors appear ordinary, with floral-patterned spreads and stuffed animals on the beds, crucifixes and images of saints on the walls and the aroma of home cooking wafting from the kitchen. These businesses rely on classified advertisements and mobile telephones, the two elements that also explain the boom in independent workers who run businesses from home.

- Near the vast plantations where Europe's vegetables and fruits are grown under plastic, two kinds of sex venues coexist. The first is of luxurious bars with private cubicles located directly across from the plantations, where clients are from the managerial class and sex workers come from Eastern Europe and the former Soviet Union. The second consists of poor rental housing located up inconvenient or nonexistent roads, where customers are undocumented migrants from northern and western Africa and sex workers are Nigerian women offering a domestic ambiance.

- Businesses along highly developed tourist coasts display the effects of expatriate cultures and hybridity. Brochures on commercial sex include sections for Gay Bars, Swapping, Private Establishments, Contacts and Sex Shops. A plethora of clubs, bars, party rooms and flats advertise, mentioning as specialities piano bars, saunas, jacuzzis,

Turkish baths, dark rooms, go-go shows, striptease, escort services, bilingual 'misses', private bars, dance floors, a variety of massages, private booths 'with 96 video channels', gifts for stag and hen parties, latex wear and aphrodisiacs. [67]

Equivalents of such locales exist everywhere, varying according to local norms and legal contexts. Some of these businesses may demonstrate 'McDonaldisation', in which efficiency, rapidity and standardisation are primary.[68] Others are more customised, traditional or even *pre*modern. Working conditions vary enormously: giving a blowjob inside a car, or in an alley in the rain, is not the same as doing it as part of a shift inside a comfortable club. People also perceive jobs in different ways: some find working in a brothel less alienating and isolating (than working from home or being a live-in domestic); others prefer working from the street because they feel more independent. Every job is easy for some people and impossibly difficult for others. Many work only part-time or occasionally. As in every sector, workers feel confident and in command of their work when they have more experience. Generalisations about 'sex work' and 'prostitution' can only mislead.

At the heart of many jobs are social relationships with a physical or sexual element. 'Sex acts' are sometimes imagined to be executed by everyone in more or less the same way, and sometimes they are divided into 'natural' and 'unnatural'. But those who sell sex discover the multiplicity of human desires, tastes and preferences, as well as the variability of ideas about naturalness. Vendors learn how to perform sexual and emotional acts in order to satisfy customers, as well as how to manoeuvre and manipulate so as to receive the greatest amount of money for the least amount of work. Since workers are also individuals with tastes and values, when possible they seek out work sites where they can at least tolerate the acts required of them.

Many critics who consider exploitation and violence to be inherent in the sale of sex point to the figure of the 'pimp', traditionally a man who closely controls the movements of street workers, taking their money and threatening them physically in exchange for protection services. Although this classic figure does exist in some times and places, he is unknown to most workers, while other kinds of intermediaries may be conventional (and are often women). Workers who give money to friends or lovers, whether they provide protection or not, widely repudiate the term 'pimp', asking how their relationships differ from others in which one partner gives money to the other.[69] Of course, some of these relationships would be called dysfunctional or abusive by some psychologists, but so would many ordinary marriage relationships. 'Pimps' are imagined to be inherent to street work, but coercive inter- mediaries can be found throughout the sex industry – inevitably, given the lack of regulation of businesses. With the growing presence of migrant workers in Europe, the figure of the 'trafficker' has come to replace the 'pimp', with similar suppositions made about relationships between migrants and those who facilitate their employment. Certainly there is evidence that some people force migrants to work and take their money, but the 'trafficker' label tends to be pinned on an array of intermediaries who form part of migrants' own networks.

'Different' Identities: Gender, Age, Ethnicity

Not only women sell sex. Activists who condemn 'prostitution' as patri- archal violence focus on women (and children) and usually imply that men who sell sex are intrinsically different and few in number. Certainly, the stereotypes concern women, and women are those overtly stigma- tised and targeted for rescue. However, male workers abound; researchers and outreach workers estimate they exceed women in some places and times; and men have been called *more* stigmatised because their presence is not even acknowledged.[70] Those seeking women in 'prostitute' uniform in the streets walk straight past soliciting men without seeing them. Transsexual, transgender, transvestite and intergender people are also abundant in the industry, the most well-known being those labelled men at birth and who are changing to, or express, a more feminised state. Some of these identify as women and some as transsexuals; some have had their genitals modified through surgery; others maintain their genitals while modifying the rest of their appearance. In the sex industry, gender issues are extremely complex and subtle.

Outside commentators may be misled by notions of 'sexual orienta- tion'. In non-commercial relations, people seek partners to fulfil their own desires, but in commercial relations, they may offer services to anyone. Labelling causes more confusion than enlightenment, as when men who sell sex are called by ambiguous terms like 'male prostitutes' or 'masculine transsexuals'. Women who sell to men may identify as lesbians in their private life; men who sell to men may identify as heterosexuals; female-appearing unoperated transgenders may identify as homosexuals; transvestites may identify as hetero-sexuals and so on. Outsiders who insist on imposing set categories forget that there is gender identity, but also gender play and experimentation.

According to the UN Convention on the Rights of the Child (1989), any person under eighteen years of age who works is engaged in 'child labour', which is prohibited. The ILO, finding it difficult to advocate total elimination of child labour in the face of economic and cultural realities around the world, focuses on what it calls the worst forms of child labour, one of which is selling sex. Many activists in this cause prefer to speak of the 'sexual exploitation of children'.[71] Philippe Ariès describes the development of the west's current construction of child-hood as a long, innocent period needing protection,[72] but this development did not happen everywhere in the world. When advocates attempt to impose this notion on other cultures, they may come into conflict both with societies that distinguish between pre- and post-pubescent youth, allowing the latter to have sex, wed and assume responsibilities, and with societies that routinely put all able children to work. Europeans who decry the presence of young-looking migrants selling sex, who at sixteen or seventeen may be considered adults in their *own* home cultures, say that they cannot have consented to what they are doing (even if they say they have).

Those who attempt to speak up for the rights of children and adoles-cents in this matter tend to be stridently condemned, and for this reason nearly everyone states at the beginning of any discussion that they oppose children selling sex. Nevertheless, things get complicated when children speak about their own activities and desires. Heather Mont-gomery points out that forcing children to accept that they are 'prostitutes' (or 'exploited' or 'abused' sexually) denies 'the skillful way that they use what very small amount of control that they have'.[73]

There are no colour or ethnicity barriers *per se* to getting any sex industry jobs, and people who have travelled from small towns on other continents can be found working in sophisticated venues. To arrive there, they need the right contacts and skills. Monthly incomes like €5,000 allow migrants to repay debts quickly, and while not everyone makes so much, everyone knows someone who does. Money and ethnicity – or simply a foreign appearance – are intertwined in different ways according to local conditions. A report in the *Economist* revealed:

- A Latvian woman who worked in Riga in the bar of a luxury hotel for US$200 per service, for an average of US$5,000 a month.

- 'Gypsies' or Ukrainians who worked with truck drivers on the highway between Prague and Berlin for US$10 a service.

- A London call girl who specialised in investment bankers for £1,000 a night.

- Dozens of workers who charged DM50 (€25) per service in an *eros centre* in Kiel, Germany.

- Women native to the Gulf States who could earn US$2,000 per service with 'aristocratic' Arabs. Europeans charged less; Thai and Philippine women even less. Given the preference, there were Moroccans learning the local Gulf dialect in order to try to 'pass' for natives, while Russian women with 'Middle Eastern' features were studying Arabic.[74]

This list illustrates how the values assigned to human types are not fixed but change according to context (which may stimulate migrations). Where the industry is uncontrolled, migrants who have no permission to work at anything may, paradoxically, be employed in any job at all. In the case of transgenders, having ambiguous bodies allows them a clientele sometimes seeking exactly that kind of difference.

The Argument for Labour Rights and the Problem of Migration

Traditional legal proposals associated with the sex industry are called 'systems to control prostitution': abolitionism, prohibitionism, regulation, decriminalisation, tolerance and legalisation. These regimes, which focus on 'prostitution' and no other forms of commercial sex, neither recognise the work nor consider workers' demands. Today, rights activists propose that sex work be recognised as an occupation, with labour rights for those who wish to do the jobs and help to get out for those who don't.[75] In October 2005, 120 workers from twenty-six European countries endorsed a Sex Workers in Europe Manifesto that affirms sex work as a service in the market economy[76] and demands labour rights and the right to organise. Beyond that basic tenet, ideas are diverse:

> If the status of prostitutes were raised by repealing the archaic laws surrounding it, street walking would be eliminated and prostitution could take place in properly controlled establishments, as girls could work in the safety of their own place or flat, with police consent and protection in pleasant, discreet, hygienic conditions which would be better for both the prostitute and the client.[77]

> All forms of sex work are equally valid, including dancing, stripping, street or indoor prostitution, escorting, phone sex or performing in pornography.[78]

> I would like to work with more protection ... less hypocrisy. I would be happy, for example, working in a window, with some kind of security.[79]

Workers differ about how to achieve acceptance of their rationalising proposals. Here, I limit myself to noting some effects of these proposals for migrants (many of whom attended the 2005 conference). Organising for rights requires assuming, if only strategically, a professional identity ('stripper', 'prostitute', 'sex worker'). Many people who dislike or despise selling sex, or who see it as a temporary means to pay off debts, are unwilling to claim such an identity. Some are afraid of coming out to families:

> The greatest fear you have is that your family will find out ... That's why we watch out for ourselves, we don't trust anyone and avoid letting anyone from our country recognise us. There have been cases where they end up blackmailing you: 'If you don't pay – I'll tell!' (Latin American woman in Europe)[80]

> I would never publicly support a political struggle for prostitutes' rights. I wouldn't do it because it would destroy my discretion. No one in my family knows that I work in this. (Colombian woman in Spain)[81]

Some workers feel they perform an art, a therapy or a rite and welcome calling themselves sex workers. Others feel selling sex is analogous to typing or running a machine and see benefits from being called sex workers. But many, including migrants, even when they do not want to stop selling sex, don't think of themselves that way.

> God has to understand that what I do is out of necessity. I know I am doing something bad and that makes me feel bad, but I need the money.[82]

European sex workers focused on normalising their own positions sometimes accuse migrants of lowering the value of services by charging less, behaving less professionally and muddling the claim that sex workers are upstanding and autonomous through their involvement in illegal activities, perhaps even 'trafficking'. The interests of migrants who have no right to work and are concentrating on accumulating as much money as they can as quickly as possible may conflict with the interests of Europeans who want to legitimise the industry. Since the most important fact conditioning migrants' lives is having or not having residence and work permits, they often feel that proposals about sex worker rights are irrelevant to themselves.

Laws in both Germany and the Netherlands, where some sex businesses are legal, prohibit the granting of work permits to non-EU citizens in this sector.[83] Migrants who sell sex may well not have permission to work at any job, may be using false documents, may be working while on tourist visas or may have permission to work at a specific other job. Those who want to support migrants should not forget that most knew they would be travelling and earning money illegally, which neither calling them victims nor normalising sex work can overcome. Given their irregular status and vulnerability to police harassment and deportation, as well as the stigma attached to sex work, most are loath to draw attention to themselves. Many lead an itinerant lifestyle, do not join groups (in some countries they are forbidden from doing so) or feel no interest in politics. Associations of legal migrants, overwhelmingly dominated by men, have not been eager to espouse the cause of those who sell sex.

On the other hand, migrants who do regularise their situations may become interested in normalisation later on.

> No one brought me or deceived me and I never had bad experiences ... I take care of myself, I have a private insurance policy and Social Security. My work life has been very tranquil, in flats ... I'm not proud of what I do but I do it as a job. It's the fastest way to make money. (Colombian woman in Spain)[84]

> It makes me laugh when they think that I am not an honest woman because I do this job. Of course, as a job it's ugly, and I don't understand why in Italy they don't let us do it in organised places; I don't understand what is bad about selling love for money ... With this job I have made it possible for all my brothers to study and I have supported my mother, so I am proud of being a prostitute. (Nigerian woman in Italy)[85]

> I put an advert in the newspaper with my telephone, they call, I tell them the price ... I don't have to share the money with anyone ... I have no schedule, I work when I want to. I work only in the daytime, at nine or ten at night I turn off the telephone ... because the night is for my son. (Colombian woman in Spain)[86]

> We should work with the media so they don't view this in such a drastic way. (migrant in Spain)[87]

The single in-depth, large-scale research carried out on the sex industry concluded that workers' situations can only be improved if governments include businesses in their formal accounting systems.[88] Under this plan, states would tax and license establishments, which would then be required to comply with normal workplace regulations and grant benefits and rights to employees. This proposal bypasses rhetorical and moralistic arguments about whether selling sex is work or exploitation and proceeds to a pragmatic solution.

I frame the three kinds of services considered in this chapter together – domestic, caring and sex – because they are the ones Europeans are willing to pay migrants to do in large numbers. I do not say they comprise a category of life or work or that they should be seen as somehow the same. Instead, I am interested in how the demand for people to do these jobs constitutes a real migratory 'pull factor' towards Europe, and how seemingly progressive European discourses fail to address adequately the *European* context of these migrations, in which families, gender relations, sexualities, consumer attitudes and ideas about acceptable work are changing.

The Demand for Services

Western societies have long employed people outside the family to help with housework and home nursing, and sex has been paid for outside the home as far back as historians can go. So why do these jobs continue in feudal conditions when progress toward rationalisation characterises other work? To understand this, I consider contemporary ideas about the family, sex and consumption.

In parts of Europe, middle- and upper-class families still prefer to hire live-in maids, to be available from morning to night to perform a wide range of tasks, some of them quite intimate. Sometimes, this is a holdover from the past, when a belief in social hierarchy was conventional, and families commonly decided to forgo intimacy in exchange for having constantly available servants.[89] On the other hand, all societies in which both partners or spouses leave the house to work stimulate the bringing-in of outsiders to care for those left at home (unless states are able to provide unlimited services to their citizens). As extended families are reduced to their nuclei, extra aunts and grandmothers are no longer available to take on these tasks, and daughters now expect to educate themselves for work outside the home.

Gender politics is also changing the shape of the nuclear family or committed couple, with the movement toward equity seen most obviously in women's entry into labour markets once closed to them. They used to be

> in charge of children, elderly, and the ill; maintaining personal relationships; offering emotional support, personal attention, and listening; embodying (or so it was understood) sexuality ... As women move

increasingly into the world of paid work, many of these traditional intimate tasks are being performed in relationships that include the explicit movement of money. Paid child care, nursing homes for the elderly, talk therapy and phone sex are just a few examples.[90]

Yet while women have moved into the so-called public sphere, men have moved much less into the private. So if demand remains steady for cleanliness and order inside the house, either women must do double labour or someone must be hired to come in. Equal gender relations between both parties in western couples therefore may *rely* on the employment of a third person.

Traditionally, the family was assumed to be the site of love and commitment, and sex to be properly located only there:

> In the family history literature, family usually means a grouping of kinsfolk ... who *should* be living together inside of households. I want to argue that we need to focus on the 'should' ... to reveal a key structure crucial for the understanding of ideology ... Because people accept the meaningfulness of family, they enter into relations of production, reproduction, and consumption with one another ...[91]

Nowadays, more kinds of relationships are accepted as meaningful, or 'familial'.[92] Although these changes are not universal and vary by generation, class and ethnicity, it is fair to say that in Europe many concepts of family now extend beyond the walls of houses (living together not required) and increasingly do not include blood or formalised relationships. Some feel that 'communities' acting through social movements have more symbolic meaning than families.[93] Families are not impermeable, and loving a wife or husband does not impede having sex with, or loving, other people.[94]

The loosening up of important relationships may help explain some of the demand for sexual services. Anthony Giddens calls 'pure' those relationships claiming to be sexually and emotionally free and equal, supposedly formed without interests, characterised by a sexuality freed from reproduction and continuing only as long as both people involved feel satisfied.[95] Discourses of gender equality and individuality encourage heterosexuals to look for relationships that suit their own personal emotional needs,[96] and discourses of nonheterosexuality emphasise the right to form families and unions. Yet, for many people, the romantic ideal of finding the perfect mate has not been achieved, or is not sought, or has failed, but they still want intimacy and sex. In this context, paying for it occasionally looks less significant. Moreover, research reveals that commercial relationships usually considered superficial may involve warm emotions as well as fantasies and lies.[97]

The ideal of sexual and gender 'liberation' has been active in the west for four decades, evolving and proliferating to include women, gays, lesbians, bisexuals, trans, the disabled, and so on. The liberation concept, originating with Herbert Marcuse, Wilhelm Reich and other theorists of the 1960s, follows the hydraulic model of drives and repressions that must be set free;[98] accordingly, all persons have the right to discover themselves both physically and emotionally. The link made between personal identity and sex and the construction of a new concept, sexuality, was a central theme of Michel Foucault's *History of Sexuality*.[99] The paradoxes of the search for sexual identity – its possibilities for limiting as well as expanding personal potential – have been the subject of much theorising since then, but the attainment of self-knowledge continues to be highly valued. For R. W. Connell, the individual's personal narrative makes the sexual persona.[100] For Jeffrey Weeks,

> Self-identity, at the heart of which is sexual identity, is not something that is given as a result of the continuities of an individual's life or of the fixity and force of his or her desires. It is something that has to be worked on, invented and reinvented in accord with the changing rhythms, demands, opportunities and closures of a complex world.[101]

So the sexual search, with its experimentations, is considered necessary, and since experimentation is considered perverse and criminal *inside* western families, it must happen outside. The desire to leave home and relate to other people intimately is deemed positive, and if there were no hegemonic condemnations of promiscuity, infidelity and paid sex, there would be no contradictions here. However, these are all still censured, and those who buy sex rarely admit it publicly (although speaking about it privately can contribute to the construction of heterosexual masculine identity).[102] Changes in attitudes about sexual behaviour look different through the lens of gender: girls are denounced for promiscuity, not boys. There is resistance to the idea that women might want to watch others have sex, have multiple sexual partners, engage in public or anonymous sex or pay for sex – as well as be paid for it.[103] Eric Ratliff discusses advertising and entertainment messages that 'effectively communicate the ideals of personal improvement' as well as sexuality as an 'expression of self' for rural women migrants working as hostesses.[104]

The hydraulic-drive model of sexuality has been the subject of debunking for some time,[105] particularly the idea that men have great sexual 'needs', which is called a myth oppressing women.[106] Nevertheless, the discourse of sexual liberation is still strong, and the contemporary proliferation of sexual images and opportunities is often ascribed to a 'de-repressing' of the population – continuing the notion that we are progressing towards complete sexual enlightenment. In this context, commercial sex appears to be part of today's wide-open, sexy consumerism.

Weeks believes that 'choice of lifestyles is central to radical sexual politics; choice to realize our sexual desire, choice in the pattern of sexual relationships, choice in our general ways of life'.[107] Could this choice on behalf of sexual identities apply to commercial sex? Is being a 'client' or 'sex worker' an analogous identity to those based on sexual orientation or gender? If identities are multiple, shifting and temporary, perhaps so. In contemporary capitalist markets, objects, experiences and services that not long ago were unavailable now multiply before our eyes; consumers are urged to buy products that enhance their personal lifestyles, and entrepreneurship is celebrated for providing an immense explosion of spaces where we can be entertained and served in new ways. There is nothing economically mysterious about the increase of sexually oriented shows and services on offer.

Urry classifies tourist gazing, a form of consumption, as collective, when the presence of other people adds to the experience, and romantic, when privacy is important.[108] Both are available in the sex industry, where clients drink, eat, dance, relax, take drugs, meet friends, do business, impress partners, watch films, travel, and pay for sex.

Everything seems to indicate that sex clubs are little by little becoming places where the role of sexual demand is giving way to a tissue of more complex interactions ... [These places] are assuming a new role, that of a social place to which groups of men go without specifically seeking a sexual relationship with the women they find there, but rather having fun amongst themselves until early morning hours.[109]

Elizabeth Bernstein describes this commercial sex as recreation as 'a reconfiguration of erotic life in which the pursuit of sexual intimacy is not hindered but facilitated by its location in the marketplace'.[110] Nonetheless, the question repeatedly heard about this consumption is framed as individual aberration: 'Why do men buy sex?'

The Motivation to Buy Sex

Why is asked about *this* purchase as it is about few others. In polemics against 'prostitution', clients are described as exploiters, colonisers, victimisers, perverts, people with sexual or psychological problems or simply as immoral (the past's libertines).[111] Westerners questioned in Thailand and the Caribbean expressed disagreeable, disrespectful, power-oriented, colonialist and racist attitudes about women to one research team,[112] and there is no doubt that men sometimes say these things. But another researcher found tourists who feel victimised by women they paid,[113] and tourists' concerned and affectionate letters to women left behind paint yet another picture.[114] The context for such remarks must always be considered: who asks the questions, where, in front of whom – a spectrum of methodological and ethical issues influencing how people react to being questioned that are crucial when sexual issues are at stake.

Studies of client motivation that consider ideas about masculinity in different cultures question the separating of sex industry sites from hostelry and entertainment sectors (taverns, bars, discotheques, cafés, restaurants) and the health and well-being sector (saunas, massage parlours, body therapies). Martha Stein observed more than a thousand clients and 64 call girls, concluding that clients used these occasions for stress reduction and counselling.[115] Anne Allison's study of Japanese middle-class businessmen reveals the importance of homosociality among male work colleagues who spend time together away from rigid workplace hierarchies;[116] Alyson Brody questions the Cartesian separation of mind from body as inadequate for understanding Thai notions of maleness.[117] In an ethnography with older street workers and their clients in Spain, Angie Hart demonstrates the fullness of their relationships.[118] Paul Lyngbye reveals the cognitive dissonance between the conventional denunciation of clients and their own feelings about what they are doing.[119] Roberta Perkins, in a study of 1,000 clients of sex workers in Australia, finds them to be no different from everyone else, across age, social, labour, religion and marriage categories.[120] In research on gentlemen's clubs in the US, where dancers offer nude dancing, company and conversation but no touching, Katherine Frank shows how regular patrons want to indulge in fantasies about sex in spaces where gender relations are not like daily life.[121]

Replies to the question 'why do you pay for sex?' are nonplussing.

I didn't do anything different with my wife from what I did with whores. What was the difference, then? With my wife there was the problem of obligation, the fact that being married we couldn't go back, [so] the idea of being able to choose was liberation.

It's something I do as a distraction. To do something different from . . . I don't know . . . going to a film.[122]

It keeps my marriage together. My wife won't try anything different, so I go to prostitutes.

I've never liked going out drinking with groups of lads, clubbing it, looking for girls. I find it difficult and a hassle to go through all the chatting up and all the trying to get off with them. This is easier.

It's so exciting partly because I shouldn't be doing it.[123]

It's different to lovemaking. It's lust and it's great to have something new and different whenever you want it.[124]

There are sailors or businessmen who want a quick fuck. Others have matrimonial problems or don't like lasting relationships. There are people who don't look good, or who are handicapped. But there are also people who simply like to vary, or who want to enjoy sex in their own way.[125]

I came to these places occasionally even though we had a good sex life
in the sense that my wife was well satisfied and so was I. Like most
males, every now and then I have a need, a craving, for a different
female.[126]

Could this be all there is to it? Or is there a problem in the directness of
the question, which assumes the interviewee is engaged in doubtful, if
not reprehensible, activities? Knowing that so many condemn clients'
desires as the eroticisation of poverty or race, violence, perpetuation of
the madonna/whore dichotomy or a need to feel masculine and powerful, it is no wonder that clients are reluctant to talk about deeper desires
and fantasies (if they have any). And of course, it may be that most
people asked the question 'why do you – ?' do not know the answer
themselves.

The desire for sex is often compared to the desire for food:

It is said that people who go in for sex without love are missing a lot.
That may be true, but it provides not the slightest argument for never
having it without love. You might just as well say that because the
pleasantest way to eat was with friends at dinner parties, no one
should eat in any other.[127]

Carol Pateman and others dismiss such arguments as reducing commercial sex relationships to contracts, without considering the power
structures in which they occur.[128] Some say the difference between a
demand for most services and a demand for domestic and sexual ones lies
in the buyer's interest in 'the person' of the worker – in his or her distinct
personal identity and appearance.[129] But many consumers think about
these when they select other kinds of human service-providers, too.

Then there is the question of the size of demand for sexual services. A
French report calculated in 1977 that an average of 40,000 men a day
had sex with 'prostitutes'.[130] In 1996, a Spanish NGO speculated that
300,000 'prostitutes' might have three clients a day, making a million
men buying sexual services every day in Spain.[131] The media, national
governments, the European Parliament and the UN continually cite high
figures for both 'trafficking' and 'prostitution', most of which are crude
extrapolations from estimates that were unreliable in the first place. The
calculations of one Roman street worker in 1988 are more specific:

Rome was known to have 5,000 prostitutes. Let's say that each one took home at least 50,000 lire a day. Men don't go more than once a day. That means that for someone who asked 3,000 lire in a car, to arrive at 50,000 she had to do a lot, maybe twenty or so. Figure it out, 20 times 5,000 comes to 100,000 clients. Since it's rare for them to go every day, maybe they go once or twice a week, the total comes to between 400,000 and 600,000 men going to whores every week. How many men live in Rome? A million and a half. Take away the old men, the children, the homosexuals and the impotent. I mean, definitely, more or less all men go.[132]

The extent of demand can be presumed also from the probable presence of hundreds of thousands of migrants selling sex in Europe. The point is, given such a large market, that customers cannot be exceptional cases or technically 'deviants'. Even an attempt to generate a profile for men who buy sex from children found that proper 'paedophiles' form a tiny subgroup of conventional social characters (seamen, businessmen, migrants, aid workers) who pay for sex opportunistically and ignore the ages of the people they buy it from.[133] The only conclusion possible is that in all cultures and countries, many males consider it permissible and conventional to buy sex.

Buying Services Away from Home

Development workers, international civil servants, representatives of multinational corporations and diplomats, often with large incomes, employ housekeepers, maids and nannies for little money and grant them few rights.[134] Some employers treat these employees as chattels, 'bringing them along' when they move.[135] But despite these widespread abuses, 'sex tourism' receives all the attention and alarm. Many paying for companionship and sex in countries other than their own repudiate the term, as do people who provide services.

'Sex tourism' causes scandal as the patriarchal, imperialist and racist exploitation of poverty, but this is oversimplified. To begin with, it is impossible to separate this kind of tourism from others; many who seek out interludes of paid sex have other agendas, such as ecotourism or seeing cultural monuments. The activities exist everywhere, not only on sunny beaches.[136] Some travellers consciously seek out sex, while others passively let it seek them out.

Many western travellers celebrate the sexual and affective possibilities in poorer countries, complaining that women are too feminist and commercial sex is overly industrialised in the west, where timekeeping and pricing-per-item are the norm.[137]

> It's by the hour, like a taxi service, like they've got the meter running ... Here it's different. They're not professionals. They enjoy sex, it's natural to them ... they're affectionate ... They even kiss you. A prostitute in Europe will never kiss you. (Canadian man in the Dominican Republic)[138]

> The women reach maturity earlier here ... the very climate makes them behave differently. (Portuguese man in Brazil)[139]

> Oh, the Italians, you can't say anything to them, everything offends them, the Italian woman has a conflict of identity, they're full of feminist ideas. (Italian man in Brazil)[140]

These travellers value the open-ended, ambiguous sexual relations that can be slipped into on holiday, which suggest friendly gift-giving more than contracts.

> The foreigners are different, as far as caring is concerned. In the experiences I've had, sex wasn't just sex ... There was caring, that exchange, conversation. (Brazilian woman in Brazil)[141]

> They know how to make a man feel looked after. Squeezing the toothpaste onto the brush so it's waiting for you when you go into the bathroom in the morning, that's what I call caring. How many women in England would do that? (Englishman in Thailand)[142]

Some tourists know that their new friends are only pretending affection but don't mind, because they see themselves to be pretending as well.[143]

> In the club, they were granted safety from the struggle to attract 'real' women, from the necessity to form 'real' commitments and from the demands of those 'real' women on their time and emotions.[144]

> It doesn't matter if they really like me or not, but if they want to receive drinks or a tip they have to pretend that they enjoy my company and I have to believe it ... I don't really care to have a long-term

relationship at this time, but I *do* want to believe that such a relationship is possible. (US man in the Philippines)[145]

Cohen explains how emotional labour is essential to making brief touristic experiences satisfying:

> Purely commercial attitudes on the part of the hosts … rob the tourists' relationships with them of much of their attractiveness. Professionalisation in tourism … finds one of its expressions in the ability of the service personnel to provide 'personalised service' – a form of 'staged authenticity' in which relationships based essentially on economic exchange are camouflaged to appear as if they were based on social exchange.[146]

Besides this staged authenticity or emotional labour, those working with foreigners offer flexibility, working as guides, drivers, cultural and linguistic interpreters, sport and dance instructors and protectors against swindles. Touristic sites attract people from other parts of the country, who then make up an informal market in crafts, dance, local sports, religious rituals, typical food and drink, hair-braiding and beach massages, as well as drugs and sex. Many service-providers, as well as their clients, resist being labelled as objects of sex tourism when sexual contact is only one service among many.[147]

While governments may denounce 'sex tourist' practices or native 'prostitutes' who bother tourists, host countries generate images of themselves as beautiful, friendly and natural through advertising *and* through assuring that friendly subjects are actually present in tourist environments. Malcolm Crick's guide in Kandy sums up the flexible local:

> Felix had a short list of addresses of tourists with whom he had been friendly over the years … Most on this list were women with whom he had been on trips around the island. At the start of such trips, he would state the price of his company, but if he grew to like his companion, he would tell them at the end that they could give him whatever gifts they liked. Of course he would have enjoyed several days' travel, good food, good accommodation and probably sex, but he made a qualitative distinction between such relationships and a simple business arrangement. As has been recognised in other cultures, such relationships with foreigners can have a profound

psychological significance, which terms like 'tout' or 'prostitute' do not adequately convey.[148]

Though there has been some attempt to position women tourists' search as romantic rather than sexual,[149] most research rejects this distinction.[150] Opportunities open up for male natives, and gay tourism is no different.

> Though the boys prefer girls of their own age, they do understand that older women often find themselves in a more secure economic position and of a better purchasing power, which makes them highly attractive as sexual partners promising a ticket to a better life ... [151]

> The boys had refused money in return for their sexual favours. But since it was assumed that some form of reciprocity other than free lodging was to take place, he and Alexander had decided on the shopping trip, where they would buy their tricks a number of goods. 'Stuff here is so cheap for us anyway. It's really no problem.'[152]

The issue of emotional labour arises here, too.

> The thing is, it is a particular skill, that's why they're in the bars – they can do the necessary play-acting, they can convince the punter that he's what they've been waiting for all their life. And because you are at the centre of your own life, you don't think 'Oh she'll be doing the same thing with somebody else tomorrow or next week.' You think you're special or different.[153]

> When I find out what the customer wants, then that is who I am. If he likes someone to talk to, then I can do that; if he wants someone to be like his girlfriend then I can do that too. I am good at figuring out what others want from me. (Filipina in the Philippines)[154]

Local people may also be genuinely assisted and cared for by tourists.

> He was very traumatized, to see the situation in which I lived ... He said he would help me while he was here ... I told him I was alone ... and that there was no one I could leave the boys with. So we waited until the boys went to sleep and ... we became intimate. After that, he visited every day. He gave me money, bought us food, and many other necessities. This was a beautiful situation but only lasted for about 20 days because he had to return to Italy. Before he left, he gave me 500 dollars ... (Cuban woman in Cuba)[155]

Caribbean women in times of structural adjustment have been described as making do, trading in the informal economy and in sexual relationships, manipulating and switching partners, selling sex, resorting to relationships of convenience or getting involved with other women's men.[156] Young people's relationships with older men and women that involve sex, money, security and protection are documented in many African countries and in Japan, Taiwan and other parts of Asia,[157] in traditions well outside anything called 'prostitution'.

Sexual cultures can be understood as comprising a continuum of relationships in which sexual labour is present, without differentiating absolutely between marital and extramarital sex. Many people who sell sex do not see it as separate from other activities or as directly commercial. In different parts of the world, relations combining feelings, sex and money are considered conventional, and both sides of the relationships may have names.[158] Viviana Zelizer analyses the myriad ways that money intersects with intimacy:

> Different forms of payment signify differences in the character of the social relations currently operating. To label a payment a gift (tip, bribe, charity, expression of esteem) rather than an entitlement (pension, allowance, rightful share of gains) or compensation (wages, salary, bonus, commission) is to make claims about the relationship between payer and payee. Negotiation, then, runs in both directions: from definition of social ties to selection of appropriate payments, from forms of payment to accepted definitions of ties.[159]

These multi-faceted relationships exist in wealthier countries as well. In Liverpool, in the 1980s:

> The women typically spend the evening drinking and dancing with the same client, before accompanying him back to the ship for the rest of the night ... it is not uncommon for a woman to spend up to several weeks without leaving the docks at all, working, eating, and sleeping on board then moving on to the next ship. For some, it is like a holiday, free food and drink, plenty of money, and parties on board every night.[160]

Although there are few shipboard parties in Liverpool these days, this tradition is alive and well in many ports. On a trip to Colombia,

Nicaragua and Costa Rica, I encountered such ship culture, with local intermediaries advising women when boats come in and ferrying them out for parties lasting days. Many of those who spend time with seafarers do not see themselves as sex workers but rather describe themselves as 'good-time' or party girls.

> Kiwi ship-girls [exchange] sex with foreigners they find attractive or agreeable for money, meals and drinks, rather than an agreed upon fee-for-service arrangement. If a woman decides to spend a night with one of the men, he will, at the very least, give her enough money to cover her taxi fare home, and pay for child-minding expenses.[161]

Some feminists in Europe, too, have long been aware that the difference between marriage and 'prostitution' is imaginary[162] – a topic too large to go into except in one small way.

Marriage

Marriage (and now, in some countries, civil union between people of the same sex) is still one of the easiest ways for migrants to acquire legal status in Europe and thus access to all kinds of jobs. A brochure for potential Latin American migrants, *Alemania ¿Un paraíso para mujeres?* (Germany, A Paradise for Women?) dedicates several pages to the topic.[163] Increasingly, potential spouses must put on a very good show for immigration officials, living together for some time and demonstrating a convincing affective history; at the same time, marrying migrants is now a standard way to demonstrate solidarity among (especially, younger) Europeans. Some marriages last; in others divorce is planned from the outset. In some cases, migrants begin to sell sex, which may have been foreseen (or not), involve coercion (or not) and benefit both partners (or not).[164] Sometimes observers lump all such situations together as exploitative, but such a conclusion masks the diversity, resourcefulness and flexibility found among migrants themselves. Annie Phizacklea mentions the bride who 'has calculated that marriage will be the easiest and possibly only legal route of gaining employment commensurate with education and qualifications'.[165] The melding of sexual, domestic and labour necessities that characterises this chapter may find its epitome in this kind of migrant marriage.

'Anti-prostitution' discourses frequently condemn matrimonial agencies that use catalogues and websites. Although intermediaries have always arranged conventional marriages in cultures across the world, there is no doubt that some of them now advertise potential mates using the same techniques that sex businesses use. There is also no doubt that some would-be husbands are looking for wives who will be more submissive than they believe western women are. But it is impossible to distinguish between abusive and non-abusive matrimonial agents by simply looking at their catalogues, and many women married through such agencies reject the derogatory label 'mail-order brides', considering themselves to be actively looking for good partners.

Research on matchmaking reveals a variety of unions arranged commercially: trade marriages, blind marriages, arranged marriages, love marriages and marriages of convenience.[166] Some of these arranged marriages turn out well, others not. Many women creatively use marriage abroad to avoid oppression at home and create new possibilities for themselves.[167] And westerners are hardly alone in looking for spouses abroad; consider a recruiter of Japanese husbands for Thai women:

> They don't stay long or come too often. Husbands we choose for ourselves are not as nice as this. To marry a man from the village is to suffer. This way, we don't get tired and we don't have to worry. We only want money. What's more, if we go into prostitution, we're at risk from disease ... It's like having a husband who works abroad to send us money. We are faithful to them ... They are happy to support us.[168]

When people buy sexual services in Europe, or get into holiday romances where they pay a local for spending time with them, or marry someone willing to be a 'traditional' spouse, the relationships often occur across cultural, ethnic, class and age boundaries. For many participants in the 'prostitution' debate, this point is definitive, proving that the male service-buyer is not only sexist but racist. Some studies of the sex industry rely on an analysis of imperialism and globalisation that makes the west's rapaciousness in the third world as sexual as it is economic.[169] In most of these works, women, darker people and the poor are positioned as powerless beside men, whiter people and the rich. A desire to relate to exotic Others may characterise many commercial sex relations, but the vendor may be whiter than the buyer, and the buyer may be the foreigner or migrant.[170] Besides, clients don't all have the same ethnic prejudices.[171] For managers of businesses, it is important to have a variety of phenotypes and nationalities on offer:

> The difference is with the clients, if they tell me 'a Spanish woman' then I send a Spanish woman; it's not racism because I have some girls as blonde and white as the Spanish and they don't work ... 'I won't give my money to a foreigner', and a foreigner can be white, from India or from wherever you like, but she's foreign ... There's something for everyone here, it's a boutique. (Dominican woman manager of a flat in Spain)[172]

Some years ago, when migrants selling sex in Europe were mostly Asians and Latin Americans, a colour-based analysis seemed plausible, but nowadays large numbers of light-coloured people from Eastern Europe and countries of the former Soviet Union are selling sex, under similar conditions and subject to similar discourses of victimisation and agency. If we substitute ethnicity for race, we find that everywhere societies create hierarchies of social value for nationalities, ethnicities and regions. 'Whiteness' may be ranked, as in the Greek comment that 'Russians and Ukrainians [are] at one end of the scale and Albanians at the other'.[173] These distinctions change according to cultural context: Albania and Greece share borders, which means they share rivalries, prejudices and jokes and know each other's histories, whereas at the other end of Europe, in Spain, say, Albania and the Ukraine may seem to be two undifferentiated countries in 'the east'. And workers are just as prejudiced as customers:

> Normally in a club they don't accept more than three or four Africans, because they have a very bad way of working. They approach a client and if the client doesn't want anything they just stay and stay until the client leaves ... The Russians have messed up the job. They do whatever they are asked, anywhere and in front of anyone. (Colombian woman in Spain)[174]

Studies of sexual relationships between European colonists and the peoples they colonised reveal a complex of social, cultural, psychological, economic and symbolic elements[175] that also need to be investigated if we are to understand how the exotic functions in commercial sex relations.

Contemporary westerners tend to believe that work constitutes a unique way to realise personal identity, but this belief is not universal. Doing low-prestige service work can, for many, be the instrument to realise other ends, even other identities. I end this chapter with the words of a Filipina domestic in Switzerland:

> We look at migration as neither a degradation nor improvement ... in women's position, but as a restructuring of gender relations. This restructuring need not necessarily be expressed through a satisfactory professional life. It may take place through the assertion of autonomy in social life, through relations with family of origin, or through participating in networks and formal associations. The differential between earnings in the country of origin and the country of immigration may in itself create such an autonomy, even if the job in the receiving country is one of a live-in maid or prostitute.[176]

To understand how discourses developed that so uniformly disqualify this kind of testimony, I started reading about the past. And there I found the answers I was looking for.

NOTES

1   Mechanised and industrial cleaning (as in office buildings and plants) and hospital nursing are other markets.
2   Folbre 1991; Folbre and Wagman 1993; Agustín 2003d
3   Tilly and Tilly 1998: 22
4   Bose 1987: 101
5   Ironmonger 1996: 39–40
6   Anderson 2000:14. It should also be pointed out that many European employers of domestic labour consider many employees incompetent at the most basic of tasks, in need of training, lazy and so on (Colectivo Ioé 2001).
7   Parreñas 2001: 155
8   Bakan and Stasiulis 1995: 325
9   Benería 1981; Chadeau 1985; Bose 1987; Waring 1988; Folbre 1991
10   Levitas 1998: 8
11   Smart and Smart 1978: 3
12   Folbre and Nelson 2000: 7

13   Bubeck 1995: 129
14   Ironmonger 1996: 55
15   Parreñas 2001: 117
16   Anderson 2000: 114
17   Chadeau 1985: 241
18   Anderson 2000: 119
19   Dinnerstein 1976; Gilligan 1982; Chodorow 1978; Hochschild 1983; Wouters 1989; Abel and Nelson 1990
20   Tronto 1987: 652
21   Tadiar 1998: 938
22   Hochschild 2000a
23   Parreñas 2001; Hochschild 2000b
24   Kellner 1999: 21, citing figures from *Economic Trends*
25   For example, Shrage 1994; Alexander 1995; Chapkis 1997
26   Barry 1979; Dworkin 1987
27   Simmel 1978: 377
28   Pateman 1988: 562
29   Chancer 1993:145
30   Marx [1857] 1986: 202 and Engels 1884
31   Bailey 2002: 2
32   Bailey 2002: 12
33   Perkel website
34   Good summaries of the array of ideas are given in, for example, Barbara Sullivan's 'Rethinking Prostitution' (1995), Jo Phoenix's *Making Sense of Prostitution* (1999) and Belinda Carpenter's *Re-Thinking Prostitution* (2000). The sheer quantity of analyses produced in this area is striking.
35   See also Agustín 2004a and Weitzer 2005.
36   Linda Singer shows how the AIDS industry commodifies health in the same way (1993: 58).
37   Daly 1978; Leidholdt and Raymond 1990; Jeffreys 1997
38   Sedgwick 1990: 25. See also Rubin 1984; Vance 1984; Califia 1994.
39   Bernstein 2001: 402
40   Sullivan 1995: 184
41   Lever and Dolnick 2000: 86
42   Oso 2000
43   Høigård and Finstad 1986: 54
44   Oliveira 2004: 157
45   Casal 2001
46   Dahles 1998: 30
47   Bunzl 2000: 88
48   Hochschild 1983; Wouters 1989; Chapkis 1997
49   'While some [flight attendants] distance themselves from the job by defining it as "not serious", others distance themselves from it in another way ... They use their faces as masks against the world; they refuse to act. Most of those who "go into robot" describe

it as a defense, but they acknowledge that it is inadequate: their withdrawal often irritates passengers, and when it does they are forced to withdraw even further in order to defend themselves against that irritation' (Hochschild 1983: 135).

50   Lever and Dolnick 2000
51   Diplomacy is necessary toward a client unable to perform sexually (Kong 2006: 420). Other kinds of emotional labour involve the use of humour (Sanders 2004) and setting boundaries (Ho 2000; Kong 2006).
52   Ho 2000: 16
53   For example, Sanders 2005
54   World Sex Guide, PunterNet and other online fora for clients
55   Agustín 1995
56   Murphy and Venkatesh 2006: 149
57   Ratliff 2004: 43
58   frauenlesbenfilmkollectif 2002: 5
59   Ho 2000: 9
60   Cabiria 2002: 286
61   Gülçür and İlkkaracan 2002: 415
62   CATS 2006: 7
63   Riopedre 2004: 222
64   Laskowski 2002, from notes to *Bundestagsdrucksache* 14/5958. The *Economist* gave a figure of US$20 billion a year worldwide in 1998. An Indonesian figure was US$1.2–3.3 billion, or 0.8–2.4% of the Gross National Product of the country (Lim 1998). There are no standard rules for these calculations.
65   Lim 1998: 9
66   Lim 1998
67   *Encuentros* 2002; also see *Ocio* 2004.
68   Hausbeck and Brents 2002
69   For example, Mukherjee 1989; Sleightholme and Sinha Indrani 1996; Hart 1999; Cheng 2002; Davies 2006
70   Comment by sex worker Elisabeth Molina, public lecture, Quito, Ecuador, March 2005
71   The definition for the term 'sexual exploitation' used by the Coalition Against Trafficking in Women says: 'A practice by which a person achieves sexual gratification, financial gain or advancement through the abuse or exploitation of a person's sexuality by abrogating that person's human right to dignity, equality, autonomy, and physical and mental well-being; i.e. trafficking, prostitution, prostitution tourism, mail-order-bride trade, pornography, stripping, battering, incest, rape and sexual harassment' (CATW 1991).
72   Ariès 1962
73   Montgomery 1998:146-7
74   *Economist*, 14 February 1998
75   Bindman 1996
76   See www.sexworkeurope.org
77   IUSW 2000: 3; see also Lopes 2006

78 Sex Workers in Europe Manifesto
79 CATS 2006: 13
80 Polanía and Claasen 1998: 105
81 Riopedre 2004: 223
82 Bonelli et al 2001: 94
83 Challenges to this prohibition were brought by sex workers from countries with Association Agreements with the EU (European Communities 2002); also see Laskowski 2002.
84 Oso 2000
85 Kennedy and Nicotri 1999: 32
86 Oso 2000
87 CATS 2006: 14
88 Lim 1998; see also Agustín 2007
89 Oso 1998; King and Zontini 2000
90 Folbre and Nelson 2000: 1
91 Rapp et al 1983: 235
92 Stone 1977; Davidoff and Hall 1987; Sorrentino 1990; Bourdieu 1996; Silva and Smart 1999
93 Weeks 1995: 44
94 Consider a long erotic tradition associated with maids (Stallybrass and White 1986; McClintock 1995). In addition, they are often urged to feel they are 'one of the family'.
95 Giddens 1992
96 Nelson and Robinson 1994
97 Frank 2002
98 Gagnon and Simon 1973; Weeks 1982; Plummer 1982
99 Foucault 1979b, 1985, 1986
100 Connell 1987
101 Weeks 1995: 38
102 Allison 1994; Bird 1996; Leonini 1999
103 Irigaray 1977; Snitow et al 1983; Nead 1988
104 Ratliff 2004: 40
105 Connell 1987; Berger et al 1995
106 McIntosh 1978
107 Weeks 1995: 45
108 Urry 1990
109 Sequeiros 1996: 62
110 Bernstein 2005: 108
111 Barry 1979; Dworkin 1987; Høigård and Finstad 1986
112 O'Connell Davidson and Sanchez Taylor 1999
113 Seabrook 1996
114 Walker and Ehrlich 1992
115 Stein 1974
116 Allison 1994

117 Brody 1999
118 Hart 1999
119 Lyngbye 2000
120 Perkins 1999: 46
121 Frank 2002, 2005
122 Cutrufelli 1988: 24
123 Campbell 1997: 49
124 Perkins 1999: 44
125 Gerrit Bloemen quoted in Fundación Esperanza 1998: 62
126 Bailey 2002: 4
127 Richards 1980: 199-200; see also Ericsson 1980: 335
128 Pateman 1983; for a more recent argument, see Miriam 2005.
129 O'Connell Davidson and Anderson 2003
130 Crimi 1979
131 Hernández Velasco 1996
132 Cutrufelli 1988: 26
133 O'Connell Davidson 2001
134 Cheng 1996; Anderson 2000
135 SOLIDAR; Kalayaan
136 See, for example, Bunzl 2000
137 World Sex Guide website
138 O'Connell Davidson and Brace 1996: 16
139 Piscitelli 2004: 20
140 Piscitelli 2004: 22
141 Piscitelli 2004: 16
142 Seabrook 1996: 38
143 Frank 2002; Ratliff 2003
144 Frank 1998: 189
145 Ratliff 2003: 157
146 Cohen 1982: 415; see also MacCannell 1973
147 Phillip 1999; De Albuquerque 1998; Cabezas 1999; Hanson 1998
148 Crick 1992: 142
149 Pruitt and LaFont 1995
150 De Albuquerque 1998; Phillip 1999
151 Dahles 1998: 30
152 Bunzl 2000: 74
153 Seabrook 1996: 22
154 Ratliff 2003: 122
155 Cabezas 2004
156 Kempadoo 1999
157 Kuate-Defo 2004; Ueno 2003; Ho 2003; Cornwall 2002
158 Consider 'mistress', on the one hand, and 'sugar daddy', on the other.
159 Zelizer 2000: 826
160 Matthews 1990: 78

161 Hanson 1998: 16

162 Goldman 1917; Beauvoir 1953

163 Amnesty for Women 1998

164 Wijers and Lap-Chew 1996; Skrobanek et al 1997

165 Phizacklea 1997: 5

166 Lu 2005

167 Wilson 1988; Domingo Tapales 1990; Wijers and Lap-Chew 1996; Tolentino 1996; Robinson 1996; Constable 2003; Lu 2005; Davin 2005b

168 Hobson and Heung 1998: 132

169 Truong 1990; Barry 1995; Bishop and Robinson 1998

170 Kempadoo 1995: 75-6

171 Lyngbye 2000; O'Connell Davidson and Anderson 2003: 20-23

172 Agustín 2001a

173 Laziridis 2001: 86

174 Bonelli et al 2001: 83

175 Stoler 1995; McClintock 1995

176 Hefti 1997

4

THE RISE OF THE SOCIAL –
AND OF 'PROSTITUTION'

This chapter reveals the beginnings of social interventions aimed at helping people considered needy and unable to help themselves. In today's Europe, non-European migrants may be the group perceived as most needy, problematic, threatening and in need of control (and the subgroup 'migrant prostitutes' most of all). In the nineteenth century, 'the poor' were perceived this way, and 'prostitutes' perhaps most of all. As part of a phenomenon known as the Rise of the Social, a newly empowered bourgeoisie set out to define how society ought to be constituted and how citizens should live; in the process, our contemporary understanding of 'prostitution' was fashioned and philanthropy was carved out as a women's sphere of work. The Rise of the Social began around the time of the French and US revolutions and forms part of the Enlightenment; today, the social is a major element of governments. In this sense, *the social* refers to the way social problems, social reform and social welfare are formulated and managed. The concept derives substantially from the work of Jacques Donzelot, who closely links the social with conscious efforts at philanthropy.[1] The role of female philanthropists, both voluntary and paid, is crucial to the later formation of states' assumption of social services, programming, planning and other technologies.

I do not mean to imply that there was no stigmatisation, harassment, regulation or suffering of women who sold sex before the social period. Rather, the social caused what it called 'prostitution' to be viewed in a different way, and, more important, designated a class of people with a mission to do something about it.

> Whereas earlier Victorian writings had emphasised pauperism as a failure of the moral will, they now relocated the locus of poverty, putting it within the homes and bodies of the poor themselves. Whether victims of environmental or biological determinism, the poor would remain the poor, unless extricated from their fate by the transforming power of heroic investigators and reformers.[2]

The Rise of the Social occurred all over Europe — although local commentators may not describe it the same way — over the late eighteenth to early twentieth centuries. On 'prostitution', studies demonstrate general European trends from the Middle Ages on.[3] I concentrate on evidence from France and England, since both theory and evidence on the social are abundant there. The French evidence chiefly concerns the setting up of a state system to control 'prostitution', while the English mostly concerns how a work sector was created to control individual 'prostitutes'.[4] The two histories are intertwined, since the French system was almost extended to Britain (as it was to other parts of Europe), but energetic campaigners fought against it.[5]

I do not think a recounting of chronological events is the best way to understand the simultaneous and contradictory, the ebbing and flowing, waves of sentiment about sex. People with reforming, repressive and regulatory theories and projects have existed throughout human history. I take a genealogical approach to the discourse on 'prostitutes' *as well as* to that of helping them, following Judith Butler's concept of genealogy as investigating the 'political stakes in designating as an origin and cause those identity categories that are in fact the effect of institutions, practices, and discourses with multiple and diffuse points of origin'.[6] I am particularly interested in how new social theories of how to help were entangled with helpers' own needs and desires, and I relate these to changes in the patterns of women's work, which are documented Europe-wide.[7]

The subject of helping is usually treated as benevolent, as the entry of capable women previously excluded from nondomestic work into the field of philanthropy. Martha Vicinus seeks to correct a version of history that did not respect 'charity work':[8]

Women had always been active in charity, willingly giving of their time and money, but the increasing wealth and leisure of middle-class Victorians freed even larger numbers of women to take up the cause of the poor ... Charitable organizations united middle- and upper-class women and gave them greater access to poor women and children; since women were less identified with economic exploitation and political power, they were more readily accepted into the homes of the working class and the poor ... By the end of the century an upper-class woman who did not do some kind of volunteer work would have been an anomaly among her friends. And for single women, such work had become a respectable alternative to idleness. But boredom alone cannot explain why so many women willingly visited the slums, week after week.[9]

I do not deny the charitable impulse but want to consider other motivations, such as the desires for autonomy, status and money. In this period, people interested in the management of human life shifted their focus from the sovereignty of rulers to the art of government. A new entity, the 'population', was perceived to have problems that must be solved. For Foucault, the goal of government consists

not in the act of governing as such but in the improvement of the condition of the population, the increase of its wealth, longevity, health, etc.; and the means that the government will use to attain these ends are all in some sense immanent to the population, all of them pertain to the population itself on which government will intervene either directly through large-scale campaigns, or indirectly through techniques that will make possible, without the full awareness of the people, the stimulation of birth-rates, the directing of the flow of population into certain regions or activities etc.[10]

Power-knowledge is exercised over individuals through controlling institutions: schools, asylums, reformatories, penitentiaries, prisons and armies. This power is carried out through interlinked 'regimes of practices' known as punishment, medicine, education, protection and so on.[11] Discourses, practices and acts are inseparable; the machinery produced by efforts to govern are varied; governmentality theory can help us understand not only what social agents were thinking but also what they were doing, as well as illuminate the cult of domesticity and attached ideas of moral reclamation and regulation.[12] My work reveals not only the discourse but the tangible practices of those who tried to do something about 'prostitution' by controlling women who sold sex.

Before the Invention of 'Prostitution'

Though not a very honorable profession, no disgrace was attached to the person practising it. The professional prostitute was a free-born independent woman and the law protected her economic position.[13]

To understand the historic development of prostitution we need … to examine its relationship to the sexual regulation of all women in archaic states and its relationship to the enslavement of females … It is unfortunate that most authorities use the same term to cover a broad range of behavior and activities and to encompass at least two forms of organized prostitution – religious and commercial – which occur in archaic states.[14]

According to Gerda Lerner's analysis of patriarchy, historians have unjustifiably melded 'cultic sexual service' with commercial sexual service when writing about ancient worlds, creating a cause–effect relation that cannot be proved. Here, among scholars considering human customs many thousands of years old, we find a fusion of distinct cultural activities into one supposedly encompassing term. Lerner's sources are encyclopedias and historical works, the earliest dated 1858, William Sanger's *A History of Prostitution*. The date is not coincidental, falling squarely in the period I explore. The following are some suggestive points.

In general, before the late eighteenth century, commercial sex was treated as one of an array of offences to be managed, without any special moralism. Between 921 and 939 AD, an English decree required that certain wrongdoers be banished or killed, among these wizards, sorcerers, perjurers, conspirators to murder and 'vile, polluted, notorious *horewenan*', a word comprising whores, fornicators and adulterers.[15] By the eleventh and twelfth centuries, the clergy had much to say about the buying and selling of sex, theologians arguing, after Saint Augustine, that women who sold sex were a necessary evil (the 'sewer in the palace')

who needed only to be contained. Later, both monarchs and municipalities attempted to suppress commercial sex as one of several kinds of
vice; projects ranged from curfews and expulsion of sex vendors outside
the city walls to the assigning of them to designated districts and
municipally run brothels, but all evidence shows that sex was sold at
every place and hour and that those selling it were 'an integral part of
urban life in the Middle Ages'.[16] City authorities were interested in legal
issues related to selling sex, but they did not usually isolate this
particular problem from a range of others.[17] The recurring concerns
were (1) juridical (what crimes to punish and what methods to use) and
(2) town planning (where to allow this sex to take place). There was
always a minor discourse of religious reclamation as well, but, in the
premodern world-picture, every object and being was believed to
occupy its proper place for a reason, and large-scale attempts to change
fate did not make sense.

Leah Otis, in her study of the Languedoc, believes that modern concepts of deviance and marginality cannot apply to the medieval period,
'when prostitution was a recognized, if not particularly respected,
profession'.[18] Mary Perry, describing sixteenth- and seventeenth-
century Seville, writes that the common maxim of the day that whores
were moral cesspools had the effect of integrating them into society
'because it saw them as necessary vessels for human filth, sinners who
could divert others from the more serious sins of homosexuality, incest,
adultery, and propositioning honorable women'.[19]

The issue is less whether those selling sex were considered part of
society or not and more whether they were considered to have a dis-
tinguishable identity. Although laws were passed to regulate whoredom,
the category 'whore' itself was never defined.

> The connection of sexuality, greed, and commerce permeates the
> view of gender relations presented in late medieval English as well as
> Continental literature. If prostitutes in real life were marginalized by
> their treatment under the law, the institution of prostitution was
> integral to medieval English culture's concept of what it was to be a
> woman, for all women threatened to introduce sex into the world of
> commerce. The prostitute presented that threat most forcefully, but
> she was not so different from the married woman.[20]

Although Ruth Karras uses the word 'prostitute', there was no word or concept which signified *exclusively* the sale of sexual services until the social period. 'Whoring' referred to sexual relations out of marriage and connoted immorality or promiscuity without the involvement of money, and the word *whore* was used to brand any woman who stepped outside current boundaries of respectability. The emphasis was on the behaviour, not the personal identity.

Jacques Rossiaud believes that there was a general change toward further social integration of those selling sex from the fifteenth century on,[21] but the evidence points both ways: toward a greater acceptance and normalisation and also toward a more moralising rigour. In the early sixteenth century, a severe syphilis epidemic swept Europe, preparing the way for further repression.[22] Edward Bristow suggests that 'for conventional moralists of the late seventeenth and early eighteenth centuries, sexual misconduct was a serious matter; but there was no reason to single it out as the ultimate in wickedness'.[23] But as the eighteenth century went on, repressive movements grew, in France related to denunciations of the hedonism of nobles and royals, and in Britain associated with the evangelical Protestant revival. Vice and the obscene were to be rooted out on the stage, in books and in a general reformation of manners. Improper sexual relations formed part of this general concern, but there was still a lack of consensus on how to frame the problem itself. Most attempts to control it referred to disorder, public scandal or indecency, in which nonsexual offences were included with sexual. Although homes for reformed harlots had existed in other parts of Europe earlier, linked to the Catholic Church, history showed that such attempts usually failed, and women took up their old occupation. Despite accusations of popishness, reformatories began in Britain during this time.[24]

Again, tendencies can be seen both ways: towards repression and towards acceptance. In the eighteenth century, when James Boswell was keeping track of his sexual encounters in London's open spaces, and vice societies were attempting to stop such behaviour, the first modern argument for officially regulating and surveying commercial sex was published in London.[25] Both regulation and reform shared the logic of the social: identifying subjects to be rounded up and placed in buildings where programmes would work on them and authority figures would watch over them.

The Rise of the Social – and the Family

In the late eighteenth and early nineteenth centuries, societies in northern Europe were discrediting the idea that monarchs had a divine right to rule. Self-appointed observers and commentators consciously set out to consider social questions: of poverty, of the effects of industrialisation and of the growth of cities. Beyond the ages-old belief that destiny proclaimed some people unlucky or depraved, thinkers began to consider the possibility that destitution and depravation could be prevented. Philosophers and new social experts began to define the virtuous way for people to live and how to bring this about. Foucault described this task as involving not only 'upwards continuity', in which the governing person must first govern his own conduct, but 'downwards continuity', in which good governing principles are transmitted to families and to individuals. Government's purpose became not simply to govern but to assure the *welfare* of the population.[26]

Women who sold sex constituted one of the groups targeted for attention from this time.[27] This is not to claim that no such attention had ever been paid before or that the values were completely new. Some of the difference lies in the moral charge assigned to these values, the sheer number of people proclaiming them and a shift in the sex of who was doing most of the proclaiming. But a good part of the innovation lies in new ideas about the relationship between those making proposals about social problems and the people considered to *be* problems.

During the Rise of the Social, the bourgeoisie were finally achieving the power and status they had long sought. For the nobility, lineage and pride were secured through guaranteeing that property stayed in the family; noble persons were invested automatically with right and respectability – the principle of *noblesse oblige*. For the bourgeoisie, the nuclear family was to be society's central unit and 'family' had more emotional meanings – a way of life, domesticity, 'the home'.[28]

When the man and woman of the people live in disorder, they often have neither hearth nor home. They are only at ease where vice and crime reign free. But on the contrary, once a man and a woman of the people, illicitly joined together, are married, they desert the filthy rooms that were their only refuge and set up their home. Their foremost concern is to withdraw their children from the hospitals in which they had placed them. These married fathers and mothers establish a family, that is, a center where the children are fed, clothed, and protected; they send these children to school and place them in apprenticeship.[29]

Ariès emphasises two essential changes in this new vision of family: the development of the notion of privacy and the concept of childhood. Before, all of life was permeated with sociability, home and work were not considered separate, married couples with their children lived amidst larger households, and houses themselves were not separated into the rooms and functions we know today. The formulation of childhood as a time of innocence requiring long years of protection and instruction meant that particular people had to be assigned these tasks; families required supervision and spiritual nourishment in a specific place of their own.[30] Women were considered uniquely gifted with virtue and affection and therefore called to carry out these tasks, if not directly then through correct supervision of servants. Women's work was increasingly regarded as the 'emotional labour motivated (and guaranteed) by maternal instinct'. Conveniently, her domestic role contributed to bourgeois wealth and power.[31]

Donzelot shows how eighteenth-century French 'policing' extended its power through the family and how the home as a feminine domain became the new focus of respectability and virtue.

This great discovery: woman, the housewife and attentive mother, was man's salvation, the privileged instrument for civilising the working class. It sufficed merely to shape her to this use, to furnish her with the necessary instruction, to instill in her the elements of a tactics of devotion, in order for her to stamp out the spirit of independence in the working man.[32]

Some historians emphasise how, in this new domesticity, women became modest and passive, their sexuality dormant and their fate isolation and loneliness,[33] while others show how management of a household was

raised to the level of a science. Theories of hygiene, nutrition and regulation of personal behaviour were turned into a series of norms intended
to prevent the family from falling apart, now widely called the Domestic
Ideology.[34]

During the Rise of the Social, the bourgeoise believed it had a duty to
civilise the working class, as the aristocracy before believed it had in
relation to the bourgeoisie.[35] And in the same period that European
explorers thought that natives in faraway places would benefit by being
colonised, so did the 'more enlightened' class think the working class
would benefit by intervention in their affairs. The middle class
proclaimed the right way to live to everyone else, placing the bourgeois
woman in a position *vis-à-vis* the working-class woman in which 'a new
continuity was established for the bourgeois woman between her family
activities and her social activities. She discovered a new missionary
domain in which to operate.'[36] Not by chance, there was a sizeable social
area that needed her. As Engels pointed out in his study of Manchester,
the bourgeois capitalist system created an ideal of home and family life
that was impossible for the workers to attain:

> The various members of the family only see each other in the
> mornings and evenings, because the husband is away at his work all day
> long. Perhaps his wife and the older children also go out to work and
> they may be in different factories. In these circumstances how can
> family life exist?[37]

In France, Jules Simon published popular works (*L'Ouvrière* 1861, *La
Famille* 1869) railing against women who worked as 'impious' and
'sordid', no longer women. They represented disorder, when order was
defined as family and maternity. In Britain, bourgeois residents moved to
oust brothels from their environs.[38] As Weeks sees it, 'The more ideology
stressed the role of sex within conjugality the more it was necessary to
describe and regulate those forms of sexuality which were outside it.'[39]

With the identification of families as virtuous and normal, large
numbers of people were discursively converted into social misfits:
people without proper places in a domestic structure. Not only flagrant
beggars, homeless children and criminals but people who spent too
much time in taverns, who gambled, who bought meals outside the

home, who weren't interested in marriage and who liked to dawdle in the streets: all were peered at through a lens that sought to know *why* they did these things and how they could be prevented. Non-conforming individuals, those outside the hearth, were seen as threats to normal society who had to be steered toward a right way of life, cared for, protected from their erring ways.[40] This meant setting up machinery of social control that included investigation, surveillance, codes of dress and behaviour, definition of acceptable pastimes and vocations as well as techniques for classifying and recording the information collected. Donzelot calls this *philanthropy*:

> not to be understood as a naively apolitical term signifying a private intervention in the sphere of so-called social problems, but [to] be considered as a deliberately depoliticising strategy for establishing public services and facilities at a sensitive point midway between private initiative and the state.[41]

The discourse of problem groups necessitated the creation of jobs for those who would carry out the projects. 'Prostitutes', once viewed as miscreants who assaulted men in the street and offended good taste, were now seen as pathological, capable of contaminating good citizens and needing to be controlled.

The Drive to 'Do Something about Prostitution'

According to Tony Henderson, what the eighteenth-century London poor said about themselves (as opposed to what the non-poor said about them) indicates that 'prostitutes, both individually and collectively, were perhaps as much an accepted part of plebeian London as any other identifiable group', and they appeared to have had little difficulty in moving into other roles.[42] But the Vagrancy Act of 1822 *named* 'prostitutes' as one among other stigmatised groups who could be arrested.[43] Even so, efforts to count and locate offenders were frustrated by the impossibility of agreeing on their definition. Henry Mayhew, in *London Labour and the London Poor,* classified 'prostitutes' with vagrants, professional beggars, cheats and thieves, and subdivided them into 'park women', 'female operatives', 'maid-servants', 'ladies of intrigue', 'keepers of houses of assignation' and 'cohabitant prostitutes'. But Mayhew himself said that 'literally every woman who yields to her passions and loses her virtue is a prostitute, but many draw a distinction between those who live by promiscuous intercourse, and those who confine themselves to one man'.[44] Lynda Nead cautions us to read the term 'prostitute' not as

> an objective description of an already-determined group; rather, it actively constitutes a group which is both socially and economically specific. In the nineteenth century this process of categorization was produced through various social practices, through legal and medical discourses, religious and cultural forms.[45]

That the term did not have a firm meaning is reflected in the following excerpt from the trial of a woman picked up under the Contagious Diseases Acts:

Q. You know the man who goes by the name of William Simmons?
A. Yes.
Q. Have you lived with him for some time?
A. Yes, for six or seven years.
Q. As his wife?
A. Yes.
Q. And you are not a prostitute?
A. No; only to the one man.
Q. Only to Simmons, you mean?
A. Yes.
Q. You mean that you are not a prostitute, other than as living with one man without marriage?
A. Yes, that's what I mean.[46]

The difficulty in counting and locating the right women, rather than throwing doubt on the project, incited more discourse, more investigation and more surveillance. But the dangerous connection to sex was certain; sexuality was becoming 'a continent of knowledge, with its own rules of exploration and its own expert geographers'.[47] In France, investigators affiliated with the Académie des Sciences Morales et Politiques, charged with researching factory life, were like 'travellers in foreign lands, [journeying] from city to city, recording in minute detail the new and strange sights they had seen'.[48] Their reports were reprinted and their views were cited as scientific evidence for programmes, but

> Programmes presuppose that the real is programmable, that it is a domain subject to certain determinants, rules, norms and processes that can be acted upon and improved by authorities. They make the objects of government thinkable in such a way that their ills appear susceptible to diagnosis, prescription and cure by calculating and normalising intervention.[49]

So the social invented not only its objects but the necessity to do something about them, and thereby its own need to exist. Before, various kinds of authority figures, including kings and clergy, pronounced and decreed about promiscuity, commercial sex and adultery, and there was no contradiction in the fact that members of the royalty, nobility and clergy themselves bought sex and ran brothels, and that some nuns sold sex.[50] The relationship between those doing the decreeing and those being decreed about was hierarchical and judicial, those above deciding what the duties and faults were of those below, without any self-reflexion on their own roles.[51]

The question is not whether 'prostitution' had long been simultaneously deplored, combated and tolerated, because it had; the whore stigma had been severe and the punishment at times horrific (as it was for many crimes). But what appears in histories prior to the social consists mostly of municipal authorities' dictates on how to deal with problems of crime and public scandal, with the clergy providing pious reasons in support. Discourses changed little over hundreds of years. Some phenomena were condemned, but they were thought to exist inevitably, through a 'great chain of being', God's will or Destiny (which didn't stop some individuals from trying to alter fate). But when problems began to be viewed as interdependencies within the social fabric, a different relationship arose between the person considering a problem called 'prostitution' and the 'prostitute'.

Érica-Marie Benabou draws a detailed picture of the situation in Paris before the Revolution, when a system of policing the sex trade was already in place. The *police des moeurs* (morals police) were more interested in finding out about aristocratic clients than in penalising

women who sold sex.[52] In 1769, Restif de la Bretonne published his
'utopian' plan, which suggested placing 20,000 women in state-
regulated houses, with older, former workers in charge, for the better
convenience and delight of the clientele. One element of his proposal
recommended mandatory medical exams for the women, whom he
called *filles de joie* – gay girls.[53]

Filles de joie or *putains* (putrid women): the schizophrenic nature of
ideas about women who sold sex is not easily explained. At the
beginning of the social period, the most widespread image was the 'vile
harlot', whose body was a stinking sewer threatening society but who
was also carefree, pleasure-seeking and seductive. An alternative image
saw her as a victim of circumstances, and this image came to predominate as time passed (in tandem with the rise in helping professions).
Nead devotes a good part of her *Myths of Sexuality* to images of the
'prostitute' and theorises the metamorphosis from dangerous to
victimised as a mechanism allowing outsiders to feel pity rather than
fear: 'Pity deflects the force of that group and redistributes power in
terms of a conventional relationship organized around notions of social
conscience, compassion and philanthropy.'[54] The various 'prostitute'
images were never perfectly distinct from one another but rather acted
at one minute as the symbol of lighthearted pleasure, and at the next as
vile, contaminating or damaged – a tendency that still exists.

Considered the bearer of syphilis, the woman selling sex was associated with excrement, dead meat and decay.[55] To the French police, she
was a member of the 'dangerous' classes, irrevocably associated with the
crime and criminality that obsessed Parisians early in the nineteenth
century. A police report published in 1828 summarised the actions
required to solve the city's problems:

> (1) Put a stop to usury, which is becoming excessive; (2) Curb the
> bailiff's rapacity; (3) Expel five-sixths of the beggars still here;
> (4) Clear Paris of a crowd of vagrants who do nothing but spread
> theft and crime; (5) Halt the proliferation of common prostitutes.[56]

Through a series of administrative decisions that responded to the spirit
of the time, rather than the passing of any law, the Paris police prefecture
imposed both state regulation and mandatory medical examinations on

'prostitutes', together comprising what came to be known as the French System whose essential principles were: (1) create an 'enclosed *milieu*'; (2) supervise it constantly; (3) compartmentalise this space according to distinct perceived types, in a hierarchy. Corbin's work demonstrates how these principles facilitated both the surveillance and the disciplining of those selling sex and how they form part of a typical Enlightenment project to 'destroy confusions' of categories.[57]

The social investigator who produced the necessary knowledge was Alexandre-Jean-Baptiste Parent-Duchâtelet, who had already investigated Parisian sewers when he took on 'prostitution'. Considered the chief authority during the nineteenth century, his Paris research and ideas were emulated all over Europe. He took the regulatory system to be a natural development towards the new concept of *public health*, and through his presentation of extensive statistics approved what the police had already done. But Parent-Duchâtelet's research produced another kind of result. Interviewing thousands of Paris women, he was unable to prove that there was a 'prostitute' type, a regional tendency or a predisposing professional life. Although he began his work believing the 'prostitute' had immoral proclivities, he ended by seeing her as a victim of poverty and as a member of the urban proletariat.[58]

Writing of the nineteenth century, Jill Harsin calls the *police des moeurs* a 'creeping bureaucracy', an administrative department with a huge budget, while a military corps of *gendarmes royales* was required to accompany them on their rounds.[59] Registered brothel-keepers became one sort of civil servant, brothel inspectors another. Dispensaries dedicated to the business of examining women's vaginas employed doctors who used a new metal apparatus, the speculum. The studies and diagnoses they made 'legitimated all kind of intrusions into women's lives – observation, classification, supervision – in the name of research',[60] and each form of intrusion provided intruders with employment.

In nineteenth-century Britain, commercial sex was a burning issue, and London was believed to have more women selling sex than any other European capital. 'From three o'clock in the afternoon, it is impossible for any respectable woman to walk from the top of the Haymarket to Wellington Street, Strand'.[61] The reigning image was of a woman who falls into degradation, torturing guilt, drink, failing looks, syphilis and suicide, within just a few years (Nead's 'myth'), and various serious texts reproduced it without question.[62] William Acton, inspired by Parent-Duchâtelet's work in Paris, published the first British study, in 1856, aimed at debunking the myth, his chief finding being that 'prostitution' was a transitory occupation.[63] This led him to advocate regulation as the best way to reduce the harm done to women and to society.

The move toward regulation in Britain came with the Contagious Diseases Acts of 1864, 1866 and 1869, which mandated the medical examination of 'prostitutes' in England's garrison and port towns, to protect the armed forces.[64] Nonuniformed police officers selected women for examination; those found to be suffering from venereal disease were isolated. But Acton's findings provided ammunition to campaigners against the Acts, since if 'prostitution' was not a pre-destined tragedy, then it *could* be done away with.

Occupied by Women: Cross-class Accounts

The vast surge of proposals and actions on behalf of problem groups was often motivated by a desire to prevent unhappiness and injustice. Women and men often took up the social banner because they were in sympathy with or angry about the lot of the poor; they spent time theo-rising, debating ideas, forming associations, as well as doing practical work.[65] While middle-class women were seen as helping the working class, histories of philanthropic movements show that the benefits were questionable or nonexistent for the people they aimed to help. The benefits to the helpers, on the other hand, in terms of experience, satisfaction and future prospects, were significant, both for themselves as individuals and for capitalism. The moral reformation of the working class encouraged workers to spend time at home, where they would eat, sleep and bathe at certain hours in certain ways, in order to be fresh and able to perform in the workplace. Nancy Armstrong notes how 'the notion of charity was inexorably linked to the female role of household overseer'.[66]

For a complex of demographic and social reasons, there were now more educated women with time to spare and/or the desire or need to work for a living: widows, unmarried daughters, wives without access to their own property, and leisured women. At mid-century in Britain, women with money to pay an attorney could denounce violent husbands, but only through laws passed in 1870 and 1882 did they get the right to keep their own earnings after marriage.[67] In France, 'women who wished to improve their position in society through work were obliged to sacrifice their private lives', and an 1880 study of female postal workers showed a majority had chosen financial and professional independence rather than marriage.[68] Perhaps the most famous such woman was Florence Nightingale, who defied her upper-class parents and became a nurse. The museum dedicated to her honour says that her greatest achievement was the raising of nursing to respectability; she was awarded the Order of Merit and herself never married. Some extremists said such 'redundant' women should be shipped to the colonies.[69] The supply of women needing or wanting to earn a living was growing, but how could they maintain respectability?

It is risky to impose contemporary ideas about class on the past. In the nineteenth century, women's relationships with men mostly determined their class status,[70] but once a woman went out to work, she confused categories. The only occupations long considered compatible with respectability were lady's companion, governess, teacher — jobs carried out by living inside a real home, by the side of real respectable ladies. Governesses were ideally meant to be gentlewomen. At the same time, they shared the taint of forbidden sexuality the bourgeoisie ascribed to all house servants,[71] which means that even the respectable occupations were considered dubious.[72] One middle-class lady considered engraving, drawing patterns and needlework to be suitable tasks; another said her work was running a household, writing letters and seeing callers; while a third believed her work was crocheting bonnets for friends.[73] These ideas reflect what the bourgeoisie considered correct.[74]

The jobs widely available for women in the nineteenth century were in textile manufacturing and domestic service, but women worked in a wide array of other jobs. In England, they were dressmakers, needlewomen, milliners, washerwomen, charwomen, milkmaids, nurse-maids, circus women, shoebinders, mantua makers, satinstitch workers, glove makers, straw bonnet makers, stay trimmers, hat binders and chambermaids. Women worked in the jute industry, as machinists in mills and as hawkers, flower sellers, message girls and match girls. They brewed and sold beer; they managed lodging houses and brothels; they tended silkworms. Outside the cities they kept vegetable gardens and animals, carried loads on their backs and picked strawberries and hops. Flither girls gathered limpets and birds' eggs, and women hauled coal in the mines. Later in the century, more women did 'white blouse' work (school teaching, shop assistance, office work and nursing) and were waitresses and attendants in toilets. Many jobs became available because of the rise of social projects: cleaning, maintenance and policing. Some women in all jobs *also* sold sexual favours at some time, to tide themselves over or to supplement income.[75] Petty theft and picking pockets were other sources of income.

Natalie Zemon Davis lists women's jobs in sixteenth-century France, apart from domestic service, as ferrying people across rivers, attending in bath-houses, digging ditches and carrying loads at construction sites.[76] Joan Landes writes of French women's widespread desire to go on the stage, this being 'one of the few professions in which a woman could hope to earn a living, practice a craft and achieve some measure of social acclaim'.[77] In 1836, when Parent-Duchâtelet published his survey of 'prostitutes', they told him they had worked in over 600 different occu-pations: *couturières*, seamstresses, breeches makers, coat makers, hair-dressers, glove makers, lace makers, artificial flower makers, day labourers, dairymaids, workers in farms and vineyards, shop clerks, street peddlers, acrobats, gauze makers, fringe makers, furriers, hatters, helmet makers, shoemakers, bootmakers, brush makers, laundresses, ironers, jewellers, clockmakers, enamellers, burnishers and polishers, engravers, stage actresses and extras, music teachers and, of course, servants.

The literary and historical writings of many middle-class men scarcely mention working women unless they sold sex. For Paris Police Prefect F. F-A. Béraud, in a book on 'public women', it did not 'take much acuteness to recognize that a girl who at eight o'clock may be seen sumptuously dressed in an elegant costume is the same who appears as a shop girl at nine o'clock and as a peasant girl at ten'.[78] Siegfried Kracauer's nineteenth-century Paris seems to be a great open-air theatre for men, against whose backdrop carefree women romp, referred to affectionately as *vedettes*, *lorettes*, *cocottes* and *grisettes*.[79] Weeks explains the male prejudice:

> Two factors were of particular symbolic importance and concern to these bourgeois intellectuals, both relating to women: their sexuality and their economic autonomy. Because of the developing ideology of woman's role in the family and her very special responsibility for society's well being, it was women working outside the home who received the most attention from the parliamentary commissioners in the 1830s and 40s. Moreover, most attention was paid not to the conditions of work as such but to the moral and spiritual degradation said to accompany female employment.[80]

Corbin argues that the woman seeking middle-class clients in Paris did participate in the new, modern, public spectacle, 'parad[ing] or exhibit[ing] herself on the terraces of the high-class cafés, in the brasseries, in the *cafés-concerts*, and on the sidewalk'.[81] But all women in public were not selling sex; a diversity of women shared the same spaces as their patrons, friends, harassers, potential targets and boyfriends: parks, taverns, markets, theatres and streets. Women also liked to dance, drink, take walks, make money and have sex. 'Although the male ruling class did all it could to restrict the movement of women in cities, it proved impossible to banish them from public spaces. Women continued to crowd into the city centres and the factory districts.'[82] Elizabeth Wilson discusses the contradictions between ideology and the possible reality of women's confinement to the domestic sphere, and disputes, as I did in Chapter 2, the argument that female *flâneurs* (itinerant urban observers) were impossible. Bourgeois women may not have been 'permitted' to spend time in public until special areas with shops were built (the Arcades) and shopping became an acceptable activity,[83] but working women were already there when the respectable arrived: working, not working class. There were women of middle-class status working to support themselves, women of the lower class skilled enough to improve their financial and social status,[84] and women from a higher class who did jobs considered beneath them.

Chance, serendipity and personal desire entered into the search for jobs. In many late-eighteenth- and nineteenth-century novels written in Northern Europe, the story depicts individuals' attempts to break out of oppressive destinies and improve their lives. The classic *Bildungs-roman*[85] described a young, familyless man from the country arriving in Paris or London to make his fortune, learning, loving and in some way triumphing at the end; the familyless young woman trying to do the same was often doomed to disaster and death. Not safely ensconced in a home, she encountered enemies everywhere, some of the fiercest being members of polite society who preferred to see a woman dead rather than unmarried and pregnant, or married but realising herself outside the home. Nevertheless, many significant novels from this time reveal that another plot was waxing, in which marriage was not enough for a bourgeois women and a woman who worked was not punished or doomed to lose respectability.[86]

Superficially, women were not considered working class if they presented a genteel image, but in histories of the Contagious Diseases Acts, over and over we are told that researchers erred when trying to identify 'prostitutes' and that police officers kept mistakenly arresting 'decent' women. The sole fact of standing on a notorious street corner, a bare head, 'garish' dress, a loud voice or 'rowdy' behaviour could incriminate. Olive Schreiner, a writer and exponent of women's rights, drew attention by not wearing gloves while out walking with a male friend.[87] Patriarchy's desire to distinguish between good and bad women is as old as written history: those who engage in pre- or extramarital sexual activity have to be *detectable*. The problem for those charged with ferreting out vice arose when 'the way women dress today they all look like prostitutes', a policeman's complaint.[88] In fact, mainstream fashions are often initiated by women who sell sex, a phenomenon particularly lamented during the social period.[89]

In the lower classes, sexual relations between engaged couples and common law marriages were conventional, but in this epoch distinguishing between pure and impure women became extremely important to the bourgeoisie. Good women were seen as biologically capable of sexual abstinence, morally superior to men and naturally domestic, while men were thought to have an inborn need for frequent sexual relations and a predisposition to vice, which led them to leave home for bars, streets, gaming houses, brothels and theatres. Girls were assumed to have no need for sex, and married women to want it only with their husbands (and, some thought, only in order to have children). 'Suffer and be still' may have represented the most extreme vision of proper womanhood, but in a myriad of other ways society told respectable women that sexual desire should be overcome. Women were expected to sexually wait until men were in a position to marry and provide for a family, but men were expected neither to wait until marriage nor to inhibit their desire after it. In order for some women to remain 'pure', then, other women had to behave 'impurely', whether they were married ('adulteresses'), servant girls ('seduced virgins') or professionals ('prostitutes'). Later, morally fervent crusades on behalf of purity recognised these contradictions about sexuality and proposed that men assume a 'woman-like' chastity, which they linked also to the eradication of syphilis and the vote for women. New waves of evangelical Protestanism reinforced these ideas. In France, the term *femmes isolées* (isolated, or stranded, women) was used for both women wage earners living alone in furnished rooms and for women selling sex without being registered at a brothel. The authors of the Paris Chamber of Commerce's *Statistique de l'Industrie* (1847–8) associated 'dissipation' and 'disorderly conduct' with workers, in the same way that Parent-Duchâtelet targeted 'vanity and the desire to glitter' as causing women to sell sex.[90] Issues of gender and class are inextricably intertwined in the story of how bourgeois women came to occupy a new sphere in the labour economy.[91]

The Creation of Suitable Jobs for Women

Social investigators, statisticians, police, missionaries, hospital and penitentiary staff, teachers, lecturers, members of committees, tract writers, clergy, campaign activists, clerical workers, doctors, nurses, civil servants: jobs for those engaged in stamping out immorality and imposing virtue abounded, and though many worked as volunteers, as time went on more came to be paid. 'Social' work carried a certain prestige and began to be considered a dignified, suitable job for middle-class women; the highest posts were usually assigned to father figures, but the very nature of the project meant there had to be mother figures as well.[92] The middle class's certainty of their ability to help may be understood as part of the period's belief in social evolution:

> All living societies were irrevocably placed on … a stream of Time – some upstream, others downstream. Civilization, evolution, development, acculturation, modernization … are all terms whose conceptual content derives … from evolutionary Time.[93]

During the Rise of the Social, a theory of *self*-government also arose, but it was thought only possible for people with sufficient capacity for rational thinking and, where that was lacking, other people had to govern. Considered 'as an aggregate', 'the poor' were to be treated differently from individuals capable of 'specular morality', the ability to reflect on one's own moral character.[94] The bourgeois way of life was considered advanced, and the poor's like primitive tribes', backward. Women were considered inherently inferior to men, but bourgeois women were seen as naturally superior to poor women.[95]

Whereas eighteenth-century salon hostesses, a prestigious social group of intellectual women, had moral authority because of their 'disinterestedness and generosity, an eloquent concern for the public welfare', virtue was now defined by respectability.[96] Middle-class women were seen to have a natural duty to care for the incapable poor, a 'civilising mission', which,

> when appropriately applied, not only would give the family a happier and better life, but also would help to eliminate the most grievous wrongs of society. Philanthropy had traditionally been women's par-ticular concern, and its definition during the … century … was broadened to include virtually every major social problem. It is from the narrow base of woman's special duties and obligations that women in the nineteenth century came to expand their fields of action and their personal horizons.[97]

The virtuous domestic woman came to be accepted as knowing what was best for everyone;[98] at the same time, anxiety grew about women working outside the home, potential 'prostitutes'. To the social sector, there was 'only one cure for sexual licence and that was control'.[99]

> As superintendents of the domestic sphere, (middle-class) women were represented as protecting and, increasingly, incarnating virtue ... their economic support tended to be translated into a language of morality and affection; their most important work was increasingly represented as the emotional labor motivated (and guaranteed) by maternal instinct.[100]

Women wanting to work outside the home could claim a vocation, 'lifting up' the poor: reclaiming, restoring, rehabilitating, redeeming and (re)integrating them into society. They would inculcate protestant principles of thrift, individual responsibility and domesticity.[101]

> The moral decay of the working class was seen above all in terms of its deficient pattern of family life, the apparently absent values of domesticity, family responsibility, thrift and accumulation. Hence the growth of the paradoxical phenomena of leisured middle-class ladies encouraging the education of working-class women in the virtues of housewifery, with the development of sewing schools, cooking classes and so on.[102]

A phrase of the time, 'woman's mission to women', contradicted the masculine idea that pure women should not know about the 'vile' things that happened to less fortunate ones.[103] It was argued that women magistrates and women police should be introduced to work with women[104] and that workhouses should be supervised by women, who would inject 'the law of love'.[105] For some women it was important that the rescue project be called a 'home', and its inmates located through house-to-house visits by women.[106]

> It has been felt that no efforts on behalf of the fallen were likely to be so successful as those which were made by their own sex. They are able better to enter into their feelings, to sympathise with them, to receive from them their tale of sorrow, and to advise them for their present and eternal welfare.[107]

Mary Higgs, for the pamphlet *Three Nights in Women's Lodging Houses*, posed as a poor woman in order to find out what went on in places where streetwalkers lived, and proposed that 'girls such as this should be passed on to some agency that would "mother" them. It is easy to see how a little indecision, and the pressure of hunger, might anchor a girl to sin.'[108] Frank Mort, quoting the Reverend Frederick Maurice on the 'softening, humanising, health-giving influence' of lady visitors to hospital wards for the poor, notes they

> could supervise and reinforce the medical regime, administering medicines, scrutinising the nurses, reporting their behaviour and above all inquiring into the moral habits of poor patients – factors which were now known to play such a crucial role in the spread of disease.[109]

Some believed that religious sisterhoods should take charge so that ordinary women would not lose their respect for men.[110]

Even extremists among the moral reformers, the 'stampers' and 'watch committees', shared a gender concern that Lucy Bland urges us not to lose sight of: 'the evangelical emphasis on personal morality and a moralising role for women within the home gave women a language and a voice with which to demand moral behaviour from those within that home, including their husbands'.[111] To understand, Corbin's comment on men's attitudes is useful:

> It is important to decipher the meaning of the laughter that rocked the Chamber of Deputies in 1895 when it tried, unsuccessfully, to discuss a legal proposal on prostitution. One can imagine watching a Marshall Sahlins, returned from Tahiti, resting his anthropological gaze on this group of males with bulging bellies, the majority of which were clients of prostitutes, as they shook with irrepressible laughter.[112]

Ann Laura Stoler suggests that Foucault insufficiently understood the extent to which European sexualities were formed in, not merely transmitted to, their colonies, and the role that race played in this formation.[113] The usual view is that European elites used the colonies as their sexual playground, but

> those same elites were intent to mark the boundaries of a colonizing population, to prevent those men from 'going native', to curb a proliferating mixed-race population that compromised their claims to superiority and thus the legitimacy of white rule. In colonial

societies as in Europe, 'racial survival' was often seen to be precariously predicated on a strict adherence to cultural – and specifically gendered – prescriptions.[114]

Europeans may be said to have carried the message about civilising women to the colonies, but this involved, more than colonialism, the creation of 'a series of hegemonic projects'.[115] On her arrival in Sydney in the late 1830s, Caroline Chisholm set out to round up single women immigrants and find them temporary employment and permanent marriage.

> If Her Majesty's Government be really desirous of seeing a well-conducted community spring up in these Colonies, the social wants of the people must be considered. If the paternal Government wish to entitle itself to that honoured appellation, it must look to the materials it may send as a nucleus for the formation of a good and great people. For all the clergy you can despatch, all the school-masters you can appoint, all the churches you can build, and all the books you can export, will never do much good without what a gentleman in that Colony very appropriately called 'God's police' – wives and little children – good and virtuous women.[116]

During the French colonising of Shanghai (the 'Paris of Asia'), systems of regulation, tolerance and eradication of 'prostitution' were all tried out and found to fail.[117] Tahiti was another site for trying out the French system.[118] A system of regulation already existed in Hong Kong when the British exported the Contagious Diseases Acts to India, where Josephine Butler, even while campaigning against them, believed that Britain had a Christian responsibility to protect and civilise. In Vron Ware's analysis, Butler hoped that Indian women would someday be capable of taking on the role of moral guardian, but first they would have to be freed from the laws and practices that oppressed them. British women were positioned as spiritual mothers, with Indians their daughters.[119] When in the late nineteenth century the middle class became aware of large numbers of European women emigrating to seek their fortune in countries such as Argentina, where they worked in brothels, they called them victims of 'white slavery' who should be protected for their own good.[120]

Many women reformers also mentioned class and cultural differences in arguing about who was in the best position to implement
helping. Ellen Ranyard ran the Female Bible Society on the principle that
'the poor could best be encouraged to help themselves if they were
initially helped by another like themselves', and helpers supplemented
the distribution of bibles by assisting with household tasks.[121] Octavia
Hill founded a charitable society based on the belief that 'personal
relations between rich and poor would bring the deserving ones out of
habits of dependence and thriftlessness'. She bought tenements and sent
out female home visitors to collect rents and supervise domesticity.[122]
Linda Mahood describes the treatment of 'prostitutes' in Glasgow's
penitentiaries as

> organized around the premise that inmates could only be reformed if
> order was put into their lives and a strict regime of 'mild, whole-
> some, paternal, and Christian discipline' was enforced ... [W]hat is
> striking ... is the overall 'gentility' and similarity to the manner in
> which middle-class women might spend their evenings. The emphasis
> on gentility reflects how closely penitentiaries associated middle-
> class manners with reform.[123]

Institutions, including penitentiaries, varied, of course. Those run by
Anglican nuns have been called 'therapeutic communities' that offered
shelter to many types of female victims who entered voluntarily.

> ... penitents were taught instant obedience to orders and to curtsey
> when passing sisters ... The reformation of the body included
> cleanliness, 'modest refined ways,' and good manners. The sisters'
> hope was to render the penitents psychologically unfit for their
> former lives; success was achieved when formerly acceptable
> manifestations of working-class speech and behaviour filled reformed
> penitents with 'shock and disgust'.[124]

For the religious, rescue work could be explained with the parable of the
lost sheep.

> Significantly, the privilege and responsibility of seeking to bring those
> termed wandering sheep home to the Good Shepherd's flock was
> seen to be immeasurable. By returning the lost sheep ... to the

heavenly fold the redeemers not only saved a soul but also notched up a point for themselves on some heavenly tally.[125]

So a whole sphere of tasks came to be considered not only appropriate and dignified work, but also particularly suitable and natural to women. These were respectable, paid occupations, something that had not existed before. There was now employment for women in charitable, educational and correctional institutions. New jobs included social investigator, district visitor, rent collector, sanitary inspector, Poor Law guardian, fundraiser, public speaker, settlement house worker, superintendent, matron, manager, probation officer and adult education teacher. Some women worked as unpaid career administrators and planners; affluent women undertook roles of patronage[126] (in France called *dames patronesse*). In convents, routine tasks were carried out by paid female employees.[127]

These kinds of posts multiplied as social causes did. Later, there would be a move to professionalise, train and struggle for recognition, but at the beginning, amateurs were the rule. Many women began as volunteers, defying ideas that their only place was the home. Charity work, especially the rescue of victimised children and women, was a way to move into the public world. F. K. Prochaska documents the significant rise in numbers of women on charity subscription lists, in women's financial contributions to charities, in women's district visiting to the poor, in women's participation on management committees and in women as managers and volunteer helpers in a variety of situations from lying-in hospitals to village bazaars.[128]

In London, 279 charities were founded before 1850, and 144 more during the following *decade* alone.[129] In Aberdeen, with a population of fewer than 70,000 in the 1840s, rescue organisations included local branches of the Association for the Promotion of Social Sciences, the British Ladies' Society for Promoting the Reformation of Female Prisoners, and the Association for the Promotion of Social Purity, as well as the Aberdeen Association for Reclaiming Fallen Females and the Aberdeenshire Association of Ladies for the Rescue of Fallen Women.[130] In France, groups campaigning for the end of regulation proliferated from the 1870s, and by the turn of the century, there were at least 1,300 associations devoted to the 'raising up' of girls.[131]

In terms of religious institutions, in the early 1840s there were few penitentiaries for fallen women, but the first Anglican sisterhood was founded in 1845, after which the number increased quickly (there were places for 400 women in 1840 and 7,000 by 1893).

> Two needs coincided in the 1840s: the number of former prostitutes desiring some form of institutional care was growing rapidly, and the newly established Anglican sisterhoods, seeking a means of justifying and defending their vulnerable institutions, saw the provision of refuges for fallen women as an irrefutable vindication of their own existence.[132]

New theories emerged, such as the concept of prevention: 'The work of the reformer is not with the outcast, the Magdalen, but with the causes that make outcasts – better save future generations than twenty fallen women.'[133] The evolution of theories and the maturing of discourses meant the creation of new projects and increasing numbers of workers. The movement was diversifying, and, as societies expanded, some homes became specialised. The Rescue Society ran a home for the fallen, another for invalids and a third for girls in danger. The Female Mission to the Fallen, which sent out lady missioners to approach women who sold sex in the streets and workhouses, also helped those who attempted suicide and sponsored two homes for unmarried mothers and their babies.[134]

The Work of Helping 'Prostitutes'

Foucault suggests we examine how 'forms of rationality inscribe themselves in practices or systems of practices, and what role they play within them'.[135] Here I show how helping played out on the ground day to day. Both the English and the French responses to 'prostitution' used the principle of incarceration: brothel, hospital, 'home' and prison were all institutions to which women were to be confined, providing a structure for women believed to lack one. The French system envisaged four distinct spaces for the surveillance and discipline of 'prostitutes': the house (where sex was sold), the hospital (where venereal diseases were treated), the prison (where wrongdoers were kept) and the refuge (where repentant women were rehabilitated). Some specialists advocated concentration of these activities in a panopticon system: prison, dispensary and hospital in one enclosure next to a red-light district.[136] In 1822, a Female Factory was opened in Parramatta, Australia, which functioned as both prison and workplace. Women were divided into three classes according to their moral and immigration status. Incarceration was meant to spare them the 'enforced whoredom' that was the fate of so many women arriving in Australia, yet the factory operated openly as both brothel and marriage market.[137]

Many people laboured inside the institutions where women were kept,[138] and much of the work was maintenance (cleaning floors, preparing food). But most of the interned women did not want to be there; escape attempts were rife (and often successful), so policing had to be carried out. Locking the door on people who want to get out is a concrete task. Requiring people to have a particular appearance means taking their own clothes away, cutting their hair. Forcing people to do laundry (the standard work imposed on inmates) means supervising it. Reading Bible lessons and other improving texts to people who didn't ask to hear them is a chore, as is teaching one kind of domestic economy to people who already know another.

> For the good influence of the *dame patronesse* to have an effect, the prostitute must be prevented from keeping up any relationships with her family and friends. The madam, the policeman and the police doctor, and the *dame patronesse* are the only people with whom the imprisoned prostitute is to be allowed to communicate.[139]

Employees kept women from their families and friends through surveillance, locked doors and a deaf ear to pleas. Consider the posted 'Rules for the conduct of the women' in York Female Penitentiary at mid-century:

> I. The directions and orders of the Matron shall at all times be promptly obeyed.
>
> II. The women shall preserve a decent deportment, and a becoming silence, especially while at work. Reproaches for past irregularities,

railing, and all angry expressions, are strictly forbidden; and if repeated after admonition from the Matron, shall be reported to the committee, and punished at their discretion.

III. Lying, swearing, dishonesty, repeated disobedience, and gross misbehaviour, shall be punished by the Committee with expulsion, unless circumstances should induce them to mitigate the punishment.

IV. No woman shall leave her employment without the Matron's permission.

V. The father, mother, or other near relation, (being known to be such,) may be permitted to see and converse with any of the women, at the discretion and in the presence of the Matron, between the hours of eleven and twelve in the morning, and two and three in the afternoon (Sundays excepted.) – But no such person, whether male or female, shall be admitted into the wards.

VI. No letter shall be conveyed to or from the house, without the inspection of the Matron.[140]

The rationale for this treatment rested on the conviction that working-class women would be improved by their incarceration: these were reformatories aiming to transform offenders, not punish wrong acts. Reformers need to get access to wrongdoers first, establish a relationship through coercion and constraint.

Time-tables, compulsory movements, regular activities, solitary meditation, work in common, silence, application, respect, good habits ... ultimately, what one is trying to restore in this technique of correction is ... the obedient subject, the individual subjected to habits, rules, orders, an authority that is exercised continually around him and upon him, and which he must allow to function automatically in him.[141]

Concern was often expressed that the staff in some institutions exercised their authority in an inappropriate tyrannical manner, and managers were urged 'not to imagine that the dulcet tones used to them (by the matrons and other staff) are the same as the penitents experience'.[142]

The use of penitentiaries for 'prostitutes' belongs to the new kind of discipline and punishment Foucault identified in prisons, asylums and other institutions from the eighteenth century onwards. The object was not to requalify inmates as subjects with rights but to turn them into docile domestic servants or wives – not the autonomous subjects that educated women were themselves struggling to become.

> In asserting a particular feminine point of view, women philan-thropists made an indirect contribution towards the emancipation of women of their own class. However, their philanthropic initiatives were often diametrically opposed to the emancipation of women in the social classes beneath them. [143]

In 1851, 42 per cent of British women aged 20 to 40 were un-married, and two million of a total six million women were self-supporting: one third of the female population. [144] Ladies who had to work for a living were pitied. By 1861, women represented more than one third of the labour force, one fourth of these being married women. [145] By 1914, middle-class working women, a respected and self-respecting group, were an essential part of the country's labour force. [146] The opening up of the social sector for women played a large part in this change.

> Through their work with the poor, the reformers discovered many of the elements from which they would forge their own class and sexual identity, still ill-defined and diffuse in 1850; women, particularly, strengthened their role as dictators of domestic and familial standards for all classes ... [147]

Our contemporary interest in the voice of the subject had no place in this scheme.

The Voice of the Subject

In my account of the Rise of the Social, I focus on how the construction of the slippery category 'prostitution' provided work for those intent on eradicating it. A central irony of this story is that these middle-class women's occupations aimed at doing away with many working-class women's means of support. While formulating their own desire for independence and participation in the culture of individual work, many joined campaigns to repress and limit opportunities for other women.

Social investigators and morals police looking for 'prostitutes' ignored them when they said they did not see themselves as immoral or did not wish to be rescued. In the testimonies of social agents, one rarely encounters the actual words of working-class women, yet those could be compelling.

> I was a servant gal away down in Birmingham. I got tired of workin' and slavin' to make a living, and getting a _____ bad one at that; what o' five pun' a year and yer grub, I'd sooner starve, I would. After a bit I went to Coventry, cut brummagem, as we calls it in those parts, and took up with soldiers as was quartered there. I soon got tired of them. Soldiers is good – soldiers is – to walk with and that, but they don't pay 'cos why they ain't got no money; so I says to myself, I'll go to Lunnon and I did. I soon found my level there.[148]

This voice demonstrates several points. First, that the pay and working conditions of respectable domestic service were considered insulting. Second, that women made their own decisions about how to improve their lives. Third, that selling sex was not seen as different from other jobs. Fourth, that money was important. Fifth, that personal enjoyment was important. Sixth, that risks were taken to find one's personal 'level'.

The issue of remuneration was supremely important.

> The standard of living of prostitutes was perceptibly higher than other working women. A prostitute, even a sailor's woman, could earn the weekly wages of a respectable working woman in a day, at a shilling a 'shot'. Prostitutes had a room of their own; they dressed better; they had spending money and access to the pub, the principal facility in the working-class neighborhood that provided heat, light, cooked food, and conviviality.[149]

For social agents of the servant-employing class, the only truly approved job for regenerate 'prostitutes' was domestic service. Anne McClintock relates how the colonial middle class in South Africa expressed outrage at the fact that women were allowed to work in the mines, while servants in their own houses often worked longer, more exhausting hours for a tiny wage, were isolated from family and community, and 'emotionally and physically at the mercy of the men of the house-hold'.[150] The effort to turn interned women into domestic servants, however, succeeded in few cases.[151]

Since the 'prostitute' of middle-class imagination didn't actually exist, it shouldn't surprise us to find that, for helpers and savers, the centre of the discourse was themselves. They believed their help was intrinsically different and better than the policeman's or the judge's because of their class, education and sex. But like the work of the policeman and the judge, theirs depended on defining others as wrong-doing, mistaken, misled, deviant. When reformers refused to accept the information, obtained in social research, that women who sold sex did not find the life uncongenial, they paid no attention. This refusal was self-serving; after all, without people to rescue, they could be out of a job.

While bourgeois women's demands did not talk about pleasure and desire, their own desires did impel them, whether for love, freedom, happiness, tranquillity, independence, money or adventure. They concentrated on gaining liberties and legal rights from the state (their own property, the right to divorce) and on detaching woman's fate from man's (the right to work). During this period, these women's campaigns and moves were also bound up with ideas of their own virtue. The paradox is that the victim they constructed, who needed saving from her fate, already enjoyed a great deal of what middle-class women desired: a looser concept of marriage, more access to public spaces, the right to enjoy common pleasures, and more varied and flexible jobs. All research, beginning with Parent-Duchâtelet's, shows that those constructed as 'prostitutes' were nothing more than poor women taking up the one employment opportunity that offered independence and decent money. They often lived in ordinary lodging houses; they led sociable lives; their neighbours and lovers did not exclude them. Selling sexual services, often an occasional or part-time activity, did not provide an identity. Women who sold sex had a difficult life, but they lived within communities.

By the late nineteenth century, helping projects had isolated these women, given them a totally negative identity and yet failed to achieve what reformers had set out to: the end of commercial sex, the eradication of poverty, the attempt to make women domestic, a regime of chastity rather than promiscuity, the prevention of women's entrance into increasingly 'unfeminine' job spheres. In Britain, 'Nothing had been done for the women who were exploited by prostitution,'[152] and in France, 'Despite the frequency of reregistrations, the high number of disappearances and discrepancies between the strictness of the procedures and actual behavior demonstrates quite clearly the failure of the regulationist project.'[153] In other words, what the social *said* they were doing was *not the same as* what they were actually accomplishing: 'The domain of effects in the real cannot be read off the programmes of government themselves.'[154]

By the end of the nineteenth century, the image of the 'prostitute' as vile and disgusting had been replaced by the figure of the victim, an ordinary working-class woman who needed rescuing. Some believe that the imagery and discourse had little influence in the end, since commercial sex remained a problem of public order rather than spiritual damnation.[155] It is also true that there was enormous resistance to helpers' interference. Nevertheless, the damage done was real, since the stigmatising victim discourse remained, as did the machinery of social control that I go on to study in the present.

NOTES

1   Donzelot 1979. The concept is much wider than our modern 'social work'.
2   Walkowitz 1994: 30
3   Richards 1992; Abrams (1988) on Germany; Corbin (1978/90), Benabou (1987) and Harsin (1985) on France; Gibson (1986) on Italy; Vázquez García and Moreno Mengíbar (1998) on Spain; Mahood (1990) on Scotland; Luddy (1997) on Ireland and Walkowitz (1980) on England
4   The development of movements for women's rights and integration in France are usually agreed to have been impeded by the series of social upheavals during this period (1793, 1834, 1850, 1871).
5   The Paris police received requests for copies of the Parisian regulations from all over Europe (Harsin 1985: 80).
6   Butler 1990: ix
7   Scott and Tilly 1975
8   'Philanthropic labor filled a vacuum' in the lives of bourgeois women, writes Platt in *The Child-Savers* (1969).

9   Vicinus 1985: 211–12

10   Foucault 1979a: 17–18

11   Foucault 1978. We may call these regimes *programmes*, signifying they are more formal, evolved or institutionalised, or *projects*, when they are more personal, limited or spontaneous.

12   Concepts of governmentality include government as more than state machinery: all forms of governing (such as of the family, of oneself); the study of government as a way of ruling; and government-mentality.

13   *Slavery in the Ancient Near East*, Mendelsohn 1949: 131–2

14   Lerner 1986: 124

15   Henderson 1999: 77

16   Richards 1992: 116

17   Karras 1996; Otis 1985

18   Otis 1985: 2

19   Perry 1985: 143

20   Karras 1996: 95

21   Rossiaud 1988

22   Richards 1992

23   Bristow 1977: 20

24   Bristow 1977

25   *A Modest Defence of Public Stews: Or, An Essay Upon Whoring, As it is Now Practis'd in these Kingdoms* (Mandeville 1724). On Boswell, see Boswell 1982.

26   Foucault 1979a

27   Foucault did not include the 'prostitute' with his identified pathologised subjects of the period (the masturbating child, the hysterical woman, the Malthusian couple and the perverse adult) but this figure operates in the same way.

28   Barber 1955

29   1840 resolution of the French Academy of Moral and Political Sciences supporting civil and religious marriage among the poor, cited in Donzelot 1979: 32

30   Ariès 1962

31   Poovey 1988: 10

32   Donzelot 1979: 36

33   Perrot 1990

34   Armstrong 1987

35   Elias [1939] 1994

36   Donzelot 1979: 46

37   Engels [1845] 1958: 145

38   Simpson 2006

39   Weeks 1981: 32

40   Foucault (1979a) described this as pastoral power, a version of earlier Christian ideas about ministry now in a secular form.

41   Donzelot 1979: 55

42   Henderson 1999: 44

43   'All common Prostitutes or Night Walkers wandering in the public Streets of public

Highways, not giving a satisfactory account of themselves, shall be deemed idle and disorderly Persons;and it shall and may be lawful for any Justice of the Peace to commit such Offenders (being thereof convicted before him, by his own View, or his, her or their own Confession, or by the Oath of One or more credible Witness or Witnesses,) to the House of Correction, there to be kept to hard Labour for any Time not exceeding one Calendar Month.' 3 Geo.IV, c.40, 1822. This 'temporary' Act was superseded by the all-encompassing Vagrancy Act of 1824; see Self 2003.

44   Mayhew 1851: 215

45   Nead 1988: 94

46   Josephine Butler Collection, Women's Library, cited in Walkowitz 1980

47   Weeks 1981: 12

48   Scott 1987: 129

49   Rose and Miller 1992: 183

50   Roberts 1992; Bullough 1987

51   Foucault's upwards continuity

52   Benabou 1987

53   The word *fille* was so closely associated with selling sex (*filles soumises* for women registered with the regulatory system, *filles en carte* for women registered and working independently, outside the houses) that 'respectable' girls had to be called specifically *jeunes filles*.

54   Nead 1988: 139

55   'As the century progresses, the growing fear of contamination is given medical justification by theories of degenerate heredity and syphilitic infection. In the imagination of a Huysmans, the entire organic world is diseased and decomposing, and the syphilitic prostitute is the morbid emblem of this collapse. Confronted by this pathological erosion, the writer must construct art against nature, against woman, against the organic. Such constructions of artifice and reflexivity signal the birth of modernism, which, I suggest, is inscribed on the prostitute's wounded body.' (Bernheimer 1989: 2).

56   Chevalier 1973: 267: n17

57   Corbin 1990: 9

58   Harsin 1985: 96-130

59   Harsin 1985: xvii

60   Coffin 1982: 92

61   A police officer, quoted in Pearson 1972: 23

62   'A woman who has fallen like a star from heaven, may flash like a meteor in a lower sphere, but only with a transitory splendour. In time her orbit contracts, and the improvidence that has been her leading characteristic through life now trebles and quadruples the misery she experiences. To drown reflection she rushes to the gin palace, and there completes the work that she had already commenced so inauspiciously. The passion for dress, that distinguished her in common with her sex in former days, subsides into a craving for meretricious tawdry, and the bloom of health is superseded by ruinous and poisonous French compounds and destructive cosmetics...' (Mayhew 1851: 214). See also Tait 1840; Logan 1843; Greg 1850 and Sanger 1858.

63   Against this debunking, Frances Finnegan (1979) analysed archives in York and claims
      that the myth was true, and Acton the one making a myth.
64   During the Crimean War, William Howard Russell's dispatches 'enlightened the public
      to the fact that the British army's most implacable opponent was disease' (Bristow
      1977: 79). The regimes imposed by and associated with the Acts are described in
      Walkowitz (1980) and Mahood (1990) and the movements to abolish the Acts in
      Bristow (1977), McHugh (1980) and Walkowitz (1980).
65   Leach 1980; Ferguson 1992; Walkowitz 1994
66   Armstrong 1987: 133
67   Humphreys 1997
68   Perrot 1990: 255; see also Levine 1990: 46
69   William R. Greg called redundant those women who were not fortunate enough to
      marry, 'who in place of completing, sweetening and embellishing the existence of
      others are compelled to lead an independent and incomplete existence of their own'
      (1876: 276). Paintings of the time showed 'the reduced gentleman's daughter', 'the
      poor teacher', the 'fortune hunter', 'the seamstress', 'the fallen woman' (Roberts
      1972). The surplus of middle-class women is usually ascribed to the emigration of
      men, the differences in mortality rates of men and women, and the tendency of
      middle-class men to marry later than women.
70   Levine 1990: 158
71   Davidoff 1979; Donzelot 1979
72   It may be that any paid occupation for women was tainted, as nursing was (Holcombe
      1977: 69).
73   Davidoff and Hall 1987: 183–9
74   Mary Wollstonecraft was known to comment that respectable women were the most
      oppressed members of society.
75   This tradition was so long that Daniel Defoe complained of the 'amphibious' lifestyle of
      women who moved to and fro from domestic service to bawdyhouses (Defoe 1725: 7).
76   Davis 1975
77   Landes 1988: 75. For Jean-Jacques Rousseau, who believed there was no correct life
      for women outside retirement and domesticity, acting was the most odious of all
      'public' existences they could have.
78   Béraud 1839: 51
79   Kracauer 1937
80   Weeks 1981: 58
81   Corbin 1990: 205
82   Wilson 1995: 61
83   Wilson 1995: 72–89
84   Kanner 1972: 191
85   Novel of personal development or education
86   A short list illustrating the two tendencies includes *Jane Eyre, Ruth, Madame Bovary,
      Middlemarch, Nana* and *Tess of the D'Urbervilles*.
87   Schreiner [1885] 1988
88   Peiss 1983: 78

89   Nead 1988: 180

90   Scott 1987: 122

91   For some suggestive treatments of race issues, see Davidoff 1979 and McClintock 1995.

92   In the British system, the hospital director was male, but the day-to-day overseer of operations was a matron. The French system used women as *dames de maison*, or brothel managers, and as submistresses carrying out the actual business.

93   Fabian 1983: 18

94   Poovey 1995: 34

95   Some tried to prove through anthropometry that women who sold sex were biologically degenerate, born with a constitution and disposition to this particular evil; see Lombroso and Ferrero 1895.

96   Glotz and Maire, quoted in Barber 1955: 14-15

97   Vicinus 1977: x

98   Armstrong 1987

99   Scott 1987: 123

100   Poovey 1988: 10

101   'The same logic that allowed women to carry the skills they possessed as women into the new world of work would eventually provide the liberal rationale for extending the doctrine of self-regulation and, with it, the subtle techniques of domestic surveillance beyond the middle-class home and into the lives of those much lower down on the economic ladder. It was not uncommon for nineteenth-century conduct books to put forth a rather explicit theory of social control' (Armstrong: 1987, 133)

102   Weeks 1981: 32-3

103   Walkowitz 1994

104   Bland 1992: 400

105   Louise Twining, quoted in Nead 1988: 199

106   Ryan 1990: 122

107   Charles 1860: 4

108   Higgs [1905] 1976: 281

109   Mort 1987: 43

110   Mumm 1996: 2

111   Bland 1992: 403

112   Corbin 1987: 213

113   Stoler 1995

114   Stoler and Cooper 1997: 5

115   Cooper 1997: 409

116   Chisholm 1847, quoted in Summers 1975: 300

117   Henriot 2001

118   Howell 2000

119   Ware 1992: 156

120   Guy 1992

121   Poovey 1995: 46-7

122   Walkowitz 1994: 54-5

123 Mahood 1990: 78 and 84
124 Mumm 1996: 9-10
125 Bartley 2000: 33
126 Kanner 1972: 186
127 Bartley 2000: 61
128 Prochaska 1980
129 Humphreys 1997
130 Mahood 1990: 116
131 Corbin 1990: 280
132 Mumm 1996: 2
133 Quoted in Leach 1980: 295
134 Bristow 1977: 70
135 Foucault 1991: 79
136 The panopticon was a design for prisons proposed by Jeremy Bentham in 1791, a circular building with cells around the outside and a central surveillance point, from which an observer could see all prisoners.
137 Summers 1975: 280-82
138 In 1860 there were about 65 such homes in Britain, accommodating about 1,300 women (Bristow 1977: 70).
139 Corbin 1990: 15
140 Reproduced in Finnegan 1979: 173
141 Foucault 1978:128
142 From 'Seeking and Saving', quoted in Bartley 2000: 62
143 Summers 1979: 33. Mary Wollstonecraft led a life of personal sexual freedom, influenced men of the French Revolution on the subject of women's rights, published what some call the first feminist treatise (1792) and yet exhorted women in general to stay home and be pure.
144 Poovey 1988: 4-5
145 Holcombe 1977: 10
146 Holcombe 1977: 20
147 Stansell 1982: 311
148 'Swindling Sal', quoted in Bracebridge Hemyng, 'Prostitution in London', in *London Labour and the London Poor*, Mayhew [1851] 1968: 23. Also quoted in Walkowitz 1980.
149 Walkowitz 1977: 76
150 McClintock 1995: 114
151 Bartley 2000: 58
152 Mort 1987: 113; see also Bartley 2000. However: 'On its own terms … [rescue work] was far from failing. As the Church Penitentiary Association pointed out in 1862, "the Mission of the Association is to rescue individual souls; and if, out of the number who annually leave the Penitentiaries, between two hundred and three hundred are permanently rescued, who can dare to say that little is done?"' (Bristow 1977: 70)
153 Corbin 1990: 35
154 Dean 2002: 120
155 Henderson 1999: 91

5

GRASPING THE THING ITSELF:
METHODOLOGY

The curious double position of the European, as participant-observer, makes it possible to experience the Orient as though one were the visitor to an exhibition. Unaware that the Orient has not been arranged as an exhibition, the visitor nevertheless attempts to carry out the characteristic cognitive maneuver of the modern subject, separating himself from an object-world and observing it from a position that is invisible and set apart. From there, like the modern anthropologist or social scientist, one transfers into the object the principles of one's relation to it and, as Pierre Bourdieu says, conceives of it as a totality intended for cognition alone. The world is grasped, inevitably, in terms of a distinction between the object – the *thing itself* as the European says – and its meaning, with no sense of the historical peculiarity of this effect we call the *thing itself*.[1]

Timothy Mitchell's idea is useful to an understanding of what the social researcher does when conceiving and arranging objects of research. In my case, I am the participant-observer in an exhibition of social agents, both implicated in the exhibition and struggling to see it from a critical vantage point while remaining visible to the people researched. Nor do these represent any totality. But I do think it is useful to turn this European kind of gaze onto Europeans themselves: a temporary exhibition, as it were, of traits assumed to be normal. In this chapter I relate how I did my field work.

How I Came to This Subject

My study of the issues raised in this book began in my own social-type work in the mid-1990s: in a paralegal project on the Mexican border with Central Americans and Cubans seeking asylum in the US; in a Caribbean NGO doing HIV/AIDS prevention among people selling sex and often travelling to Europe; and with projects in Chile, Argentina and Brazil to understand tourism and migration. Everyone I met spoke the same way about travel and work, including selling sex: pragmatic, resigned, perhaps sad but also unwilling to consider migrants victimised; on the contrary, many in NGOs and doing community organising were thinking about migrating themselves and had family members abroad. When I came to Europe, however, I found that the services, programmes and projects reaching out to migrants discussed them in a very different way, especially if commercial sex was involved; migrants were seen as victims. The gap between these two ways of talking – why it exists, how it works, what keeps it going – motivated me to turn my questioning gaze away from the objects usually studied (poor women, 'prostitutes', migrants) to those engaged in 'helping' them.

I also wondered, after reading a great deal and participating in activist networks for some time, why so much passion and effort had not managed to improve life for people who sell sex. The social sector dedicated to helping them has grown and diversified, and some of the rhetoric has changed slightly, but the situation for the subjects themselves is largely unchanged: abolitionism continues to be the central moralising idea in hegemonic arguments, debate centres on how to 'control prostitution', unpredictable local toleration predominates, police abuse is endemic, commercial sex is blamed for spreading sexually transmitted diseases, thriving networks facilitate workers' mobility and entrance into commercial sex, which pays far better than any other job available to women, male and transgender workers are overlooked, and research focuses repeatedly on individual motivations for buying and selling sex. There is an energetic campaign to counter these traditions worldwide, but progress is impeded by angry reactions from those favouring eradication of commercial sex. Sex workers, in studies that record their opinions, indict a broad range of authorities including police, judges, doctors, lawmakers and researchers for their reinforcement of the 'whore stigma' and their direct or indirect collusion in the persecution of sex workers.

Discussing homosexuality, Weeks describes the historical problem as how to

> explain the various sources of the social stigmatisation of homosexuals and the individual and collective response to this broadly hostile regulation. But the way to do this is not to seek out a single causative factor. The crucial question must be what are the conditions for the emergence of this particular form of regulation of sexual behaviour in this particular society?[2]

In the previous chapter, I reveal some of the conditions making possible the conceptualising of a class of victims that mandated a class of rescuers, as well as how helping practices exacerbated the stigmatising of victims. Since stigma is now continually blamed for the problems of sex workers, understanding how it is reproduced is useful, beyond the usual accusations at the media and police (though these are deserved). I limited the field by focusing on Spain, where the area of helping migrants, and 'migrant prostitutes' as a subcategory, was more recently identified than in some European countries. The smaller, emergent field in Spain made it easier to see the formation of the discourse, the steps taken to create projects, and the people who took them on. From my observations over a long time in other European countries as well, I can say that what I observed in Spain is not unique.

Why Do Field Work?

I did field work in order to gather information until now absent from most discussions of commercial sex, on the practices of social agents attempting to help people who sell sex. I had to go beyond helpers' own descriptions of their projects, which involved participation over time within the social sector, examining the texture and atmosphere, as well as the words and gestures, making up their practice.

I chose anthropological theory and methodology for the field work, because I questioned the validity of frameworks that begin with moralising views at the outset by labelling the buying and selling of sex as deviance, victimisation or violence. Since these attitudes reproduce what drove me to undertake research, I wanted a theoretical space that would allow me to resist moralising as well as western cultures' claim that its values are best. Cultural relativism avoids judging the object of study and provides insight into practices that may be incomprehensible unless researchers shed their assumptions.[3] Relativism holds that a missionary may arrive in Samoa and begin teaching the concept of shame to naked natives by obliging them to cover their bodies, but an anthropologist should arrive there to observe and record existing customs, trying to abstain from imposing her own values. For me, anthropological settings provided a space where I could not only think but talk aloud about taboos, contradictions and stigmatised subjects related to sex, without having to announce my personal stance or condemn anyone else's. It allowed me to study migrants and helpers, their words and actions, in the same kinds of ways, evaluating these within their own groups' logic.

Studying 'Up'

In 1969, Dell Hymes said that if anthropology didn't exist, it would not need to be invented. But possibly the academic work anthropology has produced would not have existed had its authors been sociologists, historians or psychologists. Ethnography, the method which came to define anthropology, provides results that, if not more truthful than others, offer insights of its own. The term is used both for the research process and for its written product, the opening chapter of Bronislaw Malinowski's *Argonauts of the Western Pacific* (1922) usually cited as beginning the tradition. Ethnography is not simply *not* quantitative and does not pretend to provide a complete picture. Traditionally, it was used to study 'down', at cultures the west considered primitive.

By the 1960s, these assumptions were being questioned; Hymes's collection, *Reinventing Anthropology*, was published in the aftermath of 1968. In widespread discussions on the relevance of academia, some anthropologists faced the cruel facts of their tradition: that it had often been racist, colonialist, west-centred, self-serving, frivolous and the running dog of imperialism and espionage (in the past for the British, in the present for the US). Much of this is documented in Hymes's collection: William Willis suggests taking these skeletons from the closet, turning to urban ethnography and using 'frog perspectives' (Richard Wright's term for the effort he wanted white people to make, looking up from where coloured people live);[4] Eric Wolf prescribes 'educating ourelves in the realities of power';[5] and Laura Nader articulates the principle of studying up:

> What if, in reinventing anthropology, anthropologists were to study the colonizers rather than the colonized, the culture of power rather than the culture of the powerless, the culture of affluence rather than the culture of poverty? Studying up as well as down would lead us to ask many common sense questions in reverse. Instead of asking why some people are poor, we would ask why other people are so affluent ... How has it come to be, we might ask, that anthropologists are more interested in why peasants don't change than why the auto industry doesn't innovate, or why the pentagon or universities cannot be more organizationally creative? The conservatism of such major institutions and bureaucratic organizations probably has wider implications for the species and for theories of change than does the conservatism of peasantry.[6]

Anthropology's imperialism was explicated in more detail in Talal Asad's 1973 collection *Anthropology and the Colonial Encounter*. Studying up proposed a solution to many students' doubts and showed how traditional academic fields could expand and intersect with others; an anthropology that stayed at home shared interests with urban, community, family and organisational studies. Studying up continued to rely on detailed observation of human beings, but now western metropoles could be field sites and the people observed could be educated, privileged, powerful or simply those living everyday lives in the first world. Many such studies have now been carried out about scientists, businesspeople, religious figures, doctors, police, lawmakers, educators and, I expect, most possible categories.

In my field work, I studied culturally middle-class people participating in social projects with the disadvantaged. I use the term social agents to mean individuals who work in the social sector, which takes in research (including academic research), theorising, lobbying, policy making and direct services. Social agents work for government or private bodies; they include agency directors and highly placed political appointees, outreach volunteers, bureaucrats, doctors and religious figures. All receive salaries and/or funding. I will refer to organisations, mostly, but sometimes describe the practices of individuals on behalf of organisations.

In mainstream discourses, these people are positioned as normal, their behaviour is usually unquestioned and their voices *are* much heard in the media, government and NGO events and policy documents. But I wanted to study more than what these figures *say* they are doing, flat statements like 'We treat sick people,' 'We provide information on services.' My goal was to look at their everyday practices, believing with Foucault that 'People know what they do; they frequently know why they do what they do; but what they don't know is *what* what they do does'.[7] Helping projects say their aim is migrants' welfare but often seem unaware that they are not succeeding, and, if they are aware, they tend to externalise the problem and blame others. One of my earliest publications was entitled 'They Speak, But Who Listens?', reflecting my concern that bringing out marginalised voices is not enough if those who need to hear them are not listening.[8]

Standpoints

The issue of which direction research takes – down, up, sideways – belongs to a wider debate in the social sciences around the idea that a detached observer can do objective research. Feminists dispute this idea, proposing instead the need to 'situate knowledge',[9] understanding the importance of every researcher's *standpoint*, or personal location. In her critique of objectivity, Sandra Harding argues that everyone has a stake in their own research results, white men as well as blacks, women and any other interest group.[10] Other theorists suggest that women have knowledge that is unavailable to men, notably about ordinary social relations. Earlier ideas focused on women;[11] later ones include many oppressed groups and issues of power and class; black feminists argue that white women cannot perceive issues of heterosexism, racism and class exclusion.[12]

The last twist on standpoint relevant to my research relates to the researcher's status as 'insider' or 'outsider' in the group studied, the assumption being that groups are cohesive enough for the researcher's status to be of crucial importance. Thus, if the researcher is an insider, she is presumed to understand the group's social relationships and subtleties in their concerns. But the idea of a dichotomy between inside and outside has been thoroughly questioned,[13] since one's status as insider to a group such as 'black women' could be compromised by one's other status as an academic, if the group being investigated were not composed of academics. Or one might be a member of an ecology movement in which whites predominate but be non-white. The issue of how any given researcher manages to be accepted by a group must depend in the last analysis on ineffable questions of sympathy, which sometimes occur between people who apparently have little in common. I also discovered that being an insider on sexual questions caused some academics to sneer at or ridicule my ideas.[14]

My Own (Shifting) Position in the Field

I used the traditional anthropological methodology known as participant observation. Although some use this term loosely, the traditional anthropological method implies long-time living in a place among people, in order to gain familiarity with their daily life and develop personal relationships over time in the subjects' own context. Participant observers engage in situations that they do not define, delimit or control. What they learn is different from the information provided in response to direct interview questions. Impressions are recorded as field notes, often after the experience itself is over, in a process known as interpretation.

I have done formal field work in Spain several times since 1997, lived in one city for five years and visited individuals and projects in many places. I had no special access at the beginning of my research. I approached people explaining my background and interest in the workings of projects with migrants who sell sex. Since evaluation of social projects, particularly in health, is conventional in Spain, I was accepted, and having learned the pitfalls of being identified with a particular ideology, I avoided defining my position. But early on in the field work, I was asked by the editor of a local migration journal to write an article on migrants working in the sex industry, specifying that she wanted something without the usual moralising. I complied, and was later told that the article broke the ice among people afraid to reveal their opinions publicly.[15] The word gradually got around, then, which may have affected how some people reacted to me in the field.

For a year and a half, I met everyone I could find working with people selling sex in Madrid. Most sent me their writings, invited me to visit them and gave me other names. Others I was able to introduce to each other as, despite having similar interests, they tended to work in an isolated way. I read what was published, attended seminars and conferences, accompanied outreach educators and was contracted to work with a Madrid team, Colectivo Ioé, in their government-funded research on migrant women's work, for which I researched both social agents and women in the sex industry, including field work in Pamplona. I sought out and collected large amounts of materials published by the social sector: research reports, outreach leaflets, educational booklets, conference programmes, position papers, manifestos: anything made available to someone interested in people who sell sex, migration, 'trafficking'.[16] I kept abreast of what people were talking about, not in the media but in their everyday jobs. Inevitably, I became aware of the relationships, alliances and disharmonies among organisations, and although I did not consciously research their internal workings (such as funding or management issues), I came to know quite a bit about them.

My position in the field was a mix of insider, outsider, stakeholder, political actor and researcher-with-a-self-interest, and shifted according to the conditions of the moment. At times I identified wholly with clients of health projects grateful for free services and annoyed at prying questions, while at other times I identified with researchers working hard to get decent information from unhelpful informants. My shifting position helped me understand everyone a bit better.

I had been an insider in the Latin American NGO world working with

migrants, refugees and sex workers, doing education-cum-organising
with women who sold sex, writing proposals for European funding and
carrying out field research with families receiving money from migrants
overseas. I was familiar with both health projects and those focusing on
rights; I was present at the first convention of Dominican sex workers in
1995, when an international organisation sent someone to tell them
they were exploited victims. I had worked with nuns offering shelter to
asylum-seekers on the Texas border and carried out a life-histories
project to record and publish their stories. Later, when I was investigating the possibility of doing an advanced degree, I unwittingly introduced myself to people who informed me that they were on 'the other
side' of these issues from me.[17] A sex workers' rights activist introduced
me to an influential group of militants and experts on legal and
epidemiological issues, a relationship that has gone on for ten years.
Migrancy has been my own lifelong mode, and when I lived in Spain, I
was also a foreigner, but this in itself is complicated, as there are many
aspects of Spanish cultures which I feel comfortable with and part of, yet
others that bring up feelings of alienation and 'otherness' in me (which is
true for Spaniards towards me, as well). My experience in addressing
migration issues was accepted and respected by some and doubted by
others.

   Clifford Geertz says that ethical ambiguity between anthropologists
and their informants lies at the heart of successful anthropological
research.[18] There are other power issues involved when doing ethnography where one lives among people who may see one's research
published, be in a position to support or veto future proposals, grant or
withdraw invitations and generally be people one can expect to run into
later in life.[19] Since I went on living in Spain, these apply to me, though
this particular research – on social agents themselves – may not be
translated and published there. On the other hand, some of the
international activists and academics characterised in the research will
probably see my work. I entered into the social sector's life but do not
claim to have more than a partial vision of their culture; my specific goal
is to reveal practices usually ignored. I have done my best to portray
people and events as I saw and felt them, not only in the formal field
work but in my longer study.

This can be called multi-sited ethnography, which examines the circulation of cultural meanings, objects, and identities in time and space.[20] Helen Callaway studied European women in colonial Nigeria during the period 1900–60 who lived in different parts of the country and did not constitute a face-to-face group:

> Given such diversity of activities and experience, how can these European women in colonial Nigeria be designated as a social group? They shared the signifying system of their home culture and social class – its language, values, symbolic structures, sacred and secular rituals, hidden meanings, reference points. And in Nigeria they learned the new social prescriptions that upheld the power relations of this specific imperial culture. Although they were separated from each other in both time and space, and present a polyphony of voices, they all took part in a continuing moral pageant with its implicit ordering of the social world.[21]

Contemporary people working in social programming on commercial sex and migration in Spain also share a language, values and reference points ('AIDS prevention', 'access to social services', 'health promotion', 'human rights'), the need for outside financing, the belief that their work is a duty of civilised societies, as well as a worthy occupation.

A Delicate Silence

In 1998, in a Madrid document centre specialising in migrations, I found a glaring silence where the sex industry should be. While serious research on migrant women had been going on for years, I could find no mention of the sex job market;[22] the impression given was that most migrant women were domestic servants. One academic known for work on a migrant nationality renowned for selling sex seemed to ignore one of her own findings: in a survey of previous jobs, two of her interviewees volunteered that they had been 'prostitutes', yet the author made no reference to this finding in her detailed examination of survey responses.[23] The silence was so deafening that I approached a member of the documentation centre. 'Even your own research dodges the issue,' I complained, 'How can this be?' He replied, 'No one wants to hear about it. We get paid to do research on subjects they want to hear about.'

Spanish writing traditionally focused on providing a definitive feminist analysis of 'prostitution', without doing research with actual people and without having any concrete knowledge of the sex industry.[24] Most sociological studies were carried out within a framework of deviant behaviour; a well-known example analysed life histories of fewer than twenty women working in an old and poor red-light district of Barcelona, beginning from the premise that 'prostitution' is a perversion, illness or weakness of character.[25] Only one empirical research study of any note had been carried out in Spain;[26] other research had involved either very small samples[27] or questionable methodology.[28] There were celebratory[29] and critical[30] studies about the past.

The silence in scholarly venues contrasted with a constant hubbub in the media, where news was published daily on police actions with criminals said to be 'trafficking prostitutes'. References to 'sexual slavery' and 'mafias' (gangs) were made indiscriminately, victims were characterised by nationality, and ethnic stereotyping was rampant. While the names of Spanish suspects were not published, those of foreigners were, and if the suspects were Colombian, for example, stories about other violent crimes appeared close by, apparently linking them.[31] The media focused on people selling sex outdoors in parks, parking lots, empty lots and streets.

So what I call a silence was really a kind of delicacy or discretion on the part of social figures, while the media produced scandalised brouhaha. By the late 1990s, projects to help migrants were beginning to make their presence felt.

Projects to Help People Who Sell Sex

By 2000 it was no longer possible to analyse this area of social programming in purely national terms. First, the migration phenomenon had increased such that projects to deal with it were sprouting constantly. Second, the European Commission's Daphne Programme was gaining a reputation for funding projects on migration and sex, and several other EC-funded programmes were accepting proposals; by 2000, proposals for Daphne funding had to incorporate multiple European partners. Third, a significant battle was fought between June 1998 and October

2000 in Vienna, at meetings of the UN Commission for the Prevention of Crime and Penal Justice on 'trafficking' and 'smuggling' of human beings. The Vienna meetings became the focus for lobbying efforts over both abolitionism and sex workers' rights, at stake the language of protocols to be appended to a new convention on international crime. Fourth, the use of e-mail was increasingly common. Last, transnational networks of NGOs were seeking partners.[32] So the Spanish field was expanding to include transnational experiences and influences. Within Spain, I was present at the founding of a national network of projects working in the field (health, religious, rescue, migrant aid, and research) in 2001.

My work centred on Madrid, though the same panorama of services is found everywhere: epidemiology and health promotion (the majority), assistance in leaving or rescue from sex work (difficult but often mentioned), and support for workers' (embattled) rights. Epidemiological projects receive serious funding and are integrated into mainstream social programming; rescue projects have the longest 'charity' tradition; rights projects are newest, least funded and most closely allied to movements to protect migrants' rights in general. In Madrid itself, various projects belong to each tradition. In addition to offering direct services, they also produce reports, publications and conferences.

Health projects

The main Madrid project was Médicos del Mundo-Madrid, part of an international organisation whose magazine depicts doctors helping villagers, slum dwellers and war refugees around the world. In Spain, Médicos have a harm reduction programme aimed at the 'fourth world', a concept that frames Spanish marginalised groups with migrants and that targets women who sell sex in the street, taking gynaecological services and information to them in outreach vehicles. Médicos did not give out materials but offered direct counselling to migrants who approached the vehicle. A large organisation funded by both government and private sources, Médicos has sizeable and well-equipped mobile units, though these are largely staffed by volunteers. The principle of outreach to people who sell sex was expounded some time ago in Madrid:

... foreigners in illegal situations ... collectives marginalised in these ways from general social life are usually marginalised as well from public social and health services, which they hardly use – when they exist – and if they do use them, it is without expressing openly their personal circumstances, which means that the attention [they receive] is necessarily deficient ... The social and health services must themselves approach these collectives, eliminating as much as possible the barriers that exist, in order to be used: in prostitution ghettos ... they must be located in the same neighbourhood; the services they offer shouldn't be destined exclusively to women ... administrative requirements must be flexible, since in many cases documents are missing or clients wish to maintain clandestinity ... emergency visits seem to be more effective than requiring appointments at specific times; the techniques used must be adapted to the cultural characteristics of the population, more conducive to intensive therapeutic relationships than to regular, long-term therapeutic work ... In place of placidly waiting for demand to be produced according to the manner convenient to the service's requirements ... in this case the technicians try to facilitate the capture of people at risk.[33]

By the early 1990s, Médicos used outreach vehicles. But the original project was complicated by a dramatic increase in migrants with cultural differences making standard procedures problematic: patients who would not attend clinics, who didn't subscribe to western ideas of hygiene, who were accustomed to herbal remedies or injecting themselves with cures bought in pharmacies, who didn't want to deal with doctors and who had been taught different theories of AIDS and sexually transmitted disease.[34] Migrants in Europe speak many different languages, as well, often unfamiliar to Europeans.

Several other NGOs did AIDS outreach to people who sell sex in Madrid: Fundación Triángulo with *chaperos* (male sex workers); Universida in clubs in noncentral neighbourhoods; Grupo Fénix with young people. Some groups' health activity was limited to condom distribution: Hetaira, with female and transsexual street workers in two central areas; Transexualia, with transsexuals; APRAMP, with women street workers in two central zones. Three projects did outreach in a park known as the Casa de Campo, but without coordinating amongst themselves, with the result that one could encounter multiple outreach vehicles in the same place on one day and the next day find none.

A few public clinics catered to people selling sex. The Centro Montesa had a clinic attended by a venerodermatologist who had been seeing both sex workers and their clients for twenty years, while a colleague across the hall saw HIV/AIDS patients. These and another publicly funded clinic near the Plaza de Callao did not advertise as catering to undocumented migrants or sex workers, but they were known to treat both. This tacit acceptance comes from municipalities' knowledge that if migrants and sex workers have no access to condoms and services they may agree to have unprotected sex or remain untreated. Many migrants fear that outreach and clinics will refuse them service or report them to the police, so the knowledge that clinics will accept them is important.

In many countries, health projects distribute their messages in the form of leaflets, booklets or stickers, in the hope that these will not only be kept and examined but passed on to others. An entire study could be made of the wealth of such materials provided by projects attempting to reduce harm among those having a lot of sex (the commercial aspect is not key). Printed material is less common in Spain. In 2000, the European network Tampep began to offer free a wide range of leaflets covering sexually transmitted infections, AIDS and hepatitis, pregnancy and contraception, sex change, the immune system, condom breakage and self-care, in numerous languages.[35] Other AIDS prevention materials, distributed by SOA-Bestrijding of Holland, rely on a story-board format with colours, clear photos of genital diseases, and graphic representations of sexual acts.

Two European networks collaborated to publish a guide, *Hustling for Health: Developing Services for Sex Workers in Europe*, about how to set up a health project for migrants. Translated to Spanish as *Trabajando por la salud,* the guide sat in piles in Médicos's Madrid office long after it had first been delivered in 1999, but finally copies of the guide were distributed to a few Spanish projects in 2001. In contrast, Spanish medical projects distributed a great deal of material with general descriptions of 'prostitution', migration and existing services.[36] Studies were repeatedly done on the relationship between HIV/AIDS and sex work and on access to social services.[37]

Research on AIDS is a major medical industry, many thousands attending frequent international conferences, which now include dozens of presentations related to commercial sex. Spain itself holds frequent national AIDS conferences where this theme is dominated by Médicos-Madrid and by the national AIDS plan. Funding and concern to prevent HIV transmission among those selling sex is massive, while concern over clients and other sexual partners is minimal.

Rescue projects

The best-known rescue project in Madrid was APRAMP (Association for the Prevention, Reinsertion and Rehabilitation of Prostituted Women), with offices in the Plaza de Ángel, next to a traditional red-light area. The programme included mobile outreach, crafts workshops, a recycling project, and outreach with managers of the small hotels where many women live and work. To participate, women and trans-sexuals must promise to stop selling sex, since APRAMP's mission is to save them. The director appeared often in public to argue that all women who sell sex are victims and all migrants are 'trafficked', but she probably also knew that craft making does not tempt many to give up selling sex. IPSSE (Institute for the Promotion of Specialized Social Services), a very small project similar to APRAMP, operated in another part of Madrid. Both entities concentrated on women in the street, whom they consider to be the most vulnerable.

Many religious organisations in Madrid had contact with, if not projects dedicated to, marginalised women. Some try to help women from falling into selling sex; for the Oblata nuns this means seeking out poor women in old city centres and marginal neighbourhoods, single mothers, victims of abuse, and young people considered at risk. The Adoratrice nuns had changed to focus on women who identify as 'trafficked' and want to escape commercial sex. Individual nuns supported sex worker rights, participating in public demonstrations.

Rights projects

The Madrid group dedicated to defending women's right to sell sex without being harassed or rescued was the feminist Colectivo en Defensa de los Derechos de las Prostitutas Hetaira (Collective in Defence of the Rights of Prostitutes Hetaira). Beginning with a donation in the mid-1990s, they bought a long-term lease on a large flat in an old red-light district (Calle de la Luna, Calle Desengaño, Calle Ballesteros), an area with both street work and small bars and clubs. Hetaira did outreach in the Casa de Campo, approaching women and transsexuals with free condoms and a discourse of rights and selling sex as work. When they began, the only migrants they saw were Latin Americans, so that basic communication was easy; later, language became a major stumbling block. Transexualia, a Madrid association, also focused on rights, since the marginalisation that transgenders suffer means that sex work is one of the few job options open to them. Transexualia worked on raising awareness about sexuality, gender and gender identity.

Undocumented migrants could also take advantage of social programmes and products aimed at migrants in general, such as emergency housing, food, help with bureaucratic paperwork and legal advice. When migrants need advice, they are often sent to associations of immigrant nationalities or culture groups, but migrants who sell sex may not want to show themselves, or, if they do, associations may not accept them. Of the migrant groups in Madrid that could be expected to take rights-oriented stands on migrants selling sex, none did; instead, they condemned 'trafficking' and victimisation. Migrants theoretically had access to classes in domestic work and caring for the elderly and children, but such classes were not free, and it was not clear whether taking them would increase chances of legal employment.

The preceding description of social programming related to commercial sex might sound ordinary, neutral or praiseworthy, if not examined more closely. It is this surface, which appears benevolent and constructive, that worried me ten years ago, when I worked in such programmes, and that led me to do the field work described in Chapter 6.[38]

NOTES

1   Mitchell 1989: 232

2   Weeks 1981: 98

3   Benedict 1934; Womack 1995

4   Willis 1969 on Wright in *White Man, Listen!* (1957)

5   Wolf 1969: 261

6   Nader 1969: 471

7   Quoted in Dreyfus and Rabinow 1982: 187, *my emphasis*

8   Agustín 1999a

9   Haraway 1988

10   Harding 1987

11   Smith 1974

12   hooks 1984; Collins 1990; Reynolds 2002

13   For example, Mullings 1999

14   See Hart 1999 on the difficulty of discussing her research with academics.

15   Agustín 2000b

16   See Primary Sources.

17   In 1996 I introduced myself to an academic interested in legal and postcolonial issues related to commercial sex. She took a step backward, using this very phrase, which at the time I couldn't comprehend.

18   Geertz 1968: 154

19   Forsythe 1999: 8

20   Marcus 1995: 96

21   Callaway 1987: 10

22   Marrodán et al on third-world women migrants (1991); Rivas Niña (1992), Oso and Machín (1993), Herranz Gómez (1992, 1996, 1997) and Gallardo (1995) all on Dominican women; Sánchez Hernández on women migrants (1994); Embarak López on migrant Moroccan women (1994); Tornos et al on Peruvian migrants (1997); Criado on migrants' life histories (1997); and Rivas Niña on social problems related to migrations (1997). The many articles on migration issues but not specifically touching women are not mentioned here.

23   Gregorio 1996

24   Fundación Solidaridad Democrática 1988; Osborne 1991

25   Negre i Rigol 1988

26   Gabinet 1992

27   Sequeiros 1996; De Paula Medeiros 2000

28   Jiménez and Vallejo 1999

29   Núñez Roldán 1995

30   Varela 1995; Vázquez García 1998; Guereña 1999

31   Calvo Ocampo 2001

32   Relevant funded networks of the period with Spanish members include Tampep (Transnational AIDS/STD Prevention among Migrant Prostitutes in Europe), ENMP (European Network on Male Prostitution), Europap (European Intervention Projects

AIDS Prevention for Prostitutes), European Network for AIDS Prevention Among the Subsaharan Population and Aids & Mobility. All were AIDS prevention programmes.

33   Comas and Reyero 1985: 63–4

34   Comas and Reyero 1985; Cuadros Riobó 1997; Colomo 2000

35   Tampep n/d; by 2006 the leaflets were available in Russian, French, Czech, Bulgarian, Hungarian, Spanish, English, Portuguese, Italian, Romanian, Albanian, Polish, Ukrainian, Slovak, Lithuanian, Latvian, Estonian and Thai.

36   Castillo 2000; Instituto de Salud Carlos III 1999; Castillo and Mazarrasa 1999

37   Cuanter 1998; Mardomingo 1999; Bueno 1999; Urcelai 2001; Sigma Dos 2001–2

38   It also led me to continue publishing in Spain: Agustín 2001a, 2003c, 2004b, 2004d and 2005c.

6

FROM CHARITY TO SOLIDARITY:
IN THE FIELD WITH HELPERS

In Chapter 4 I questioned benevolent nineteenth-century discourses of philanthropy that allowed people wanting to work to take controlling roles with women who sold sex. In France, social agents mostly belonged to municipal bureaucracies regulating 'dangerous' activities. In Britain, some social agents agreed with the French model and succeeded in passing legislation attempting to control poor women directly, but the majority proposed to rescue and rehabilitate them. Both systems assigned offending women to particular places (brothels, hospitals, penitentiaries, refuges) where they would be watched, corrected and persuaded to behave respectably. Competing ideas about how best to care and control were continuously debated and disputed.

Much of what was conceived in the nineteenth century is now part of state and local government programming, considered conventional management of the health and welfare of populations.[1] Knowledge is central:

> Government is intrinsically linked to the activities of expertise, whose role is not one of weaving an all-pervasive web of 'social control', but of enacting assorted attempts at the calculated administration of diverse aspects of conduct through countless, often competing, local tactics of education, persuasion, inducement, management, incitement, motivation and encouragement.[2]

The modern state consists of a vast web of devices including bureaucratic routines; techniques of notation, recording, measuring and compiling; theories and expertise; and programmes created by different agencies.[3] All evolve over time, creating new necessities. What is 'officially' governmental mixes with the 'non'governmental to such an extent that they cannot be disentangled, which is why I talk about the social sector in general, rather than the state or private sector or civil society. Some of the projects discussed in the field work belong nominally to municipal or national governments but are delegated to NGOs, while others were created by private groups who receive funds from governments to carry them out. The field work examines how social agents treat people who sell sex, migrant and non-migrant. Contradictions and diversity exist, but all the projects I studied work inside the 'prostitution' concept, whether they call it that or sex work.

I use ethnographic narratives as a technique for presenting events, actions and objects. After each narrative, I draw on other situations and ideas to elaborate my analysis. By telling stories (in a sans serif font), I also produce texts that can be analysed (in the main text font). My role as writer is pivotal in these productions, which have been called 'writing culture'.[4] However, there are places where the line between narrative and analysis is not clear, because the two are intertwined in my memories and thoughts. Quoted words were actually spoken. The narratives are also meant to bring to life some small part of the feelings evoked by the experiences. Throughout, I have changed the identifying characteristics of locations, individuals and organisations, except when references come from published material. Cases come from several sites in Spain.

A list of Primary Sources at the end of this book includes a selection of the great quantity of published material I analysed, and also suggests the breadth of projects I visited. In the narratives, I focus on a very few of the total number. The selection does not aim to create a portrait of helping culture but to reveal how social agents continuously recreate the 'prostitution' discourse. Some effects are subtler than others, but nothing described is atypical. I concentrate on public or semi-public phenomena rather than bureaucratic paperwork, accounting or interviews with individuals.

Item 1: Imposing Solidarity

For several months I had accompanied the Progresistas on their weekly rounds in a large urban park. Their aim is to let sex workers know that they accept sex work as legitimate work deserving rights and that other services and professionals are available to give advice. It's after dark when they drive up offering condoms.

Along several roads, hundreds of women and transgenders stand, alone and in ethnic, national and continental groups. There are Latin Americans (with a sizeable trans subgroup), eastern Europeans and West Africans. Men are in another part of town. Women from Nigeria, Liberia and Sierra Leone work with big smiles on their faces and go after business forcefully, stepping out in front of cars to stop them. The Latinas, in contrast, are practically nude but only wave and smile from the side of the road, waiting for customers to approach. The Progresistas call the Latinas 'sweet' (which is what clients say, too), and remark that it must be great for the 'Africans' to be in the liberated, democratic west with money to spend. A couple of times I have objected to this stereotyping and suggested that the Progresistas are missing something about migration, but when asked what I mean I say it is too big a subject to explain in a few minutes in the car.

The West Africans tend to dress alike for work, which to outsider eyes exaggerates their similarity: they are very black, very young, very tall and very strong. Nearly all are wearing shiny, skimpy bodysuits decorated with lace, in a white so white it looks blue against their black skin; many breasts are scarified; the commonest hairdo consists of hundreds of long plaits piled on top of the head like a crown. These women tend to work in large groups.

This evening, the usual scene occurs when the car pulls up at an intersection, women running up at once for their sacks of free condoms, and soon more than twenty jostle for attention. After a few minutes, I hear one of the Progresistas say 'No, I've already given to you, we can't give more than one sack to each person.' The black woman says it's not true, she hasn't received any yet and wants her fair share. The Progresista refuses and launches into an explanation about sharing, solidarity and cooperation. The black woman insists stridently, leaning on the front passenger door to stop the car driving off. The Progresista continues explaining that if they give out more than one sack now, there will be women later in the evening who receive nothing. The woman on the car is adamant she's received nothing. The Progresista asks to look inside her purse, which the woman opens to reveal many condoms but none of the Progresistas' brand. Undeterred, the Progresista accuses the woman of arriving early, getting her condoms, hiding them in the trees and then returning for more. The argument gets hotter.

I am so uncomfortable I cross the street to put distance between me and the scene. The Progresista, with her unkempt, rather jolly white person's look, repeats over and over the arguments of solidarity, in complicated Spanish. I observe how the black woman directs a hard gaze and a strong presence at the now large audience of other black sex workers.

Suddenly, the tension breaks, the woman relaxes, the Progresistas get in their car and swing around to pick me up. Everyone is talking at once. Almost immediately, we stop beside another group of black women, and the same scene is poised to begin again. When the Progresista begins her explanation of the principles of solidarity and cooperation, I lose my cool. 'Get in the car,' I say, and, to myself, 'I'll never give out condoms again.'

For the rest of the evening, while further contacts are made without incident among other West Africans, Spaniards, Ecuadorian transsexuals and thin eastern Europeans, there is confusion among the outreach workers. One is so embarrassed she wants to quit, another wants to understand what happened, while the protagonist continues to defend the politics of convincing people of the value of solidarity. She believes it's the only hope for getting them more rights and better working conditions, but also talking that way is necessary to her, it's her work. She decides the problem is language – she doesn't speak English and the Africans don't speak Spanish. When I point out that they don't 'hear' me, either, if I try to explain her position in English, she has no reply.

After the Progresistas have left, I stay on with a group of women who say they are Nigerian. They point at the Progresistas' car and ask, 'What are they doing here? They don't have anything to offer us except a few condoms. The others that come here are doctors, they can do tests, give us medicine. What good are these women?' I don't find it easy to explain what they want to know, that the Progresistas are dedicated to what they call solidarity, on behalf of which they won't give out extra condoms. The Nigerians have another question: 'Why don't the Spanish speak any other languages? Everyone speaks English. What's wrong with them?' It's hard for those who travel and learn new languages to comprehend those who don't. One of the women is hostile, feels offended by these white people coming round to help her. Pushing a flyer for a friend's grocery into my hand, she says 'There, I'm just doing the same as they are.'

I pass on to the Latinas, who do not question why the Progresistas and other outreach projects come to see them but simply take advantage of as many services as possible. They like to chat and tell personal stories: how they travelled, what happened when they arrived, where they have lived, how they are coping, what their boyfriends are up to. They don't wonder why others might be interested in these stories, either. Back home, it's common for middle-class people to contact them, for one reason or another.

Later, the Progresistas say it's true they don't have enough condoms for everyone, but also that they refuse to be duped or considered fools by women they want to work *with* (and, by the way, without being paid). They say giving out condoms is only a 'way in' to the women, who, they acknowledge, already buy their own, as well as everything else they need to do business. They see their chief offerings as their presence and ability to provide information and promote self-reliance among workers. They also say there is no difference between themselves and women who sell sex; all women are sisters. Solidarity and the desire to help are transparent, benevolent ideals to be accepted at face value. This means that if they approach people with sacks of condoms and smiles on their faces, they expect to be understood.

However, even supposing migrants understood Spanish perfectly, there is no reason to expect them to interpret any particular value in any particular way. The solidarity that the Progresistas refer to has two elements: first, their own with 'prostitutes' (the term they use), which consists of working to help get rights for them; and second, the solidarity that Progresistas want to promote *among* women who sell sex across national, ethnic, colour and gender lines. The problem is, even if the concept were to exist identically in other cultures, it is not clear that they would care about people from other cultures or countries, who they might perceive as inferior or simply irrelevant. Or some people might wish to get rid of the competition, believe that Latinos are immune to disease, for example, or any of an array of other reasons.

In Spain, references to solidarity are common and unreflexive.[5] The concept's meaning has changed a great deal since it was the subject of great debate in France in reaction to the ultra-individualism of the late eighteenth century. Emile Durkheim and Ferdinand Tönnies both used the idea of solidarity to theorise about different sorts of social bonds.[6] By the later nineteenth century, solidarity came to be seen as

> the instrument *par excellence* for securing the ideological reconcilia-tion of individualism and collectivism, bringing in its train a host of state-organised and associationist institutions calculated to repair the damage wreaked by uninhibited self-seeking without restoring the retrograde, despotic, illiberal *ancien régime*.[7]

In the present, according to Amelia Valcárcel, solidarity emerges with the realisation of the need for *mutual* help: in the case of women, that they are a collective. This solidarity is not simply a compassionate lending hand but puts collective above individual needs, occurring among equals, not in hierarchical relations.[8] But volunteers doling out condoms do not want to face the inescapable inequality of these relationships. Volunteers can withhold gifts, demand certain interactions and never risk losing their own citizens' rights, even when protesting against the state. Undocumented migrants occupy a different space entirely, where the absence of citizens' rights and the risk of deportation are only highlighted by efforts to help them with special vehicles, gift-giving and discourses of solidarity. The fact that the Progresistas *need* the condom as an excuse to talk to workers throws further doubt on the project.

How can we understand the Progresistas' desire for sex workers to show solidarity *for each other*? Maintaining that all women are the same and that 'prostitutes' are simply workers who deserve rights, they seem unaware of many feminists' critique of the notion that all women share an essence. For those historically excluded, 'homogenizing and system-atizing the experiences of different groups of women' just erases 'marginal and resistant modes and experiences'.[9] Such critiques, common in postcolonial contexts, are scarcely heard in Spain, which remains colonialist, above all with Latin Americans.[10]

Empowerment is another concept describing what the Progresistas would like to accomplish. A word used by those who view themselves as fighters for social justice, *empowerment* is the current politically correct way to talk about helping. But *empower* is a transitive verb whose subject is the person doing the empowering, a technology aimed at 'constituting active and participatory citizens' and simultaneously linking subjects with their own subjection.[11] Empowerment seeks to get subjects included in society, equipped with

the right to have rights, to be a subject by right ... to belong to a body politic in which [they have] a place of residence, or the right to be actively involved – in other words the right to give a sense and a meaning to [their] action, words and existence.[12]

Those who desire to empower sex workers must assume that they view themselves as engaged in sex work. The identity issue is crucial: while empower-ers want to valorise cultural and individual differences and give voice to the mute, if those to be empowered do not think of themselves that way then the empowerment project cannot succeed and may turn into an unwanted imposition. Many migrants who sell sex do not consider themselves sex workers.[13]

The insistence on social inclusion cannot account for people who don't mind being excluded, at least in part. When subjectivity and subjection, resistance and oppression are made into opposites,[14] there appear to be only two choices, but many people avoid the attentions of states, perhaps particularly regarding their sex lives.

'Self-esteem', another concept that aims to transform people's relationships with themselves, is frequently used about the poor and stigmatised.[15] This liberation is meant to come about through operations on our ways of being, what Foucault called a technology of the self.[16] For the Progresistas, who want to help and who have a limited vocabulary to express themselves (rights, solidarity), concepts like empowerment and self-esteem may provide more tools with which to do their job.

Item 2:   A Culture of Indignation

A grand hall is the setting for an event on 'Prostitution and Trafficking in Women for Sexual Exploitation'. The organiser of this event is a member of an international 'anti-trafficking' organisation. Few of us in the field knew about this event before the last moment, and when we found out and tried to sign up, we were told there were no places left. Meanwhile, a highly placed politician, on discovering that we had not been invited, sent out a couple of invitations of her own. I received one. All the originally invited panellists had shared a strict abolitionist line, but the politician also demanded that speakers from several local projects be included.

The hall is a large, ornate symbol of high culture in the centre of the city. Marble columns, flags, formal flower arrangements and official seals festoon the room. The height of the stage promotes a sense of great difference between those above and those below, about 300 middle-class women who work in government and mainstream NGOs. The speakers are well-known on the abolitionist circuit; many have performed together in other countries.[17] We hear that 'prostitution' is slavery, and violence against women, that in 'prostitution' men force women to have sex with them, that 'trafficking' and 'prostitution' are the same thing and that the only solutions are abolition and punishment of exploiters. For three days these ideas are repeated over and over, with rarely a word from the audience. I feel I am at a cult meeting. One speaker exhorts us to develop the capacity for indignation, establish a culture of indignation,

A psychiatrist who proclaims the universally harmful effects of 'prostitution' on women is supported by a local woman who runs a flat where troubled women can spend the night; she mentions mental retardation as a typical attribute of 'prostitutes'. A Swedish male is cut off abruptly in his presentation on why men 'use prostitutes' when he makes a slightly compassionate remark; the moderator accuses him of taking typical male advantage of the situation (it's not clear how). Another academic discusses her study of advertisements for personal services in Spanish newspapers, apparently believing literally their information about ethnicity, nationality and gender; she provides quantitative data on how many of each advertise (several people in the audience chuckle about this). For three days, Holland is referred to repeatedly as a demon, without explanation, and no Dutch speaker has been invited.

Among other telling moments during the three-day conference, a well-known US academic does a high-tech presentation of Internet pornography. When a 'rape camp' website is projected onto a large screen, many members of the audience leave their seats and hurry forward for a good look. From the back of the room, this looks like prurience. Another ghastly moment for me personally comes when a member of a large 'anti-trafficking' group describes the destructive power of people who work for rights of 'prostitutes'. Pausing dramatically, she intones, 'There might even be some of them right here in the room with us.' My blood runs cold – could she know I am here?

Near the end, wine and canapés are served in an elegant period room, all polished wood, flowers and beautiful pictures. Given the non-stop representation of poverty, misery and violence imposed by the conference, the rich setting is offensive. I speak to an enraged Bolivian woman who cannot believe what she has seen at this conference: 'Our countries are supposed to be backward, but now I realise the opposite is true. At least we say what we feel in public, we are not intimidated.' We have both noted the constant, agitated whispering occurring outside the meeting room, compared with the audience's compliance inside it.

Last-minute political pressure on the organisers leads to the inclusion of local city projects in the programme. Anti-AIDS, after witnessing the tone of the prior two days, back out on the ground that it's inappropriate for them to take a political position (nonsensical since they work within conventional discourses of social exclusion, health prevention and harm reduction). This leaves the Progresistas' repre-sentative as the lone proponent of rights. Speaking last, she is mocked and misquoted by one of the organisers. Amidst the hubbub, a desperate voice from the audience asks whether it wouldn't be possible to hear what some 'prostitute' has to say. At that, the representative of an international women's programme, wearing dark glasses, grabs the microphone and barks: 'We don't have to talk to prostitutes to know what prostitution is.'

'Consensus' is claimed at the end of the conference, when the organisers announce they are writing up a document to send to the European Commission which will represent Spain's opinion. Outraged, a well-known activist nun stalks out.

A number of symbols of cultural capital contribute to the weight of this event: the audience pampered with deluxe souvenirs and wines; their travel and five-star hotel paid with government funds; enormous flags and brilliant rich lighting in a luxurious, prestigious hall. These material conditions, like the state emblems, constitute what Pierre Bourdieu calls symbolic power, conveying to those present that correct knowledge and policy *already exist* on the topic under discussion. This, in turn, implies that there is no place for questioning or quibbling.[18] The event is not a 'conference' in the sense that many understand. Here, individuals with important titles from different countries repeat a simplistic political line made to sound like good struggling against evil. Controlling invitations and silencing difference may give the impression of solid international unity. An unwitting audience may believe this or feel as bored as I did.

Other kinds of censorship are also common. People have been shouted into silence in public settings.[19] The ideology so important to those who would censor holds that 'prostitution' is violence against women, and that even listening to other ideas is wrong.[20] These censors are moral entrepreneurs, Howard Becker's term for those who assume authority for knowing what correct behaviours are, who label others deviant and who head moral crusades against social evils.[21] Often, as at this conference, inducing indignation is an overt goal.[22]

The desire to 'abolish prostitution' represents a utopian vision of how societies should be: free of gender inequity, sexual obsession and the commodification of bodies. There is no inherent reason for abolitionists to employ tactics of censorship, personal attacks, and disinformation, and some abolitionists maintain their utopian beliefs while also collaborating on pragmatic solutions. For this reason, I do not character-ise extremist behaviour as abolitionism but as fundamentalist feminism. Elizabeth Wilson refers to secular fundamentalism when discussing the difference between understanding revolution as change and uncertainty versus understanding it as faith:

> By fundamentalism I mean here a way of life, or a world-view or philosophy of life, which insists that the individual lives by narrowly prescribed rules and rituals: a faith that offers certainty … The search for the 'new life' can be exhilarating, but it can lead to extreme anxiety and personal collapse; by contrast, the price paid for certainty is rigidity and an incomprehension and intolerance of those who do not follow the 'true way'. Those who don't believe must be either destroyed or saved.[23]

Others refer to feminist fundamentalism as the idea that woman is good (or victim) and man is bad (or perpetrator).[24] These feminists believe there are authentic roots and principles to which all feminists ought to return; they would not have been in agreement with nineteenth-century advocates of domesticity; many are vocal lesbians, believe in women's right to abortion and advocate for equal rights for women. They feel beleaguered, betrayed and at war with other feminists who see things differently from them, which explains the frequent verbal violence. Fundamentalist crusades are characterised by homogeneous, consistent, easily understood ideas.

Fundamentalists speak of 'women'; they believe in a female essence that is violated by patriarchy everywhere; they are certain of what is male and what is female.[25] This appealing notion erases differences amongst women, however, both within cultures and across cultural boundaries. Postcolonial feminists as well as many first-world women object to an inclusiveness that only reflects middle-class, 'white', heterosexual, Euramerican experiences.[26] Criticism is especially severe of the tendency to make third-world women into 'always, already' victims, passive, acted upon and not acting.

Fundamentalist feminists are not worried by this criticism; they passionately evoke a spirit of Woman that needs both protecting and liberating; signs, symbols and keywords connote that spirit.[27] Likening their campaign to the nineteenth century's against slavery, and feeling they are at war, they respond with denunciations, telling attendees at events and funders that rights activists are 'paid by the sex industry' or 'known associates of traffickers'. They maintain and circulate blacklists, denounce activists to their employers and threaten loss of funding if recipients invite the wrong people to events.[28]

In a split within feminism, some believe that the women's movement was betrayed and must return to what it was:

> a movement in which people understood the need to act with courage in everyday life, that feminism was not a better deal or a riskless guarantee but a discipline of a hostile reality. To say that the personal was political meant, among other things, that what we do every day matters. It meant you become what you do not resist.[29]

Catherine MacKinnon's piece appears in *The Sexual Liberals and the Attack on Feminism*, a collection lamenting the betrayal of women who have turned away from founding feminist principles or who have 'internalised patriarchy'.

Problems can arise when individuals influenced by such an ideology occupy for many years posts dedicated to improving the situation of women. Such jobs can involve the funding of women's projects, publications, conferences and events, and what those in charge do not like may not get funded.[30] Money may only be given to projects that define 'prostitution' as sexual exploitation and gender violence. For a year or so, one prominent campaigner held meetings of all funded projects related to 'prostitution' for the purpose of leaving no one in doubt about what positions, actions and services would be approved. The attendees at these meetings always remained silent, because, they say, they felt safer not speaking than running the risk of saying the wrong thing and losing subsidies. One project was allegedly excluded because of its director's failure to denounce 'prostitution'.[31] In this way, one campaigner has directly affected the history of a particular social movement. In Nikolas Rose and Peter Miller's terms, power 'flows' to her because she determines what gets written down, compared and evaluated.[32]

She is, however, not alone in wielding this kind of power. Another NGO concerned with migrants was partially funded by a national body to do research on 'trafficking', but when the research failed to find enough cases of victims and compared the testimonies of women selling sex with those of domestic workers, the funders boycotted the formal presentation.[33]

Item 3: The Religious Social

The house, modern, large, solid and comfortable, one of a series of lookalikes in a new *barrio*, is a safe house for victims of 'trafficking' managed by an order of Roman Catholic nuns. 'We don't go out looking for business,' says one sister. 'The police call us, or clients do, or women themselves. They have escaped from a club and gone to the police, or they are at the airport. We ask them to tell us their situations, and if they really want to get away then we go and explain what we offer.' One of the nuns' employees, a legal specialist with several languages, often goes to the first interview.

These days the majority of women in the house are from eastern Europe, the Ukraine, Russia. Participation in the project means women get help with regularising their migration status in Spain, if they want to stay, or returning to their home country. The sisters offer classes in Spanish language and culture, psychological and legal aid and help with finding work. Rules for living in the house mix discipline with culture. Take the value the nuns place on 'sharing'. Everyone, nuns and guests alike, lives in the same kind of room, and everyone eats together. The sisters want to get to know the women, and one of the mechanisms is informal mealtime conversation. Meals are often leisurely affairs in Spain, and talking during them and afterwards is assumed to be enjoyable. Nevertheless, some of the women eat without speaking and quickly leave the table when they are finished. The nuns admit to being disoriented: how will they get to know the women?

They are aware that culture infuses their work, and recount for me, as an example, how they explain the act of saying grace before meals. 'We say we are Spanish nuns and we have a custom of saying a few words before beginning to eat. In our case, we are talking to God. You may talk to whomever you like at the same time, but we ask that you accompany us in these moments.' The guest residents may be atheist, Protestant, Muslim or anything else. Once, a woman escaped during the night, which upset the sisters, since it implied that she felt like a prisoner. They were worried and afraid she had left unprepared. Since then, they stress to guests that if they are not happy they just need to say so and are free to go at any time. I say, 'Perhaps she didn't want to have that conversation with you? The conversation in which she would have to explain what she didn't like about the house, the project, you . . .' They agree this could be the case. The nuns do not present themselves as sacrificial lambs; on the contrary, they are looking for personal and spiritual fulfilment.

I have visited a project in Italy where women's mobile phones are taken from them in order to interrupt ties with traffickers, so I ask whether the sisters do this as well. No, they say, 'but sometimes we would like to smash the mobiles against the wall.' Participation in their project means starting a new life, and keeping up prior relationships gets in the way (and is also dangerous).

Their project is directed at 'trafficked' women, so I ask how they define the term. They are very clear: the women themselves must say they have been forced, obligated, coerced or deceived and want to get out. I ask the nuns what would happen if a woman decided she wanted to go back to selling sex. Puzzled, they say, 'Well, she'd have to go back, then, if that's what she wanted.'

This is the definition of 'trafficking' accepted by the Global Alliance Against Trafficking in Women (GAATW),[34] which believes that sex work and migration can be plausible projects for autonomous women. This position has little support or history in Spain, where most discourse has been polemical.[35] These same nuns have also marched in demonstrations for sex worker rights. The founder of another rescue project, upon hearing this, declared: 'You're not nuns if you do that.'

I ask these women about various papal decrees, since the Vatican condemns sex outside marriage, abortion, birth control devices, homosexuality and 'prostitution'. They want to know why the Pope is so important to me. I am bemused: to outsiders, nuns represent the Roman Catholic Church and are assumed to agree with the Vatican. They enlighten me: not only do they not agree with these papal opinions, they don't have to. Nuns are not ordained as are priests, they do not belong to the church hierarchy, and within individual orders they have considerable freedom to decide their own policies. In fact, their beliefs and practices are much more tolerant or liberal than those of many secular groups, and not only in Spain. These sisters emphasise the rights and choices of individual women, including their own. They have evolved their own feminist project, in which they realise themselves during the process of helping women who have requested help. Their stated mission is the liberation and promotion of marginalised women; they are not in the business of moral judgements.[36] One sister laments, 'When I see the Pope on television I am appalled to think what kind of image we send to the rest of the world.' So there is a We, after all.

The order was founded by a wealthy noblewoman, who during her charitable work in a hospital encountered women suffering from venereal diseases. One of these, deceived by a man pretending to want to marry her, had lost her virtue and taken to selling sex. Though the noblewoman managed to return this woman to her family, she was unable so to help the majority and therefore opened a home where they could be isolated, learn a trade, become Christians and regenerate. The home was opened in the mid-nineteenth century. For some time, the noblewoman lived in other European cities; she came to know Paris's rue de la Madeleine, famous for prostitution. The nuns place much emphasis on the story of this woman, who faced constant opposition, impoverished herself and died in order to accomplish her goal of helping.[37]

I have found a direct link to the historical phenomena described earlier: a privileged woman who doesn't need to work but wants to be useful focuses her love and energy on lower-class women who sell sex. The helper starts her project in Spain but lives in Paris several times in the years immediately following the publication of Parent-Duchâtelet's landmark study of 'prostitutes' in 1836. Homes for needy women had a long tradition in Spain, but the number of initiatives multiplied during the nineteenth century,[38] along with the number of 'prostitutes', although, as Francisco Vázquez García points out, it is not clear who was counted and why.[39] Social projects in general proliferated, with the Church a strong force,[40] but it is not until late in the century that 'social Catholicism' came into being, a new idea of pastoral care.[41]

While the Rise of the Social played out differently in Spain than in France and Britain, several key developments are familiar: an upsurge in social projects, increased preoccupation with women who sold sex, confusion about who to call 'prostitutes' and the creation of numerous projects dedicated to rescuing them. While the increase in secular, educated women needing and wanting paid work did not occur at the same time in Spain, it would not be correct to exclude religious women from feeling similar desires and needs. Accounts of all kinds of charity are incomplete if they fail to consider the spiritual and material interests of those dispensing it.[42]

Mary Nash reveals how in Spain, too, gender ideology required educated women to be devoted, domestic and maternal angels while men were public and political providers. Women working outside the home and participating in social movements provoked hostility and had to deal with extremely unfavourable work conditions and remuneration.

> Women who transgressed the norms and invaded the public sphere were likened to public women, that is, to prostitutes. The public woman, with this double connotation of prostitute and woman occupying the public space traditionally reserved for males, was subject to a specific gender repression.[43]

At the end of the nineteenth century, a gradual shift began in attitudes and efforts to overturn discriminatory laws, as in other European countries. In the picture-book story of the noblewoman helping women who sold sex, society constantly rejects her, and, at some point while being set upon by enemy forces, she changes into a black habit. The act is not explained, but we may think of it as a change to a working uniform, as well as an expression of religious devotion.

Item 4: Culture Clash

Anti-AIDS do outreach with street workers in a middle-class neighbourhood, parking at the edge of a major intersection surrounded by traffic lights, hotels, apartment buildings and shops. The large van pulls up at scheduled times, and clients for condoms begin queueing up immediately. The first time they attend, they are asked to show a document with name, nationality and birth date and are asked a few basic questions; responses are recorded on cards. From then on, attendees identify themselves by birth date (migrants change names more often than dates, it seems). The system is minimal and crude, and all the data recorded can easily be falsified, but these are the sources for published statistics. When I first tried to go out with Anti-AIDS years before, they refused, despite their proclaimed dependence on volunteers; now their policy has changed.

It's a pleasant, late summer night. Most of the medical work is over, and some of us are sitting on the edges of big planters on the sidewalk near where the mobile unit is parked. A kind of microcosm of street life has formed around the line-up of West African women and Latin American transgenders waiting to reach the big window. Vendors and one aggressive street person are bickering, and sex workers accost passing men with varying degrees of insistence, but in general there is tolerance among those occupying the street. Inside the mobile unit a woman from Sierra Leone is doing an extended interview with one of the black workers.

A busful of Japanese tourists pulls up at the traffic light next to where I am sitting, and a tourist inside points his camera through the window at a black woman resting on the kerb. Instantly the woman reaches down, picks up a large chunk of broken pavement and hurls it straight at him, hitting the window. She throws another, and another, at which point the bus driver opens the door and steps out, yelling at her. But he does not shut the door behind him, and a small figure zooms out of the bus like a tornado. It is the photographer, who throws himself screaming at the woman, pelting her with blows although she is twice his size and weight. Other black women hurry from all directions to reach the scene, and in a matter of seconds a free-for-all is under way. Among those who intercede is the young but senior Anti-AIDS employee on the unit, with seven years' experience in the job. Finally she manages to separate the parties, who are wielding weapons, pulling hair, punching and screaming. By the time the police arrive, the bus has pulled away and the brick-throwing woman has been persuaded to get out of sight. Business carries on as usual: after all, this kind of fracas is not that uncommon on the street (while it feels apocalyptic to tourists inside a bus). The outreach workers agree that 'African' women react rapidly and aggressively compared with other people, opinions diverging as to whether this is a cultural trait or the product of abuse.

Anti-AIDS did not claim to do mediation, but outreach educators, exposed to unpredictable situations, need to be flexible. Over many years and after visiting dozens of projects in many countries and cultures, I conclude that there is a type of person who makes a successful outreach worker: frank, open, proud of a nonjudgemental attitude, easy with sexual matters and gender ambiguity, not afraid to try speaking other languages, calm in emergencies, decisive, responsible. This is not a profile of social agents in general or of most Anti-AIDS bureaucrats, who rarely leave their offices, have ventured onto the mobile unit only once and who do not include outreach workers in their decision making, conferences or network meetings. The office employees would probably disapprove of the intervention described, if they were to find out about it. Their dealings with people who sell sex are limited to analysing statistics: number of women seen, country of origin, age, reproductive status, attitudes to condom use and little else. Anti-AIDS promotional material is all about extending the benefits of the welfare state to those who have been excluded, so here, too, is a discourse of social solidarity, of an ethics that draws people to give of themselves to, and care for, those who are less fortunate.

In Madrid, a school dedicated to mediation in migration contexts was founded during this period, offering basic and specialised courses in sociocultural mediation, socioeducational mediation and in immigration itself.[44] Whatever the mediation is called, it has become popular among people working with migrants and is intended to intervene when people have conflicting values. Theorists of these phenomena talk about interculturalism: Julia Kristeva writes on Europeans' behaviour toward foreigners throughout history; Will Kymlicka and Javier de Lucas examine democratic systems' ability to integrate minorities, extend human rights and maintain 'cultural pluralism'.[45] The Spanish Labour

Ministry has financed research analysing Spaniards' attitudes toward migrants, and publications on interculturalism are now routine, focusing on schools, religions, neighbourhoods. Ideas such as mediation and interculturality provide the motivation for social agents to improve themselves, attend training courses, visit other countries and apply new techniques to their work of helping.[46]

In the area of outreach to migrants selling sex, the European Tampep network promotes the use of cultural mediators, individuals familiar with more than one culture and language who can facilitate relationships between people unable to imagine each other's realities. Tampep also uses 'peer educators', who may be any nationality but must have sold sex themselves, to pass on information and 'increase empowerment' among their peers.[47] When first introduced to the national Spanish network of projects, both techniques seemed unfeasible, but several years later they began to take hold.

Although the incident between sex worker and tourist illustrates how spontaneous mediation can prevent violence, the mobile van's presence can be said to have caused the conflict in the first place. Anti-AIDS's tolerant, harm-reduction approach and excellent facility means that large numbers of foreign, black, outlandishly dressed women gather at the intersection of busy, brightly lit streets. On the night in question, two hundred women visited the van over several hours; at any one time there were always a dozen waiting to reach the condom distribution window; many worked nearby. Anti-AIDS's reaching out is aimed at preventing HIV transmission but has unacknowledged side effects, as migrants become stigmatised characters in a spectacle that underscores the difference between them and everyone else. The rage of the woman who attacked the tourist was associated with being objectified by his camera's eye, but her hostility did not arise from nowhere.

Epidemiology is the reason for Anti-AIDS's being, not outreach or condom distribution. In close collaboration with and funded by Spain's national AIDS plan, Anti-AIDS publishes information on 'prostitutes' whose major purpose seems to be classification. Statistics presented in pie and bar charts correlate 'social characteristics' and risk conduct (primarily seen as sex without condoms). A review of Spanish epidemiological research demonstrates that the social characteristics thought to

matter are: nationality, gender, age, level of education, drug use, reproductive status, housing, and work and incarceration histories,[48] banal
information of little use to anyone. Learning to evaluate epidemiological
data, I came to understand that the articles Anti-AIDS doctors publish in
medical journals recycle the same sets of statistics over and over,
tweaking the emphasis over time. In Ian Hacking's view, this kind of
production takes shape 'without anyone's wittingly knowing what they
add up to'.

> If we turn to the practice of collecting information about populations,
> each new classification, and each new counting within that classifica-
> tion, is devised by a person or a committee with a straightforward,
> limited goal in mind. Then the population itself is increasingly classi-
> fied, rearranged, and administered by principles each one of which is
> innocently put forward by this or that technocrat.[49]

Such reports can be called 'inscription devices', whose point is to
produce objects that can be evaluated, calculated, debated and
diagnosed.[50] Even when these reports actually try to understand the risk
of disease transmission, the results are uninformative, since interviewees' feelings, states of mind and calculations about the future are
omitted: How do I decide if I am safe with someone or if someone is safe
for me? Under what circumstances might I choose not being safe now to
achieve safeness later?[51] The literature on sexual risk demonstrates that
it cannot be reduced to a set of factors disassociated from culture.[52] Yet
Anti-AIDS epidemiologists continuously reproduce the same profiles,
separating active citizens, who are seen as capable of managing their own
risk, from those who require intervention and help.[53] The Anti-AIDS
organisation gets much of its prestige and financing from the existence
of groups not labelled pools of contagion, as in the nineteenth century,
but construed as high-risk. In this sense, epidemiological research and
programming belong to the machinery of security, protecting real
citizens from 'disadvantaged' foreign contagion without reaching out to
natives who buy sex. The result is instrumental care such as that offered
by Anti-AIDS.

Another kind of research sets out to discover whether higher-risk
groups use social and health services. Migrant women and transgenders

who sell sex are interviewed to find out whether they use public health services and, if not, why not. Disseminated internally and in social networks, these studies focus on ethnic and cultural ideas about health, sexual and reproductive habits and taboos in private and professional life, including body modifications. [54] The incessant asking of intimate questions and the routine assumption that Spanish culture and education are better than migrants' own is neocolonialistic; invasive questions are made to seem normal when the report is distributed under a government seal, a standard for what knowledge social agents should seek. [55] Women who sell sex are no longer likened to sewers, but AIDS's intransigent association with dark people, dark habits and the Dark Continent places a similarly heavy burden on them. [56]

Spain, like other European countries, wants to keep undocumented migrants out, but it also wants to make sure their unsafe practices do not infect real citizens and therefore sponsors research on their use of health services. Such softer studies also aim to pin down knowledge about migrants, providing an 'intellectual machinery for government' that can then be used to make decisions about them. [57]

Item 5: The Bitterness of Betrayal

I am contacted by an association for abused women in a provincial capital about giving a speech on 'trafficking' at a public seminar on sexual violence. I ask them whether they are familiar with my work, send them one of my articles on migrant women in the sex industry, and tell them I can talk about migration. They assure me that I have been recommended by someone we both know, so I accept. The lecture is announced as 'Migration and trafficking: myths, truths and a lot of ambiguities'.

It is winter in a part of Spain known for a harder, darker, more puritanical worldview. The hall where I will give my hour-long lecture is very large, and I am seated on a heavy, high-backed, wooden throne. Soon after I begin, I see tension, shock, anxiety and displeasure on faces in the audience, but it is too late to do anything but go on. At the end, I am asked questions in an acid tone prefaced with references to my supposed opinions: 'these delightful sex clubs you are so fond of', 'those respectful gentlemen you call clients', 'such a wonderful job, prostitution'. My responses all begin the same way: 'I didn't say that, I said one can make a lot of money in the clubs' or 'I didn't say that, I said that the numbers of men who buy sex mean they can't all be perverts' or 'I didn't say that, I said some people prefer selling sex to other available jobs.' A young woman asks, 'So do you think there are no harmful effects to women from being prostitutes?'

Why do they hear things I haven't said? They seem offended that I don't talk about what the media say every day, even though the organisers particularly told me that they wanted new information. But here, and now, they only want to know why I don't mention slavery, mafias, child abuse, psychological damage and violence. In fact, I *have* mentioned them, but I don't condemn anyone, and they seem dissatisfied at the lack of outraged indignation. Even when I do talk about clients, the audience feel I haven't, because they want to hear me say terrible things about these men.

Nevertheless, the organisers are polite, and during the next day and a half they show me around the city. My real hosts turn out to be not the service providers who contacted me but middle- and upper-class women interested in feminist theory and taking positions. They do not refer to the issues they invited me to speak about, but take me on a tour of a local cathedral, and when I say it is one of the most beautiful I have seen in Europe, my guide promises to send me a book about it 'in spite of everything, to show that we know how to do the right thing'. High-class manners for a despised guest. During the last meal on the way to the train station, I invite them to speak, assuring them that they do not have to agree with me. At that moment, I see how the blood boils and rises up in their leader and am glad I have given her permission to spit out her suppressed feelings. Sputtering and red-faced, she declares that 'prostitution' is always, in all situations, abuse and violence. It is imperialism, invasion of women's bodies. It is the antithesis of love. It ruins good marriages. The men are cruel, egotistical perverts who should be put in prison. No woman ever, ever wants to sell sex, she is only forced to, and if she says differently then she is lying or doesn't understand her own situation.

Later, I learn that these feminists have never studied 'prostitution'. No wonder we have a problem; inviting someone to give a lecture on 'trafficking' without thinking about the basic terms beforehand could only lead to confusion. After my visit, the association promoted a regional study project on 'prostitution', but members who brought in materials proposing any theoretical framework but violence felt silenced, and several afterward left the association.[58]

The woman whose blood boiled specialises in changing sexist language, believing that the words we use are overarchingly important to gender equity. She hates my way of talking and wants me and everyone to change our language, to instead speak in terms of *sexual exploitation* and *abuse*, making it impossible to consent to sell sex and making buyers *criminals*. Efforts to change discriminatory forms of language have long been important to social justice projects, and the push to expand definitions of violence against women is part of this. If 'prostitution' can be universally redefined as sexual exploitation, regardless of whether people say they chose to sell sex or not, then all those who purchase sexual services become, by definition, exploiters. For those who believe men are inherently and biologically aggressive and predatory,[59] this traditional battle of the sexes feels real.[60]

> The prostitute's environment is a very violent environment; its logic is silence and violence. Women detained by the police declared themselves 'in agreement'; but, in reality, they were not in agreement. From 1902, it was decided that even if the of-age person consented, there was trafficking.[61]

A contemporary French rescue project calls women who sell sex slaves who need help in order to become aware of their oppression, slave mentality and false consciousness, after which they will 'awaken', 'be able to protest, not to ask for arrangements or for the official recognition of prostitution' and 'discern their own path towards freedom'.[62] This belief may be understood as an authoritarian form of liberal government, in which those to be governed are not considered free subjects.[63] Mariana Valverde points out how, even for one of the great exponents of liberalism, John Stuart Mill, only *evolved* social subjects were considered worthy of participation in their own governance:

> Those who are still in a state to require being taken care of by others, must be protected against their actions as against external injury. For the same reasons, we may leave out of consideration those backward

states of society in which the race itself may be considered as in its nonage ... Despotism is a legitimate mode of government in dealing with barbarians, provided the end be their improvement.[64]

This colonialist notion is found today in the kind of helping that disqualifies people who sell sex from self-rule, the justification being that they have been economically forced into it, or have been deceived or sequestered or suffer from false consciousness. Many others give priority to the experiences, and therefore the words, of people actually living the situations at hand. Sandra Harding, Dorothy Smith and numerous others advocate for bringing into public discussions ideas excluded from dominant ideologies.[65] A great deal has been written about the need to bring out voices that are silenced or marginalised, but there are dangers when, as Gayatri Spivak argues, it is assumed that everyone can 'speak' in the same way.[66] This came up in debates on one of the classic films about selling sex, in which the filmmaker records the life of a Thai woman whose services he is buying:[67]

> Many feminist critics of The Good Woman of Bangkok demanded that the camera be given to the woman, so she could speak – but really this is just another demand from the West that the woman *must* speak and thus present herself for assessment and evaluation ...[68]

Believing passionately that people must tell their stories is also a governmental urge.[69] But many of the marginalised find the margins easier to live in; their friends are there; or they don't like the centre. Telling one's story, going to protests and marches, chatting with outreach workers and a host of other projects are simply not interesting to many people, whether they are maltreated by society or not.

For some people who want to help the disadvantaged, listening is essential. Homeless children in Brazil told Tobias Hecht that yes, they *could* return to a house, or that they *did* return sometimes, but that they preferred to live in the streets.[70] In Canada, young people testified to a government committee that they left home to escape from something 'impossible' to live with.[71] That children say these things, however, is unacceptable to many people who want to save them.

> If one's goal in writing about street children is to offer ideas on how to eradicate a problem one can hardly view those people seen to

embody the problem as autonomous beings in a social world. Reduced to something to be cured, street children become objects in a distant debate among adults.[72]

This is not to say that migrants, street children or sex workers will necessarily want to read publications or attend events discussing their problems but that when their own words are not taken into account, helpers (including theorists) become ventriloquists occupying the main stage while the helped sit mutely in the wings.

Item 6   Publications: Never for Women Who Sell Sex

Publication A

It looks like a conventional leaflet on AIDS prevention, like thousands of others that have been created around the world, but it is different. *¿Qué es el VIH/SIDA?* (What is HIV/AIDS?) is the product of a collaboration of an EU-sponsored AIDS prevention campaign, Spain's national health institute and a few NGOs, including West African migrants' associations.[73] The aim, to create a culturally sensitive leaflet directed at this specific group, is not mentioned in the text but is explicit in the drawings, which show brown people with particular facial features. The leaflet consists of two lists, ¿Cómo *sí entra* en tu cuerpo? (How *does* it get into your body) and ¿Cómo *no entra*? (How does it *not* get in?). Known and suspected methods appear in one or the other list, with one exception: oral sex is absent. While current medical knowledge suggests that it is more difficult for the virus to enter the body through the mouth, safer-sex practices worldwide advocate using a condom for mouth–genital contact. Moreover, oral sex is enormously common and popular, and in some sectors of the sex industry blowjobs are the most requested service.

Several meetings in a room at a public health institute have been held to decide on the leaflet's contents; I am present at the review of the mock-up before it is sent to the printer. Although I have had nothing to do with the group until now, I feel I have to intervene, so I ask if oral sex has accidentally dropped out of the text. Several sets of eyes avoid mine, but finally the project coordinator explains that this point has been discussed and left out because 'it appears that it doesn't form part of the culture of the groups to which the leaflet is directed' – meaning West Africans, but actually meaning the leaders of formal associations who have attended these meetings. The chair of the meeting looks at the doctor from the association of Ecuatorial Guineans, and I follow her glance. 'That's right,' he says, 'we don't do that.'

The decision to omit an important risk-practice from an education project is cultural relativism and delicacy taken to the extreme of subordinating epidemiological concerns. No doubt various issues of the allegedly homogeneous sexual culture of Ecuatorial Guinea could be analysed, which would question this particular authority figure's perspective as both man and doctor of western medicine, along with his position in the association and appropriateness to judge what Ecuatorial Guineans do. Possibly, all such questioning would throw doubt on his assertion. But leaving these issues aside, I want to address another aspect of this incident.

One of the most visible groups selling sex in the street in Spain are women from the western countries of Africa, and while scandalmongers talk as though all are 'victims of trafficking', the people gathered for this meeting know better. They know that women who sell sex have other identities, as mothers, sisters, girlfriends and members of the associations participating in this project. They have religious, civic, social and intellectual lives. What will a person who sells oral sex think when she sees this leaflet? That her own life doesn't count with health educators? That she engages in something unspeakable?

Though created specifically for a population called 'immigrants', the leaflet demonstrates great ignorance about migration. It does not recognise (1) that migrants have sex with people outside their community of origin; (2) that Spanish culture is saturated with positive messages about sexual liberation and experimentation; (3) that some migrants sell sex. The omission could make all people from West Africa who practise oral sex feel that they are somehow betraying their culture, whether they are paid to do it or do it for their own pleasure. Everyone involved in this publication knows that a large number of women from these countries sell sex at some time or another and therefore have probably practised oral sex, but no one mentions it. The implication is that such people no longer belong to their 'traditional culture' and therefore are not members of migrant associations. Social agents have managed to create a leaflet that stigmatises a range of people, along with a sexual practice.

A Cuban study commented that the official pretence after the revolution that 'prostitution' had been eradicated removed not only its right to exist but also 'the right of words to exist to describe it'.[74] This little AIDS leaflet does not place oral sex on the side of 'dangerous' practices, it places it nowhere – and the result is not innocuous.

Publication B

Médicos del Mundo-Madrid produced a book of resources that begins with a preface by the city's mayor:

Unfortunately, one of the realities that most worries our society, owing fundamentally to the serious personal and human deterioration that it implies, is the phenomenon of prostitution, which, in the present day, is linked, in most cases, to the existence of international networks of illegal immigration.[75]

The book goes on to outline a series of ethnic stereotypes: Latin Americans have a low cultural level, Mediterranean Europeans are usually drug addicts, and Saharans are illiterate. 'Migrant women coming from Third World countries where extreme poverty or wars ... force them to migrate ... are fundamentally trafficked, which implies forced work [and] ... working conditions in all cases unknown.'[76] The text reinforces the largely discredited stereotype of the 'classic/professional' who is induced by 'pimps' through 'dark deceit with an affectionate tinge'. No details on how the research was done are provided.

Publication C

Guía de Autocuidados para las Mujeres Inmigrantes (Guide to Self-care for Migrant Women), said to be intended for them, was published by the Ministry of Health. Although it is spiral-bound and includes drawings, the dense and semi-technical text assumes readers will be highly literate in Spanish. The book never mentions the sex industry or people who work in it – neither in the sexuality chapter nor in the list of relevant laws nor in the section of resources for migrant women.[77]

Publication D

A government newsletter is distributed before the Beijing + 5 meeting on women's issues to be held in New York in 2000, supposedly setting out all important items on the agenda. Neither sex work nor 'prostitution' appear anywhere in categories including economy and employment, education and culture, health, gender violence, feminisation of poverty, girls, decision making, human rights and armed conflicts.[78] For a long time before this, it was known that sex industry issues would be addressed.

Publication E

La prevención de la transmisión heterosexual del VIH / SIDA en las mujeres (The Prevention of Heterosexual Transmission of HIV / AIDS in Women), which is detailed and practical, simply omits references to women who sell sex. This book was funded by a national women's organisation as well as the national AIDS plan.[79]

These examples illustrate the different ways stigmatisation operates. All maintain the separation between good and bad / unmentionable women. While the Médicos booklet takes for its subject 'prostitutes', directly discrediting them racially and culturally and disqualifying them as protagonists of their own lives, the other publications stigmatise by omitting people who sell sex. In the Médicos text, selling sex fixes identity; for the others, selling sex doesn't exist. Yet migrants who sell sex are thought to equal numbers of domestic and caring workers, which means there are hundreds of thousands of them.

A good part of what's going on in these publications is neocolonialism. Most social agents see women who migrate to Europe from poorer countries as tremendously disadvantaged: poor, oppressed, coming from violent societies, having no choices. They are never described as feminists and rarely as politically active or possessing consciousness of their own situation. Research shows that European employers of migrant women in the home generally believe them to be more submissive, respectful, naturally affectionate, domestic and quiet than western women, and thus willing to accept a lower social status. They are often said to come from cultures where women have fewer rights than in Europe, so that, in a way, employers believe they are helping them progress simply by hiring them.[80] Sometimes the act of migrating earns women credit toward modernisation but they are still assumed to be backward in relation to Europeans, as neocolonialism conserves evolutionary notions in which the west represents progress and the rest tradition. But the west's self-presentation is *discursive*, not factual, called by Homi Bhabha an 'apparatus of power' whose prime function is the creation of a space for subject peoples.[81] Consider the refreshing reversal in the title of another epidemiological study: 'Prostitutes Study Truck Drivers in South Africa, Find High HIV Rate'.[82]

Item 7: A Different Morality

Another conference is held. 'Seminario Internacional Sobre Prostitución' is on the printed programme, but the banner tacked to the platform adds 'y Tráfico'. A highly placed representative of the Ministry of Labour inaugurates the event, followed by a university rector and Spain's representative at UN hearings on international crime. All condemn 'prostitution', but spend most of their time haranguing about 'trafficking' in unenlightening terms. When these august figures leave, the real conference begins, and the change of tone and terms is drastic.

Presentations are good, misleading research is not used to represent 'facts', and presenters acknowledge the complexity and variety of experiences among people who sell sex. The speakers, mostly not Spanish, are names associated with human and labour rights for sex workers.[83] As with the fundamentalist conference, the scope of discussion is narrow, most speakers making an argument for policy oriented around labour rights. My own presentation discusses the paucity of research material to back up so much theory and presents an array of situations from Latin America that don't fit into the 'prostitution' concept.[84]

Early on, in an obviously prepared action, a group of women in the audience loudly and indignantly walk out, and during the rest of the conference the director of a local rescue project paces the hall outside, manifesting disapproval. At one point, she approaches Carla Corso, an activist street worker, saying, 'You aren't a prostitute, because you don't suffer.'[85] I am struck by this comment: if the definition of 'prostitute' were changed to describe only suffering victims, perhaps the conflict over terms could be resolved. After all, the rescue director would not deny that Corso sold sexual services in the street for several decades, but Corso isn't like the women she wants to help.

Toward the end, a highly placed public functionary arrives. Obviously, neither she nor the speechwriter has been present at the conference, since she reads, 'As we have seen in the past few days, prostitution is always a form of violence against women' and more of the usual rhetoric, which, in fact, since the first morning, we have *not* heard. There are two different reactions from the audience: the foreigners exchange befuddled glances as the translated speech reaches them through headphones, while the Spanish appear to accept the incongruence without surprise. This is, after all, what is *always* said in public in Spain, so it's not strange to hear it now. Locals have probably been asking each other from the beginning how all these heretics infiltrated into a publicly funded conference in the first place.[86] The woman on the podium, eyes down on her reading, is unaware of the unrest until a sex worker from Canada stands up to object; when the translated words reach her, the official is horrified.

After the Progresista's speech, a woman in the audience launches into a tirade against her couched in the most virulent personal terms: she is a traitor to feminism. We now realise that the group that flounced out the first day is back with reinforcements. In full tilt, the heckler will not let go of the microphone, but the Progresista raises her voice to defend herself. The moderator is unable either to stop the shouting match or to make the usher wrest the microphone free. Other members of the audience jump into the fray, and the conference ends in disarray. It is a well-planned assault demonstrating firmly and visibly the moral frontier between good and evil.

This conflict resembles feminist battles over pornography in the 1980s, when one side campaigned against misogyny and exploitation while the other advocated for freedom of expression and sexual diversity.[87] Rights activists such as those at this conference avoid overt moralising but certainly feel their proposals represent a superior morality: better justice toward workers, greater humanity toward clients, healthier understanding of sexual needs and desires, more understanding of how to prevent social and physical harm.[88] This conference presented points of view seldom heard in Spain, but it also maintained the traditional boundaries between two sides of a debate. In the same way that Holland, with its regulation of brothels, was not invited to present its system at the event described earlier in this chapter, Sweden, with its criminalisation of clients, was not invited to defend itself at the second event. The organiser made no effort to bring coherency to a situation in which state officials directly contradicted invited speakers, which clearly opened the door to the ruckuses of moral crusaders. Yet these were inevitable the moment the conference was conceived.

The message of the speakers at this conference is far more complex than that of the fundamentalists. Writing of feminist campaigns against censorship in the 1980s, Lisa Duggan explains the dilemma:

> We wanted to separate ourselves from the civil liberties framework to make a specifically feminist argument in defense of sexually explicit expression. We wanted to attack many of the standard oppositions of civil liberties discourse. For instance, we did not argue that 'sex workers' have 'free choice' of occupations, but emphasized that, within a limited range of very constrained choices in a sexist, capitalist economy, 'sex work' is not always the worst option.[89]

Most present at this event, and at the others, are women. The majority of jobs in the social sector are held by women, as what was identified and carved out as a natural sphere for women long ago continues. Second, feminism is either an overt framework or implicit in woman-oriented services (for raped, battered or abused victims, for unmarried and single mothers, for employment and micro-enterprise counselling, for much psychotherapy, for self-esteem and sexuality counselling, for immigrant women, for women's health and so on). Some projects receive funding because of their 'gender perspective', as governments put in place affirmative action or equity policies. Since so many organisations exist because of the women's movement, many social agents owe allegiance to high-profile feminists in their region and may not feel able to take independent positions. Groups that survive through funded projects must write proposals within guidelines and using ideas known to please funders. At the state and international levels, where civil service rules ensure people's careers, some feminists have come to be highly placed. In these situations, the term *hegemonic discourse* takes on material meaning.

In another room, a member of Red Cross Youth brings together a number of Spanish groups in an attempt to form a national network. It takes three of us, intervening several times in rhetorical conflicts between people who have never sat down together before, just to prevent angry walk-outs. The representative from one rescue project, who cannot bear to hear people talk from medical and rights perspectives, constantly wrings her hands, inciting others to fight back. Someone asks, 'Do we all have to agree about what prostitution *is* in order to work together?'

The different morality at this conference relies on one overarching idea. In English, agency means the ability to make decisions and act, to determine what happens to some extent, even in highly structured and restrictive situations. In Spanish, there is no synonym; advocates speak of having the capacity to act, of women being protagonists and so on. The conflicts in 'prostitution' debates hinge crucially on whether poor people, migrants, women can be said to have any control over their lives, given the unjust structures of patriarchy, globalisation and capitalism they live in. Speakers at this event who advocate labour and human rights believe that even the least advantaged individuals have some power over their destiny; all poor people do not migrate, all poor women do not turn to selling sex. This vision sees individuals as creative.[90] Ultimately this argument cannot be won either way; both sides believe their view is truthful and ethical.

Item 8: Pragmatism in the Provinces

My room in the famous old hotel is next door to Ernest Hemingway's in the 1920s. Hemingway is credited with a major role in making Spain an international tourist attraction, but it is only now, seventy-five years later, that this province is seeing many black visitors on its streets, and they are not tourists. While I am in the city, a pro-immigration demonstration is held in the central plaza, with the motto 'Open Up the Wall'.[91] This province is wealthy, known for its isolation, for works of charity and solidarity and for being quirkily conservative and progressive at the same time.

The proprietor of two sex clubs, Don X, meets people in the lobbies of expensive hotels, where he seems to feel safer. He tells how at mid-life he was casting about for a more lucrative new career and hit upon opening a club for which he would bring the girls himself from outside Spain. He makes trips to Kiev via Paris and Berlin with the help of a few contacts, and since he treats his girls well they now do the 'trafficking' for him, setting things up with friends back home. He freely admits he has got rich off them and wants to open more clubs, but he rejects the idea that this makes him immoral and is offended that the media talk about people like himself as vicious criminals. He wants his workers to have normal labour benefits, which is why he approached several different social agents in the city about the possibility of getting them work permits and social security protection.

Before Don X made his move, the region's only social programming for people who sell sex consisted of traditional rescue, rehabilitation and reintegration projects. I interview the members of a religious project (for 'severely marginalised women') who are now almost out of a job. They tell me that not so long ago, uneducated Spanish women worked on the streets, took drugs, had pimps – a type now gone. The employment department of this organisation began to see increasing numbers of migrants working in sex clubs after 1995, when highway hotels began to be converted. The employment manager views the situation practically: he can look for jobs for women who come to him, but the only other work he can offer them is domestic service, which pays terribly.

Don X made a proposal to Don Y, at the Labour Ministry: X would officially register his employees as workers so that they could receive social security benefits. Y visited X's clubs and talked in private with the women. He claims to be purely pragmatic: 'Spanish women are not signing up for the job. This way everything is legal, there can't be any problems, for us or for the police. The object was to legalise these little girls.' Y's problem was what job category to register them under, since there is none for selling sex; the rubrics used by paper-fixers are artist, dancer or entertainer. But Y wants to be honest, so he chooses an older classification, *camareras de alterne* (bar hostesses, with the implication that they offer sex). Thirty women have been registered so far. The cases for regularisation being proposed by X (and now other club owners) are reviewed at weekly meetings in Y's office attended also by a police official, the employment manager from the religious organisation and an NGO worker with migrants.

The result of this completely atypical collaboration bypasses the usual moralistic confrontation of positions and debates on which system should be used to 'control prostitution' and proceeds directly to getting legal status for workers. Weekly meetings are oriented toward individual cases, the goal to reduce the number of illegal workers one by one in the province. The religious entity is interested in solving more cases of clients with problems; the Labour Ministry wants to have more legal migrants within its responsibility and the club owner wants to justify his enormous earnings by doing some good. The NGO worker is concerned to help individual women: 'I don't care if the club owner is a petty criminal, or if some people are paying and taking bribes, I just want those women to get employment protection and social security.' Only the police commissioner's motivations are somewhat obscure.

Away from centres of public debate, a pragmatic use of the concept of *sex work* is perhaps easier. In this province, leftist party proposals to change 'prostitution' law had come to nothing;[92] migrants working with no civil or labour rights did not advocate for being called sex workers or for their occupations to be recognised or legalised; no Progresistas-type project demanded rights. Yet, in the quietest possible way, the work theory was put into practice and the situation of many migrants was dramatically improved. One afternoon, I ran into two Ukrainian women from one of X's bars having tea in the main plaza, alongside middle-class Spanish and tourist clientele. Several years later I am told hundreds of women have been granted work permits in the same way.

How did this solution come about in this particular place? The answer lies with Don X, an entrepreneur from *outside* the social sector who took

the initiative to satisfy his own conscience. X was able to catalyse a different practice because his own identity and job did not depend on the
existence of a group of people he had to save. This case demonstrates that
male insiders in the sex industry may help bring about positive solutions
for workers – important, because many who work with victims cannot
conceive of working with men, whether they are business owners, clients
or intermediaries like travel agents and taxi drivers.[93] This case also shows
how social agents may participate in creative, productive solutions to
injustice.

Making Sense of the Field Work

Social programming reifies and reproduces the classic 'prostitution' discourse. Some practices blatantly attempt to control knowledge:
excluding diverse opinions from panels of experts and audiences,
censoring publications, withholding funding, discrediting people on
personal grounds, racism. Other practices appear benevolent: ending
sexist language, using rights and solidarity talk, condom distribution,
shelters, consciousness-raising on gender violence, cultural sensitivity.
Still others might seem innocuous: ethnic classifications, questionnaires
on sexual risk.

My goal is not to classify actions as bad or good or to determine
whether they 'really' help or not but to reveal how social agents and their
projects remain at the social centre of attention while failing materially to
improve the situations of people who sell sex. Helping requires a wide
array of figures, most of whom are paid a decent wage, granted positive
social status and encouraged to gain ever more knowledge about the
people they want to help: their languages, their cultural traits, their
values, details of their intimate life. Each of these produces more responsibilities and tasks for helpers to carry out, whether they are
educators, epidemiologists, doctors, editors, drivers, legal scholars,
nuns, psychologists, police, mediators, functionaries, job counsellors,
conference speakers, academics or volunteer activists. These are

> the changing discursive fields within which the exercise of power is
> conceptualised, the moral justifications for particular ways of exer-
> cising power by diverse authorities, notions of the appropriate form,

objects and limits of politics, and conceptions of the proper distribution of such tasks among secular, spiritual, military and familial
sectors. But ... also in terms of their *governmental technologies*, the
complex of mundane programmes, calculations, techniques,
apparatuses, documents and procedures through which authorities
seek to embody and give effect to governmental ambitions.[94]

More responsibilities necessitate more social programming; the
social sector expands and diversifies while the supposed aim, social
inclusion for people who sell sex, does not succeed. That the majority of
social agents continue to spend time and energy battling over the
correct feminist or moral position, or which policing regime to back,
also maintains their own importance. Many social agents turn criticism
from themselves by blaming the law, international bodies, the
communications media, violent men – never themselves. This chapter
argues that reflexivity is in order.

NOTES

1   Foucault's biopower or biopolitics (1979b)
2   Rose and Miller 1992: 175
3   These have been called both regimes of government and regimes of practices (Dean
    1999).
4   Clifford and Marcus 1986.
5   Osborne 1991; Estébanez 1998
6   See also Donzelot 1991: 172.
7   Hayward 1959: 269. 'La solidarité se développe en même temps que renaît l'espérance
    ... Jamais, peut-être, depuis l'établissment des ordres monastiques, on n'avait vu une
    telle ferveur d'union par le monde; il se fonde partout des Sociétés coopératives, des
    syndicats, des Ligues, des Compagnies, pour ne pas dire des Eglises. On n'a guère
    affaire en tous lieux qu'à des groupes au lieu de personnes.' (Paul Desjardins [1896:
    33], quoted in Hayward 1959: 267)
8   Valcárcel 1997
9   Mohanty 1991: 71
10 One hears about Iberoamérica, for example, as if it were a big happy family. When
    publicity for the 1992 celebration in Seville of the Columbian voyages of discovery
    described them as *El encuentro de dos culturas* (the meeting of two cultures), one
    comedian changed it to *El Encontronazo* (a meeting more like an annihilating collision
    for one side).
11 Agustín 2000b

12   Cruikshank 1994
13   Agustín 2005a
14   Cruikshank 1994: 31
15   Cruikshank 1993
16   Foucault 1988: 18
17   Speakers include proponents of abolitionism in international and European politics from the European Women's Lobby, the Coalition Against Trafficking in Women, the UN, the Mouvement Pour l'Abolition de la Prostitution et de la Pornographie, the US Johns Schools, the University of North London, and the Swedish parliament.
18   Bourdieu 1979: 79
19   Attested to by four experts in the field of migration
20   For a report on a similar bitter public battle see Asturias 2000.
21   Becker 1963
22   Reforming women in 1830s New York aimed to 'warn other God-fearing Christians of the pervasiveness of sexual sin and the need to oppose it' (Rosenberg 1971: 566).
23   Wilson 1992: 28
24   Bilden 1999; Meulenbelt 2002
25   To take one example, Janice Raymond's first book argues that sex/gender identity is fixed by the genitals at birth (Transsexual Empire 1979).
26   hooks 1984; Anzaldúa 1987; Spivak 1988; Mani 1990; Mohanty 1991
27   I am interested in the possible comparisons with 'Born-Again' Christianity. Evangelist churches in Appalachia are said to be 'on fire', and the charismatic passion of a leader often represents righteousness.
28   I was myself persecuted this way and lost employment; many other activists have reported similar stories and we have seen blacklists of people and groups distributed to government bodies. In nineteenth-century reformist battles, people attacked each other as 'unrespectable'. This would not make sense nowadays, so other kinds of slurs have to be found.
29   MacKinnon 1990: 3-5
30   Celia Valiente characterises this as 'institutional' or 'state' feminism (1996). According to Valiente, institutional feminism has predominated in Spain since the death of Franco.
31   Personal communications from diverse groups
32   Rose and Miller 1992: 200
33   Personal communication from the present director. The NGO had previously produced a non-research-based, polemical report on 'trafficking' but carried out real research the second time.
34   GAATW 2000
35   Fundación Dolores Ibárruri 1998; ACSUR-Las Segovias 1999; Rempe 2001
36   Proyecto Esperanza 2001, 2002a, 2002b
37   Adoratrices 1983, 1987
38   Las Oblatas del Santísimo Redentor, las Adoratrices Esclavas del Santísimo Sacramento y de la Caridad, las Dominicas de la Presentación, Hermanas de Nuestra Señora de la Caridad del Buen Pastor, Hermanas Trinitarias, Hijas de la Inmaculada Concepción para el servicio doméstico y protección de la joven and Sirvientas de la Pasión. Secular

institutions pursuing similar goals included the Patronato de Nuestra Señora de la Merced, Asociación Católica Internacional de Obras para la Protección de las Jóvenes, Villa Teresita and Cáritas. Some of these groups have changed their names during their history (Bada 1999).

39   Vázquez García 1998

40   'In 1909, of a total of 606 public welfare establishments, 422 were run by religious agents, the majority women. It should be noted that between 1851 and 1900, 64 new female congregations (orders) were born of which 44 were founded for benevolent ends'. (Varela and Álvarez-Uría 1989: 100)

41   Varela and Álvarez-Uría 1989: 100

42   Carasa Soto 1989

43   Nash 1989: 158

44   EMSI 2001

45   Kristeva 1991; Kymlicka 1995; and de Lucas 1996; see also Juliano 1993

46   This area overlaps that of 'development', in which first-world helpers travel to poorer countries to give aid and expertise, and it is similarly problematic. See Escobar 1995.

47   Tampep 1994, n/d; Associazione On the Road 1998; Signorelli and Treppete 2001. The usual example cited is that of the pregnant woman wanting an abortion who needs to pass through the decision-making and medical intervention process common in the west.

48   Estébanez 1990; Estébanez et al 1998; Llácer 1999; Belza 2000a-d; Castilla 2000

49   Hacking 1986: 35

50   Latour and Woolgar 1979; Rose and Miller 1992: 185

51   Sobo 1995; Van Kerkwijk 1995

52   ten Brummelhuis and Herdt 1995; Patton 1994; Parker and Aggleton 1999

53   Dean 1999: 167

54   Cuanter 1998; Bueno 1999; Sigma Dos 2001–2

55   Another question is whether and why people asked such questions consent to answer them, or answer them truthfully.

56   Browning 1998

57   Rose and Miller 1992: 182

58   Personal communications from the activists who originally invited me.

59   Andrea Dworkin theorised penetration by the penis of the vagina as imperialism (1987). Mary Daly said: 'If life is to survive on this planet, there must be a decontamination of the Earth. I think this will be accompanied by an evolutionary process that will result in a drastic reduction of the population of males' (in Bridle 1999).

60   I discuss the miserable nature of this tendency in Agustín 2001b.

61   Tamzali 1997: 17

62   Mouvement du Nid 1993

63   Dean 1999: 132

64   Mill [1859] quoted in Valverde 1996: 360

65   Smith 1974; Harding 1987; Stone-Mediatore 2000

66   Spivak 1988

67   O'Rourke 1991

68 Hamilton 1997: 157
69 My own contribution to bringing out voices can be read in Agustín 2005a.
70 Hecht 1998
71 Lowman 1985: 513
72 Hecht 1998: 188
73 Ministerio de Sanidad y Consumo 2000
74 Díaz and González 1997: 173
75 Médicos 1998: 3
76 Médicos 1998: 23
77 Castillo 2000
78 Consejo de la Mujer 2000
79 Velasco 1999
80 Oso 1998; Ioé 2001
81 Bhabha1983: 23
82 Agence France Presse 2001
83 Jo Bindman (1996); Gail Pheterson (1989, 1996); Jo Doezema (2000); Marjan Wijers and Lap-Chew (1996); Don Kulick (1998); Lin Lean Lim (1998)
84 Agustín 2004b
85 Note the parallel here with the comment, above, that a pro-rights nun cannot be a nun.
86 I provided a list of names of potential speakers to the organiser, with their various specialities, but they did need to be approved by the funder, so the mystery is genuine.
87 Duggan and Hunter 1995: 40
88 Bell 1994; Chapkis 1997; Nagle 1997
89 Duggan 1995: 8
90 McNay 2000
91 *Abre la muralla*; the reference being to the ancient walls that surrounded many Spanish cities
92 For example, Izquierda Unida Navarra 1999
93 Agustín 2000c
94 Rose and Miller call these 'problematics of government' (1992: 175).

7

PARTIAL TRUTHS

Belittling ideas about people who sell sex are perpetuated through police discrimination, media stereotypes, gender inequality, poverty, xenophobia and state policies on sex and migration. When I began my study, research already demonstrated the constructed nature of the 'prostitution' concept in the nineteenth century, so I set out to examine its reproduction in the present. I used the notion of a sex industry in order to embrace today's proliferating forms and changing meanings about buying and selling sex, a complexity that contrasts sharply with the usual reductionism and that encompasses more acts, places and people. First I analysed two major areas, migration and services, where migrants who sell sex ought to be discussed and studied but rarely are.

The migration discourse relies on numerous questionable dichotomies: work and leisure, travel and settling, legal and illegal. The label *migrant* goes to poorer people who are conceived as workers with no other desires or projects, but when migrants are women who sell sex, they lose worker status and become 'victims of trafficking'. The obsessive gaze on poverty and forced sex disqualifies working people's participation in global flows, flexible labour, diaspora and transnationalism. Women are victimised more, but the *migrant* label is disempowering for men, too.

Within discourse on services, cleaning and caring are treated with some subtlety, but debate on the sale of sex focuses on ideologies and moralising, despite the efforts of a minority of writers. Selling and buying of sexual services remain undertheorised and are disqualified from proposals to improve regulation and benefits for service workers.

I found the roots of these exclusions in a phenomenon called the Rise of the Social, when a newly empowered bourgeoisie came to believe that their high level of evolution and sensibility qualified them to rehabilitate inferiors. Educated women carved out an employment sphere through discovering a mission to save the less fortunate, especially 'prostitutes', who were redefined as victims. Despite a charitable discourse, many 'social' jobs were disciplinary, locating those to be rescued where they could be watched, controlled and trained in obedience. Philanthropists and helpers had good intentions, but their projects benefited themselves rather than their less lucky sisters.

In field work, I studied individuals engaged in social projects aimed at assisting particular other people. Helping discourses describe objects needing help: the poor, the disadvantaged, victims, undocumented migrants, the socially excluded. Some social agents refer to offering services, others to saving and rescue, still others to empowerment. Whether related to HIV/AIDS prevention, rescue or rights, these projects are widely considered rational and benign, and those who carry them out as charitable and solidary. The goal of the field work was to look beyond social agents' statements of missions, however, to reveal some of the tactics and practices involved in their everyday occupations. Most of these reproduce the 'prostitute' discourse and perpetuate the divide between helpers and helped, giving primacy to their own roles.

This is crucial: the social constructs its own objects in order to study, organise, manage, debate and serve them. Regimes may appear completely benign on the surface: medicine – healing, the alleviation of physical suffering; teaching – enlightenment of the ignorant; rehabilitating offenders; protecting the vulnerable from abuse; rescuing victims from violence; reducing risk and harm. But terms like *harm*, *enlightenment*, *rehabilitation* and so on are defined by would-be helpers. Those who are to be helped may well not define these terms in the same way, but their opinions are rarely taken into account.

In Europe, a fundamental contradiction accounts for the incoherent programming dedicated to migrants, as standard rhetoric on social inclusion and civil rights runs into exclusionary national immigration policies. Since so many migrants do not have permission to work legally or enjoy citizens' rights outside their home countries, the single most widely voiced help they want is *papers*: whatever bureaucratic documents are required. Very few social agents are able to help more than a few individuals in this way even if they want to, and few projects dare make this kind of help overt or public: this is a tension between goals and results that cannot be resolved.

Do I believe that those concerned with social justice and helping should sit on their hands and do nothing? Frequently asked this question, I always reply No: the desires of helpers, activists and theorists, whether utopian or pragmatic, are as valid as any other. I advocate neither nihilism nor indifference; to the contrary, I think constructive change is possible. The questions I pose to those desiring to help are: When embarking on a social project that concerns other people, how do you decide what your actions will be? Do you choose what is most rewarding to you personally? Do you try to find out what the objects of your help actually want? How do you accomplish that? What do you do if you find out that you cannot realistically provide what they desire? Or if you don't like it? In other words, who defines social projects? Consider the conversation among experts in Brussels in 1851 on the lack of separate bedrooms in houses of the poor:

Ebrington: The separation of the sexes is indispensable for morality and decency. A minister said to me: 'I have done all that I could, but the common bedroom has gotten the better of me'.

Ducpétiaux: In cases where this separation is not possible, can't we achieve the same effect by suspending bedding from the ceiling for the children?

Gourlier: One would have to separate the hammocks from the rest of the room by a kind of curtain; but it would be there one day and be taken down the next.

Ramón de la Sagra: Would you prefer hammocks, or a bed where parents and children are all brought together?

Gourlier: Supposing that this separation were not achieved, then our efforts would come to nothing. The children would see the parents from their hammocks, and thus the requirements of decency would not be satisfied.[1]

Present-day exchanges on social problems belong to the same tradition: how to prevent young girls from becoming pregnant, everyone from eating too much, men from buying sex, women from selling it. The power to define problems, terms and solutions rests with social agents, who debate how to get Others to behave differently, even save them from themselves – the disadvantaged, unruly, victimised, unhappy, offensive, addicted. Feminists of all stripes are implicated in this assumption of Knowing Best and having a duty to find proper solutions. My critique, far from implying that there are no injustices or troubles to be solved, points to the constructed character of 'social problems'. As constructions, they can change. No single objective reality or monolithic power exists; rather, we all participate in a web of dominations that are contingent on ourselves. For women's movements, part of the change requires admitting

> that not every incident and every species of women's social and historical power merits our applause … In the case of female moral reform, the laudable ability to maneuver for social influence fell short of the feminist goal … The power of women's networks, be it manifest in female moral reform or the New Right, deserves more than either congratulations or condemnation. It requires serious, critical attention to both its historical permutations and diverted feminist possibilities.[2]

Were government employees, political appointees, feminists, NGO spokespersons, academics and other social agents able to shed their certainty of knowing how everyone else should live, they might be able to dispense with neocolonialism, admit that agency can be expressed in a variety of ways, acknowledge their own desires, and accept that Europe's dynamic, changing, risky diversity is here to stay. We would also benefit from moving on from the myth of a clear boundary between commercial sex and many normalised sexual activities. Leave behind certainties, listen to Others – leave home.[3]

NOTES

1   Donzelot 1979: 44
2   Ryan 1983: 184
3   The title of this book for many years was *Leaving Home for Sex*. I develop these ideas in Agustín 2005b; see also a special edition of *Sexualities* dedicated to the cultural study of commercial sex (2007).

WORKS CITED

Abel, Emily and Nelson, Margaret. 1990. *Circles of Care: Work and Identity in Women's Lives*. Albany: State University of New York Press.

Abrams, Lynn. 1988. 'Prostitutes in Imperial Germany, 1870–1918'. In *The German Underworld: Deviants and Outcasts in German History*. London: Routledge.

Acosta, Alberto. 2002. 'Deuda externa y migración, una relación incestuosa'. *La Insignia*, 24 September.

ACSUR-Las Segovias. 1999. 'STOP: Contra el tráfico de mujeres'. Report/campaign paper and leaflet. Madrid.

Acton, William. 1856. *Prostitution: Considered in its Moral, Social and Sanitary Aspects, in London and other Large Cities: with Proposals for the Mitigation and Prevention of its Attendant Evils*. London: J. Churchill.

Adoratrices Esclavas del Santísimo Sacramento y de la Caridad. 1987. *Santa María Micaela ... desde el amor*. Paris: Rameau.

—— (Toffoli, María Milena). 1983. *Una vida al servicio del amor*. Madrid: Instituto Politécnico Salesianos-Atocha.

Agence France Presse. 2001. 'Prostitutes Study Truck Drivers in South Africa, Find High HIV Rate'. 7 May.

Agustín, Laura. 1995. Field notes from the Dominican Republic.

—— 1999a. 'They Speak But Who Listens?' In *Women@Internet: Creating New Cultures in Cyberspace*, Wendy Harcourt, ed., 149-55. London: Zed Books.

—— 1999b. 'Questioning Solidarity'. Thesis for Master's degree in International Education, University of Massachusetts, Amherst.

—— 2000a. 'Trabajar en la industria del sexo'. In *OFRIM Suplementos*, 6, 155-72.

—— 2000b. 'The Em- of Empowerment'. *Research for Sex Work*, 3, 15-16.

—— 2000c. *Action against Trafficking and Sexual Exploitation of Children*. Geneva: International Labour Organisation.

—— 2001a. 'Mujeres inmigrantes ocupadas en servicios sexuales'. In *Mujer, inmigración y trabajo*, Colectivo Ioé, eds., 647-716. Madrid: IMSERSO.

—— 2001b. 'Sex Workers and Violence Against Women: Utopic Visions or Battle of the Sexes?' *Development*, 44, 3, 107-110.

—— 2002a. 'The (Crying) Need for Different Kinds of Research'. *Research for Sex Work*, 5, 30-32.

—— 2002b. 'Challenging Place: Leaving Home for Sex'. *Development*, Rome, 45, 1, March, 110-16.

—— 2003a. 'Forget Victimisation: Granting Agency to Migrants'. *Development*, 46, 3, 30-36.

—— 2003b. 'Sex, Gender and Migrations: Facing Up to Ambiguous Realities'. *Soundings*, 23, 84-98.

—— 2003c. 'La familia española, la industria del sexo y las migrantes'. In *Sexualidades: Diversidad y control social*, O. Viñuales and O. Guasch, eds., 259-75. Barcelona: Bellaterra.

—— 2003d. 'A Migrant World of Services'. *Social Politics*, 10, 3, 377-96.

—— 2004a. 'Alternate Ethics, or: Telling Lies to Researchers'. *Research for Sex Work*, 7, 6-7.

—— 2004b. 'Lo no hablado: deseos, sentimientos y la búsqueda de "pasárselo bien"'. In *Trabajadoras del sexo: derechos, migraciones y tráfico en el siglo XXI*, R. Osborne, ed., 181-91. Barcelona: Bellaterra.

—— 2004c. 'At Home in the Street: Questioning the Desire to Help and Save'. In *Regulating Sex: The Politics of Intimacy and Identity*, E. Bernstein and L. Shaffner, eds., 67-82. New York: Routledge Perspectives on Gender.

—— 2004d. *Trabajar en la industria del sexo, y otros tópicos migratorios*. San Sebastián: Gakoa Editores.

—— 2005a. 'Migrants in the Mistress's House: Other Voices in the "Trafficking" Debate'. *Social Politics*, 12, 1, 96-117.

—— 2005b. 'The Cultural Study of Commercial Sex'. *Sexualities*, 8, 5, 621-34.

—— 2005c. 'Cruzafronteras atrevidas: Otra visión de las mujeres migrantes'. In *Mujeres extranjeras en prisión*, M.-J. Miranda, ed., 91-110. Madrid: Universidad Complutense.

—— 2006. 'The Disappearing of a Migration Category: Migrants Who Sell Sex'. *Journal of Ethnic and Migration Studies*, 32, 1, 29-47.

—— 2007. 'Fast Money in the Margins: Migrants in the Sex Industry'. In *Livelihoods at the Margins: Surviving the Streets*, J. Staples, ed. Walnut Creek CA: Left Coast Press.

ALAI (Agencia Latinoamericana de Información). 1994. *Desilusión en la tierra prometida: Latinoamericanas en Europa*. Quito EC.

Alexander, Priscilla. 1995. 'Prostitution Is Sex Work: Occupational Safety and Health'. New York: North American Task Force on Prostitution.

—— 1996. 'Trafficking v. Sex Migration'. New York: North American Task Force on Prostitution.

Allison, Anne. 1994. *Nightwork: Sexuality, Pleasure and Corporate Masculinity in a Tokyo Hostess Club*. Chicago: University of Chicago Press.

Alloula, Malek. 1986. *The Colonial Harem*. Minneapolis: University of Minnesota Press.

Almodóvar, Pedro (director). 1999. *Todo sobre mi madre*. Agustín Almodóvar/ El Deseo/Renn Productions/France 2 Cinema (Production).

Altink, Sietske. 1995. *Stolen Lives: Trading Women into Sex and Slavery*. London: Scarlet Press.

Amnesty for Women. 1998. 'Alemania: ¿Un paraíso para mujeres?' Hamburg.

Anarfi, John K. 1998. 'Migrations and Tourism. Ghanaian Women and Prostitution in Côte d'Ivoire'. In *Global Sex Workers: Rights, Resistance, and Redefinition*. New York: Routledge.

Anderson, Bridget. 2000. *Doing the Dirty Work: The Global Politics of Domestic Labour*. London: Zed Books.

Andrijasevic, Rutvica. 2003. 'The Difference Borders Make: (Il)Legality, Migration and Trafficking in Italy among Eastern European Women in Prostitution'. In *Uprootings/Regroundings: Questions of Home and Migration*, S. Ahmed et al, eds., 251-72. Oxford: Berg.

Anthias, Floya. 2000. 'Metaphors of Home: Gendering New Migrations to Southern Europe'. In *Gender and Migration in Southern Europe. Women on the Move*, F. Anthias and G. Lazaridis, eds., 15-47. Berg: Oxford.

Anzaldúa, Gloria. 1987. *Borderlands: La Frontera*. San Francisco: Spinsters/Aunt Lute Book Company.

Appadurai, Arjun. 1996. *Modernity at Large*. Minneapolis: University of Minnesota Press.

Ariès, Philippe. 1962. *L'enfant et la vie familiale sous l'ancien régime*. Paris: Seuil.

Armstrong, Nancy. 1987. 'The Rise of the Domestic Woman'. In *The Ideology of Conduct*, N. Armstrong and L. Tennenhouse, eds., 96-141. New York: Methuen.

Asad, Talal. 1973. *Anthropology and the Colonial Encounter*. London: Ithaca Press.

Ashok, Shyamala. 2002. 'Abuses against Sex Workers and Erosions of HIV Prevention Efforts Resulting from Anti-trafficking Initiatives'. http://www.nswp.org/safety/ashok-0211.html

Associazione On the Road. 1998. *Manuale di intervento sociale nella prostituzione di strada*. Capodarco di Fermo: Comunità Edizioni.

Asturias, Laura. 2000. 'Un foro de todos los colores'. *Tertulia*, 40, 3.

Azize-Vargas, Yamila, Kempadoo, Kamala and Cordero, Tatiana. 1996. *International Report Project on Trafficking in Women: Latin American and Caribbean Region*. Utrecht NL: Stichting Tegen Vrouwenhandel.

Bada, Joan. 1999. 'La iglesia católica frente a la prostitución'. *Historiar* 2, July, 62-70.

Bailey, Adrian and Hane, Joshua. 1995. 'Population in Motion: Salvadorean Refugees and Circulation Migration'. *Bulletin of Latin American Research*, 14, 2, 171-200.

Bailey, Jacquelynne. 2002. *Conversations in a Brothel*. Sydney: Hodder.

Bakan, Abigail and Stasiulis, Daiva. 1995. 'Making the Match: Domestic Placement Agencies and the Racialization of Women's Household Work'. *Signs*, 20, 21, 303-35.

Barber, Elinor G. 1955. *The Bourgeoisie in 18th-Century France*. Princeton: Princeton University Press.

Barry, Kathleen. 1979. *Female Sexual Slavery*. Englewood Cliffs NJ: Prentice-Hall.

—— 1995. *The Prostitution of Sexuality: The Global Exploitation of Women*. New York:

New York University Press.

Bartley, Paula. 2000. *Prostitution: Prevention and Reform in England, 1860–1914*. London: Routledge.

Bauman, Zygmunt. 2000. *Globalization: The Human Consequences*. New York: Columbia University Press.

Beauvoir, Simone de. 1953. *The Second Sex*. New York: Knopf.

Becker, Howard. 1963. *Outsiders*. New York: Free Press.

Bell, Shannon. 1994. *Reading, Writing, and Rewriting the Prostitute Body*. Bloomington: Indiana University Press.

Belza, María José et al. 2000a. Poster 'Social characteristics and risk behaviour for HIV in black-race female sex workers in Madrid, Spain'. Madrid: Médicos del Mundo.

—— 2000b. 'Mujeres que ejercen la prostitución en la calle: prevalencia auto-informada y conductas de riesgo para la infección por VIH'. Madrid: Médicos del Mundo.

—— 2000c. 'Características sociales y conductas de riesgo para el VIH en un grupo de travestis y transexuales masculinos que ejercen la prostitución en la calle'. *Gac Sanit 2000*, 14, 5, 330-37.

—— 2000d. 'Características sociales y conductuales de riesgo para el VIH en colectivos que ejercen la prostitución'. *Seisida*, 11, 4.

Benabou, Erica-Marie. 1987. *La prostitution et la police des moeurs au XVIIIe siècle*. Paris: Librairie Académique Perrin.

Benedict, Ruth. 1934. *Patterns of Culture*. New York: Houghton Mifflin.

Benería, Lourdes. 1981. 'Conceptualizing the Labor Force: The Underestimation of Women's Economic Activities'. *Journal of Development Studies*, 17, 10-28.

Béraud, F.-F. A. 1839. *Les filles publiques de Paris et la police qui les régit*. Brussels: Meline, Cans.

Berger, Maurice, Wallis, Brian and Watson, Simon, eds. 1995. *Constructing Masculinity*. New York: Routledge.

Bernheimer, Charles. 1989. *Figures of Ill Repute: Representing Prostitution in Nineteenth-Century Paris*. Cambridge: Harvard University Press.

Bernstein, Elizabeth. 2001. 'The Meaning of the Purchase: Desire, Demand and the Commerce of Sex'. *Ethnography*, 2, 3, 389-420.

—— 2005. 'Desire, Demand, and the Commerce of Sex'. In *Regulating Sex: The Politics of Intimacy and Identity*, E. Bernstein and L. Schaffner, eds., 101-25. New York: Routledge.

Bhabha, Homi. 1983. 'The Other Question – The Stereotype and Colonial Discourse'. *Screen*, 24, 6, 18-36.

Bilden, Helga. 1999. 'Going beyond Gender Identity – A Matter of Joy or a Matter of Anxiety?' http://www.skk.uit.no/WW99/papers/BildenHelga.pdf

Bilger, Veronika, Hofmann, Martin and Jandl, Michael. 2006. 'Human Smuggling as a Transnational Service Industry: Evidence from Austria'. *International*

Migration, 44, 4, 59-93.

Bindman, Jo. 1996. *Redefining Prostitution as Sex Work on the International Agenda.* London: Anti-Slavery International.

Bird, Sharon R. 1996. 'Welcome to the Men's Club: Homosociality and the Maintenance of Hegemonic Masculinity'. *Gender & Society*, 10, 2, 120-32.

Bishop, Ryan and Robinson, Lillian. 1998. *Night Market: Sexual Cultures and the Thai Economic Miracle.* New York: Routledge.

Black, Richard. 2003. 'Breaking the Convention: Researching the "Illegal" Migration of Refugees to Europe'. *Antipode*, 35, 1, 34-54.

Bland, Lucy. 1992. 'Purifying the Public World: Feminist Vigilantes in Late Victorian England'. *Women's History Review*, 1, 3, 397-412.

Bonelli, Elena et al. 2001. *Tráfico e inmigración de mujeres en España: Colombianas y ecuatorianas en los servicios domésticos y sexuales.* Madrid: ACSUR-Las Segovias.

Bose, Christine. 1987. 'Devaluing Women's Work: The Undercount of Women's Employment in 1900 and 1980'. In *Hidden Aspects of Women's Work*, C. E. Bose et al, eds., 95-116. New York: Praeger.

Boswell, James. 1982. *London Journal 1762–1763*, F. Pottle, ed. London: Futura.

Bourdieu, Pierre. 1979. 'Symbolic Power'. *Critique of Anthropology*, 4, 77-85.

——— 1996. 'On the Family as a Realized Category'. *Theory, Culture and Society*, 13, 19-26.

Boyd, Monica and Grieco, Elizabeth. 2003. 'Women and Migration: Incorporating Gender into International Migration Theory'. Washington DC: Migration Policy Institute.

Brennan, Denise. 2001. 'Tourism in Transnational Places: Dominican Sex Workers and German Sex Tourists Imagine One Another'. *Identities: Global Studies in Culture and Power*, 7, 4, 621-63.

Bridle, Susan. 1999. 'No Man's Land: An Interview with Mary Daly'. *What Is Enlightenment?* 16, Fall–Winter. http://www.wie.org/j16/daly.asp

Bristow, Edward J. 1977. *Vice and Vigilance: Purity Movements in Britain since 1700.* Dublin: Gill and Macmillan.

Brody, Alyson. 1999. 'Rethinking Thai Masculinity: New Perspectives on Prostitution in Thailand'. *Anthropology Matters*, October. http://www.anthropologymatters.com/journal/1999-10/alysonbrody.html.

Browning, Barbara. 1998. *Infectious Rhythm: Metaphors of Contagion and the Spread of African Culture.* New York: Routledge.

Brussa, Licia. 2000. 'Migrant Sex Workers in the Netherlands Speak Out'. In *Research for Sex Work*, 3, 19. Amsterdam: Vrije Universiteit.

Bubeck, Diemut Elisabet. 1995. *Care, Gender and Justice.* Oxford: Clarendon Press.

Bueno, Aida. 1999. 'Entrevista con mujeres inmigrantes'. In *Investigación epidemiológica de casos en población desfavorecida,* T. Calvo Buezas, ed. Madrid: CSSS.

Bullough, Vern. 1987. *Women and Prostitution: A Social History.* Buffalo NY: Promethus Books.

Bunzl, Matti. 2000. 'The Prague Experience: Gay Male Sex Tourism and the Neo-colonial Invention of an Embodied Border'. In *Altering States: Ethnographies of Transition in Eastern Europe and the Former Soviet Union*. Ann Arbor: University of Michigan Press.

Butler, Judith. 1990. *Gender Trouble: Feminism and the Subversion of Identity*. New York: Routledge.

Cabezas, Amalia. 1999. 'Women's Work is Never Done: Sex Tourism in Sosúa, the Dominican Republic'. In *Sun, Sex and Gold*, K. Kempadoo, ed., 93-123. Lanham MD: Rowman & Littlefield.

—— 2004. Unpublished manuscript, no page numbers, on file with author.

Cabiria. 2002, 2004. *Rapport de synthèse*. Lyon: Le Dragon Lune.

Califia, Pat. 1994. *Public Sex*. San Francisco: Cleis Press.

Callaway, Helen. 1987. *Gender, Culture and Empire: European Women in Colonial Nigeria*. London: Macmillan.

Calvo Ocampo, Fabiola. 2001. 'Apuntes para un análisis de prensa'. In *Tráfico e inmigración de mujeres en España: Colombianas y ecuatorianas en los servicios domésticos y sexuales*, E. Bonelli et al, eds., 51-64. Madrid: ACSUR-Las Segovias.

Campani, Giovanna. 1999. 'Trafficking for Sexual Exploitation and the Sex Business in the New Context of International Migration: the Case of Italy'. In *Immigrants and the Informal Economy in Southern Europe*, M. Baldwin-Edwards and Joaquín Arango, eds., 230-61. London: Frank Cass.

—— 2001. 'Migrants and media: the Italian case'. In *Media and Migration: Constructions of Mobility and Difference*, R. King and N. Wood, eds. London: Routledge.

Campbell, Rosie. 1997. '"It's Just Business, It's Just Sex": Male Clients of Female Prostitutes in Merseyside'. *Journal of Contemporary Health*, 5, 47-51.

Carasa Soto, Pedro. 1989. 'Beneficencia y control social en la España contemporánea'. In *Historia ideológica del control social (España-Argentina siglos XIX-XX)*, R. Bergalli and E.M. Mari, eds., 175-237. Barcelona: Publicaciones Universitarias.

Carchedi, Francesco et al. 2000. *I colori della notte: Migrazioni, sfruttamento sessuale, esperienze di intervento sociale*. Milano: Franco/Angeli.

Carpenter, Belinda. 2000. *Re-thinking Prostitution*. New York: Peter Lang.

Casal, Marta. 2001. *Inmigración femenina y trabajo sexual. Estudios de casos en Madrid, Pamplona y Bilbao*. Part of report from Universidad de A Coruña for Instituto de la Mujer, Madrid.

Castells, Manuel. 1997. 'An Introduction to the Information Age'. *City*, 7, 6-16.

Castilla, Jesús. 2000. 'Casos de sida en España en personas de otros países de origen'. *Boletín Epidemiológico*, 8, 10, 97-108.

Castillo, Susana, ed. 2000. *Guía de autocuidados para las mujeres inmigrantes*. Madrid: Instituto de Salud Carlos III.

—— and Mazarrasa, Lucia. 1999. *La salud de la mujer inmigrante en la Comunidad de*

Madrid: percepción, accesibilidad y utilización de servicios sanitarios, Instituto de la Mujer-Instituto de Salud Carlos III, Madrid.

CATS (Comité de Apoyo a las Trabajadoras del Sexo). 2006. 'Conclusiones preliminares: Profundización, a través de la investigación del trabajo sexual en calle y espacios cerrados en el municipio de Murcia'. Comité de Apoyo a las Trabajadoras del Sexo.

CATW (Coalition Against Trafficking in Women). 1991. *Report of the Meeting of Experts on the International Action in the Struggle Against Sexual Exploitation and Prostitution*. State College PA.

—— 2003. *Guide to the UN Trafficking Protocol*. Amherst MA.

Chadeau, Ann. 1985. 'Measuring Household Activities: Some International Comparisons'. *Review of Income and Wealth*, 31, 237-53.

Chancer, Lynn Sharon. 1993. 'Prostitution, Feminist Theory, and Ambivalence: Notes from the Sociological Underground'. *Social Text*, 37, 143-71.

Chapkis, Wendy. 1997. *Live Sex Acts*. New York: Routledge.

Charles, A. O. 1860. *The Female Mission to the Fallen*. London.

Cheng, Sea-Ling. 2002. 'Changing Lives, Changing Selves: "Trafficked" Filipina Entertainers in Korea'. *Anthropology in Action*, 9, 1, 13-20.

Cheng, Shu Ju Ada. 1996. 'Migrant Women Domestic Workers in Hong Kong, Singapore and Taiwan: A Comparative Analysis'. *Asian and Pacific Migration Journal*, 5, 1, 139-52.

Chevalier, Louis. 1973. *Labouring Classes and Dangerous Classes in Paris During the First Half of the 19th Century*. London: Routledge & Kegan Paul.

Chodorow, Nancy. 1978. *The Reproduction of Mothering*. Berkeley: University of California Press.

CICP (Centre for International Crime Prevention). 2003. 'Assessing transnational organized crime: results of a pilot survey of 40 selected transnational organized criminal groups in 16 countries'. Vienna.

Clifford, James. 1986. 'Introduction: Partial Truths'. In *Writing Culture: The Poetics and Politics of Ethnography*, J. Clifford and G. Marcus, eds., 1-26. Berkeley: University of California Press.

—— 1997. *Routes: Travel and Translation in the Late Twentieth Century*. Cambridge: Harvard University Press.

Clifford, J. and Marcus, G. 1986. *Writing Culture: The Poetics and Politics of Ethnography*. Berkeley: University of California Press.

Coffin, Judy. 1982. 'Artisans of the Sidewalk'. *Radical History Review*, 26, 89-101.

Cohen, Erik. 1979. 'A Phenomenology of Tourist Experiences'. *Sociology*, 13, 179-201.

—— 1982. 'Thai Girls and Farang Men: The Edge of Ambiguity'. *Annals of Tourism Research*, 9, 403-28.

COIN (Centro de Orientación e Información Integral). 1992. *Viajes al Exterior: Ilusiones y Mentiras (Exportación de sexo organizado)*. Santo Domingo: COIN.

Colectivo Ioé, eds. 2001. *Mujer, inmigración y trabajo*. Madrid: IMSERSO.

Collins, Patricia Hill. 1990. *Black Feminist Thought: Knowledge, Consciousness, and the Politics of Empowerment*. New York: Routledge.

Colomo, Concha. 2000. 'Perspectiva de la salud integral en mujeres en situación de marginalidad'. Paper presented at La Salud de la Mujer en el Umbral del Siglo XXI. Madrid: UAM.

Comas, Amparo and Reyero, Felipe. 1985. 'Atención social y sanitaria a las personas relacionadas con la prostitución femenina en Madrid'. In *Marginación social*, IRES, ed. Madrid: Consejería de Sanidad.

Committee on Migration, Refugees and Demography. 2001. Conference on the situation of illegal migrants in Council of Europe member states. Paris. http://www.ecre.org/factfile/realfacts.shtml

Connell, R. W. 1987. *Gender and Power: Society, the Person and Sexual Politics*. Stanford: Stanford University Press.

Consejo de la Mujer de la Comunidad de Madrid. 2000. 'Conclusiones de la jornada Las mujeres de Madrid ante Beijing + 5'.

Constable, Nicole. 2003. *Romance on a Global Stage: Pen Pals, Virtual Ethnography, and 'Mail Order' Marriages*. Berkeley: University of California Press.

Cooper, Frederic. 1997. 'The Dialectics of Decolonization: Nationalism and Labor Movements in Postwar French Africa'. In *Tensions of Empire. Colonial Cultures in a Bourgeois World*, F. Cooper and A. L. Stoler, eds., 406-35. Berkeley: University of California Press.

Corbin, Alain. 1987. 'Commercial Sexuality in 19th-century France: A System of Images and Regulations'. In *The Making of the Modern Body*, C. Gallagher and T. Laqueur, eds., 209-19. Berkeley: University of California Press.

―― 1990. *Women for Hire: Prostitution and Sexuality in France after 1850*. Cambridge MA: Harvard University Press. Originally published in 1978 as *Filles de noce: Misère sexuelle et prostitution aux 19e et 20e siècles*. Paris: Aubier Montaigne.

Cornwall, Andrea. 2002. 'Spending Power: Love, Money and the Reconfiguration of Gender Relations in Ado-Odo, Southwestern Nigeria'. *American Ethnologist*, 29, 4, 963–80.

Corso, Carla and Trifirò, Ada. 2003. *... e siamo partite! Migrazione, tratta e prostituzione straniera in Italia*. Florence: Giunti.

Criado, M-Jesús. 1997. 'Historias de vida: El valor del recuerdo, el poder de la palabra'. *Migraciones*, 1. Instituto Universitario de Estudios sobre Migraciones.

Crick, Malcolm. 1992. 'Life in the Informal Sector: Street Guides in Kandy, Sri Lanka'. In *Tourism and Less Developed Countries*. D. Harrison, ed., 135-47. London: Belhaven Press.

Crimi, B. 1979. 'La prostituzione in Francia'. Presentation at the Congreso Sobre los Aspectos Biológicos, Sociales y Jurídicos de la Prostitución, Rome.

Cruikshank, Barbara. 1993. 'Revolutions Within: Self-government and Self-esteem'. *Economy and Society*, 22, 3, 327-44.

—— 1994. 'The Will to Empower: Technologies of Citizenship and the War on Poverty'. *Socialist Review* 23, 4, 29-55.

Cuadros Riobó, Alfonso. 1997. 'Salud e inmigraciones: La experiencia del programa de atención sociosanitaria a inmigrantes de Médicos del Mundo de Madrid'. *Migraciones*, 2. Madrid: Instituto Universitario de Estudios sobre Migraciones.

Cuanter. 1998. 'Las notas características de la prostitución y su acceso a los Servicios Sociales'. Madrid: Instituto de la Mujer.

Cutrufelli, Maria Rosa. 1988. 'La demanda de prostitución'. *Debats*, 24, 23-30.

Dahles, Heidi. 1998. 'Of Birds and Fish: Street Guides, Tourists, and Sexual Encounters in Yogyakarta, Indonesia'. In *Sex Tourism and Prostitution: Aspects of Leisure, Recreation and Work*, M. Oppermann, ed., 30-41. Cammeray AU: Cognizant Communication Corp.

Daly, Mary. 1978. *Gyn/Ecology: The Metaethics of Radical Feminism*. Boston: Beacon Press.

Danna, Daniela. 2004. *Donne di Mondo: Commercio del sesso e controllo statale*. Milan: Eleuthera.

Davidoff, Leonore. 1979. 'Class and Gender in Victorian England: the Diaries of Arthur J. Munby and Hannah Cullwick'. *Feminist Studies*, 5, 1, 86-141.

—— and Hall, Catherine. 1987. *Family Fortunes: Men and Women of the English Middle Class, 1780–1850*. London: Hutchinson.

Davies, John. 2006. 'Explaining the Trafficking of Albanian Women'. Unpublished PhD thesis, Centre for Migration Research, University of Sussex.

Davin, Delia. 2005a. 'Women and Migration in Contemporary China'. *China Report*, 41, 1, 29-38.

—— 2005b. 'Marriage Migration in China. The Enlargement of Marriage Markets in the Era of Market Reforms'. *Indian Journal of Gender Studies*, 12, 2&3, 173-88.

Davis, Natalie Zemon. 1975. *Society and Culture in Early Modern France*. Stanford CA: Stanford University Press.

De Albuquerque, Klaus. 1998. 'Sex, Beach Boys, and Female Tourists in the Caribbean'. *Sexuality and Culture*, 2, 87-112.

Dean, Mitchell. 1999. *Governmentality: Power and Rule in Modern Society*. London: Sage.

—— 2002. 'Powers of Life and Death Beyond Governmentality'. *Cultural Values*, 6, 1/2, 119-38.

Defoe, Daniel. 1725. *Every-Body's Business is No-Body's Business; or Private Abuses, Public Grievances: Exemplified in the Pride, Insolence, and Exorbitant Wages of our Women Servants, Footmen, etc.* London.

Deleuze, Giles and Guattari, Félix. 1986. *Nomadology*. New York: Semiotext(e).

de Lucas, Javier. 1996. *Puertas que se cierran: Europa como fortaleza*. Barcelona: Icaria.

de Paula Medeiros, Regina. 2000. *Hablan las putas*. Barcelona: Virus.

Díaz Barrero, Gloria Patricia. 2005. 'Stripers, bailarinas exóticas, eróticas: identidad e inmigración en la construcción del Estado canadiense'. *Cad. Pagu*, 25.

Díaz Canals, Teresa and González Olmedo, Graciela. 1997. 'Cultura y prostitución: una solución posible'. *Papers* 52, 167-75.

Dinnerstein, Dorothy. 1976. *The Rocking of the Cradle, and the Ruling of the World.* London: Souvenir Press.

Dirección General de la Policía de Córdoba. 1999. 'Detenido el dueño de un club de alterne y once mujeres del mismo'. Press release. Córdoba.

Ditmore, Melissa. 2002. 'Trafficking and Sex Work: A Problematic Conflation'. Unpublished thesis, Graduate Center of the City of New York.

Doezema, Jo. 2000. 'Loose Women or Lost Women: The Re-emergence of the Myth of White Slavery in Contemporary Discourses of Trafficking in Women'. *Gender Studies*, 18, 1, 23-50.

Domingo Tapales, Proserpina. 1990. 'Women, Migration, and the Mail-Order Bride Phenomenon: Focus on Australia'. *Philippine Journal of Public Administration*, xxxiv, 4, 311-22.

Donzelot, Jacques. 1979. *The Policing of Families.* New York: Pantheon Books.

—— 1991. 'The Mobilization of Society'. In *The Foucault Effect*, G. Burchell, C. Gordon and P. Miller, eds., 169-79. Chicago: University of Chicago Press.

Dreyfus, Hubert and Rabinow, Paul. 1982. *Michel Foucault: Beyond Structuralism and Hermeneutics.* Chicago: University of Chicago Press.

Duggan, Lisa. 1995. 'Introduction'. In *Sex Wars*, L. Duggan and N. Hunter, eds. 1-15. New York: Routledge.

Duggan, Lisa and Hunter, Nan, eds. 1995. *Sex Wars: Sexual Dissent and Political Culture.* New York: Routledge.

Dworkin, Andrea. 1987. *Intercourse.* New York: Free Press.

Economist. 1998. 'The Sex Industry: Giving the Customer What He Wants'. 14 February.

Elias, Norbert. [1939] 1994. *The Civilizing Process.* Oxford: Blackwell.

Embarak López, Malika. 1994 'Mujeres emigrantes marroquíes en Madrid: historia de vida'. In *II Jornadas sobre fuentes orales y gráficas para el estudio de las migraciones*. Madrid: UNED.

Emerton, Robyn and Petersen, Carole. 2003. 'Migrant Nightclub/Escort Workers in Hong Kong: An Analysis of Possible Human Rights Abuses'. Centre for Comparative and Public Law, University of Hong Kong, Occasional Paper No. 8.

Empower Chiang Mai. 2003. 'Report on the human rights violations women are subjected to when "rescued" by anti-trafficking groups who employ methods using deception, force and coercion'. http://www.nswp.org/mobility/mpower-0306.html

EMSI (Escuela de Mediadores Sociales para la Inmigración). 2001. Leaflet describing courses: *Curso Básico en Mediación Social para la Inmigracion, Curso
   Especializado en Mediación Sociocultural, Curso Especializado en Mediación Socio-
   educativa, Curso de Formación Inicial en Inmigración*. Madrid: Cruz Roja Española.
Encuentros en la Costa del Sol. 2002. Benalmádena: R. A. Publicidad.
Engels, Friedrich. 1884. *The Origins of the Family, Private Property, and the State.*
   http:www.mdx.ac.uk/www/study/xeng1884.htm
—— [1845] 1958. *The Condition of the Working Class in England*. Trans. W. O.
   Henderson and W. H. Chaloner. Oxford: Basil Blackwell.
Enloe, Cynthia. 1991. '"Womenandchildren": Propaganda Tools of Patriarchy'. In
   Mobilizing Democracy: Changing the US Role in the Middle East, G. Bates, ed.
   Monroe ME: Common Courage Press
Ericsson, Lars. 1980. 'Charges against Prostitution: An Attempt at a Philosophical
   Assessment'. *Ethics*, 90, 335-66.
Escobar, Arturo. 1995. *Encountering Development*. Princeton: Princeton University
   Press.
Estébanez, Pilar. 1990. 'Prostitution and AIDS in Spain'. In *AIDS, Drugs, and
   Prostitution*, M. Plant, ed, 186-97. London: Routledge.
—— 1998. 'Un compromiso con la solidaridad'. *Trabajadora*, 6-7.
—— et al. 1998. 'A Demographic and Health Survey of Spanish Female Sex
   Workers: HIV Prevalence and Associated Risk Factors', in *J.Biosoc.Sci*, 30, 365-
   79.
European Communities. 2002. Judgment of the European Court of 20 November
   on Association agreements between the Communities and Poland and between
   the Communities and the Czech Republic—Freedom of establishment—
   'Economic activities'—Whether or not they include the activity of prostitu-
   tion. Case C.268/99. The Hague.
Fabian, Johannes. 1983. *Time and the Other: How Anthropology Makes Its Object*. New
   York: Columbia University Press.
Ferguson, Moira. 1992. *Subject to Others: British Women Writers and Colonial Slavery,
   1670–1834*. London: Routledge.
Finnegan, Frances. 1979. *Poverty and Prostitution: A Study of Victorian Prostitutes in
   York*. Cambridge: Cambridge University Press.
Folbre, Nancy. 1991. 'The Unproductive Housewife: Her Evolution in Nineteenth-
   century Economic Thought'. *Signs*, 16, 3, 463-84.
—— and Nelson, Julie. 2000. 'For Love or Money – Or Both?' *Journal of Economic
   Perspectives*, 14, 4, 123–40.
—— and Wagman, Barnet. 1993. 'Counting Housework: New Estimates of Real
   Product in the United States, 1800–1860'. *Journal of Economic History*, 53, 2,
   275-88.
Forsythe, Diana E. 1999. 'Ethics and Politics of Studying Up in Technoscience'.
   Anthropology of Work Review, XX, 1, 6-11.

Foucault, Michel. 1978. *Discipline and Punish*. New York: Pantheon Books.

—— 1979a. 'On Governmentality'. *Ideology and Consciousness*, 6, 5-21.

—— 1979b. *History of Sexuality* Vol. I, *The Will to Knowledge*. London: Allen Lane.

—— 1985. *History of Sexuality*, Vol. II, *The Use of Pleasure*. New York: Pantheon Books.

—— 1986. *History of Sexuality*, Vol. III, *The Care of the Self.* New York: Pantheon Books.

—— 1988. 'Technologies of the Self'. In *Technologies of the Self: A Seminar with Michel Foucault*, L. Martin et al, eds., 16-49. Amherst: University of Massachusetts Press.

—— 1991. 'Questions of Method'. In *The Foucault Effect*, G. Burchell, C. Gordon and P. Miller, eds., 73-86. Chicago: University of Chicago Press.

Frank, Katherine. 1998. 'The Production of Identity and the Negotiation of Intimacy in a "Gentleman's Club"'. *Sexualities*, 1, 2, 175-201.

—— 2002. *G-Strings and Sympathy: Strip Club Regulars and Male Desire*. Durham: Duke University Press.

—— 2005. 'Exploring the Motivations and Fantasies of Strip Club Customers in Relation to Legal Regulations'. *Archives of Sexual Behavior*, 34, 5, 487-504.

frauenlesbenfilmkollectif and Mucolade. 2002. *Otras vías, Migrantes en la industria del sexo* (documentary film). Berlin/Hamburg.

Fundación Dolores Ibárruri. 1998. 'Esclavas del fin de siglo XX: El Tráfico de mujeres extranjeras se ha duplicado en España'. *Mujeres en Acción*, 23.

Fundación Esperanza. 1998. *No pensé que eso me fuera a pasar: Prostitución y tráfico de mujeres latinoamericanas en Holanda*. Amsterdam: Fundación Esperanza.

Fundación Solidaridad Democrática. 1988. *La prostitución de las mujeres*. Madrid: Instituto de la Mujer.

GAATW (Global Alliance Against Trafficking in Women). 2000. *Specific Recommendations Concerning Language Related to Trafficking and Migration*. Bangkok.

Gabinet D'Estudis Socials. 1992. *Condiciones de vida de las prostitutas en Asturias*. Oviedo: Servicio de Publicaciones de Asturias.

Gagnon, John and Simon, William. 1973. *Sexual Conduct: The Social Sources of Human Sexuality*. London: Hutchinson.

Gallardo, Gina. 1995. *Buscando la vida*. Santo Domingo: CIPAF.

Geertz, Clifford. 1968. 'Thinking as a Moral Act: Ethical Dimensions of Anthropological Fieldwork in the New States'. *Antioch Review*, 28, 2, 139-58.

Georges, Eugenia. 1990. *The Making of a Transnational Community: Migration, Development, and Cultural Change in the Dominican Republic*. New York: Columbia University Press.

Gibson, Katherine, Law, Lisa and McKay, Deirdre. 2001. 'Beyond Heroes and Victims'. *International Feminist Journal of Politics*, 3, 3, 365-86.

Gibson, Mary. 1986. *Prostitution and the State in Italy.* Columbus OH: Ohio State University Press.

Giddens, Anthony. 1992. *The Transformation of Intimacy: Sexuality, Love and Eroticism in Modern Societies.* Stanford CA: Stanford University Press.

Gilbert, Alan and Koser, Khalid. 2006. 'Coming to the UK: What do Asylum-Seekers Know about the UK before Arrival?' *Journal of Ethnic and Migration Studies,* 32, 7, 1209-25.

Gilligan, Carol. 1982. *In a Different Voice: Psychological Theory and Women's Development.* Cambridge: Harvard University Press.

Global Perspectives. 2001. http://www.globalperspectivescanada.com/2001/journal-segers-484.html

Glotz, Marguerite and Maire, Madeleine. 1945. *Salons du XVIIIe siècle.* Paris: n/p.

Godfrey, Hannah. 2003. 'French Working Girls Lose Their Privileged Role'. *Observer* (UK),19 January.

Goldman, Emma. 1917. *The Traffic in Women, Marriage and Love and Women Suffrage.* New York: Mother Earth Publishing Association.

Goodey, Jo. 2004. 'Sex Trafficking in Women from Central and East European Countries: Promoting a "Victim-Centred" and "Woman-Centred" Approach to Criminal Justice Intervention'. *Feminist Review,* 76, 26-45.

Grasmuck, Sherri and Pessar, Patricia. 1991. *Between Two Islands: Dominican International Migration.* Berkeley: University of California Press.

Greg, W. R. 1850. 'Prostitution'. *Westminster Review,* 53, 448-506.

—— [1862] 1876. 'Why are Women Redundant?' reprinted in *Literary and Social Judgments,* 274-308. New York: Holt.

Gregorio Gil, Carmen. 1996. *Estudio de la red migratoria del colectivo dominicano en Madrid.* Madrid: Dirección General de Migraciones.

Guarnizo, Luís. 1992. 'One Country in Two: Dominican-owned Firms in New York and in the Dominican Republic'. PhD thesis, Johns Hopkins University.

—— 1994. 'Los dominicanyorks: The Making of a Binational Society'. In *Annals, AAPSS,* 533, 70-85.

Guereña, Jean-Louis. 1999. 'Una aproximación sociológica a la prostitución'. *Historiar,* 2, July, 12-23.

Gülçür, Leyla and İlkkaracan, Pinar. 2002. 'The "Natasha" Experience: Migrant Sex Workers from the Former Soviet Union and Eastern Europe in Turkey'. *Women's Studies International Forum,* 25, 4, 411-21.

Gupta, Akhil and Ferguson, James. 1992. 'Beyond "Culture": Space, Identity, and the Politics of Difference'. *Cultural Anthropology,* 7, 1, 6-23.

Guy, Donna. 1991. *Sex and Danger in Buenos Aires.* Lincoln: University of Nebraska Press.

—— 1992. '"White Slavery", Citizenship and Nationality in Argentina'. In *Nationalisms and Sexualities,* A. Parker et al, eds., 201-15. New York: Routledge.

Hacking, Ian. 1986. 'The Archaeology of Foucault'. In *Foucault: A Critical Reader,* D. Couzens Hoy, ed., 27-40. Oxford: Blackwell.

—— 1991. 'How Should We Do the History of Statistics?' In *The Foucault Effect,*

G. Burchell et al, eds., 181-96. Chicago: University of Chicago Press.

Hall, Stuart. 1989. 'The Local and the Global'. In *Culture, Globalization and the World System: Contemporary Conditions for the Representation of Identity*, A. King, ed., 24. Albany NY: SUNY Press.

Hamilton, Annette. 1997. 'Primal Dream: Masculinism, Sin, and Salvation in Thailand's Sex Trade'. In *Sites of Desire, Economies of Pleasure: Sexualities in Asia and the Pacific*, L. Manderson and M. Jolly, eds., 145-65. University of Chicago Press.

Hannerz, Ulf. 1990. 'Cosmopolitans and Locals in World Culture'. *Theory, Culture and Society*, 7, 2-3, 237-51.

—— 1996. *Transnational Connections*. London: Routledge.

Hanson, Jody. 1998. 'Sex Tourism as Work in New Zealand: A Discussion with Kiwi Prostitutes'. In *Pacific Rim Tourism*, M. Oppermann, ed. Oxford UK: CAB International.

Haraway, Donna. 1988. 'Situated Knowledge: The Science Question in Feminism and the Privilege of Partial Perspective'. *Feminist Studies*, 14, 3, 575-600.

Harding, Sandra, ed. 1987. *Feminism and Methodology: Social Science Issues*. Bloomington: Indiana University Press.

Harsin, Jill. 1985. *Policing Prostitution in Nineteenth-century Paris*. Princeton: Princeton University Press.

Hart, Angie. 1999. *Buying and Selling Power: Anthropological Reflections on Prostitution in Spain*. Boulder CO: Westview Press.

Hausbeck, Kate, and Brents, Barb. 2002. 'McDonaldization of the Sex Industry? The Business of Sex'. In *Mcdonaldization: The Reader*, G. Ritzer, ed., 91-107. Thousands Oaks CA: Pine Forge Press.

Hayward, J. 1959. 'Solidarity: The Social History of an Idea in Nineteenth Century France'. *International Review of Social History*, 2, 261-84.

Hecht, Tobias. 1998. *At Home in the Street: Street Children of Northeast Brazil*. Cambridge: Cambridge University Press.

Hefti, Anny Misa. 1997. 'Globalisation and Migration'. Paper presented at the European Solidarity Conference on the Philippines, Zurich, 19–21 September.

Held, David et al. 1999. *Global Transformations*. Cambridge: Polity Press.

Henderson, Tony. 1999. *Disorderly Women in 18th-century London*. London: Longman.

Henriot, Christian. 2001. *Prostitution and Sexuality in Shanghai: A Social History, 1849–1949*. Cambridge: Cambridge University Press.

Henry, Stuart. 1987. 'The Political Economy of Informal Economies'. *Annals of the American Academy of Political and Social Science*, 493, 137-53.

Herman, Emma. 2006. 'Migration as a Family Business: The Role of Personal Networks in the Mobility Phase of Migration'. *International Migration*, 44, 4, 191-230.

Hernández Velasco, Irene. 1996. 'Un millón de hombres al día va de prostitutas'.

El Mundo. Sociedad, 26, 27 December.

Herranz Gómez, Yolanda. 1992. 'Trabajadores latinoamericanos en Madrid'. *Economía y Sociedad.* Madrid: Consejería de Economía.

—— 1996. 'Formas de incorporación laboral de la inmigración latinoamericana de Madrid. Importancia del contexto de recepción'. Madrid: Universidad Autónoma de Madrid. PhD thesis.

—— 1997. 'Mujeres dominicanas en el servicio doméstico de Pozuelo-Aravaca'. In *Cuadernos de Relaciones Laborales,* 10. Madrid: Escuela de Relaciones Laborales, Universidad Complutense de Madrid.

Higgs, Mary. [1905] 1976. 'Three Nights in Women's Lodging Houses'. In *Into Unknown England: Selections from the Social Explorers*, P. Keating, ed., 273-84. Glasgow: William Collin & Son.

Ho, Josephine. 2000. 'Self-Empowerment and "Professionalism": Conversations with Taiwanese Sex Workers'. *Inter-Asia Cultural Studies,* 2, 283-99.

—— 2003. 'From Spice Girls to *Enjo-Kosai*: Formations of Teenage Girls' Sexualities in Taiwan'. *Inter-Asia Cultural Studies,* 4, 2, 325-36.

Hobson, J. and Heung, Vincent. 1998. 'Business Travel and the Emergence of the Modern Chinese Concubine'. In *Sex Tourism and Prostitution: Aspects of Leisure, Recreation and* Work, M. Oppermann, ed., 132-43. Cammeray AU: Cognizant Communication Corp.

Hochschild, Arlie Russell. 1983. *The Managed Heart: Commercialization of Human Feeling.* Berkeley: University of California Press.

—— 2000a. 'Chains of Love'. *Guardian*, 8 March. http://www.guardian.co.uk/ parents/story/0,3605,231597,00.html

—— 2000b. 'Global Care Chains and Emotional Surplus Value'. In *On the Edge: Living with Global Capitalism*, W. Hutton and A. Giddens, eds., 130-46. New York: Vintage.

Høigård, Cecilie and Finstad, Liv. 1986. *Backstreets: Prostitution, Money, and Love.* University Park: Pennsylvania State University Press.

Holcombe, Lee. 1977. 'Victorian Wives and Property: Reform of the Married Women's Property Law, 1857–1882'. In *A Widening Sphere: Changing Roles of Victorian Women*, M. Vicinus, ed., 3-28. London: Methuen & Co.

Holt, Kate. 2002. 'Once They Were Girls'. *Observer* (UK), 3 February.

Hondagneu-Sotelo, Pierrette. 2000. 'Feminism and Migration'. *Annals of the American Academy of Political and Social Science,* 571, 107-20.

hooks, bell. 1984. *Feminist Theory from Margin to Center.* Boston: South End Press.

—— 1992. *Black Looks: Race and Representation.* Boston: South End Press.

Howell, Philip. 2000. 'Prostitution and Racialised Sexuality: the Regulation of Prostitution in Britain and the British Empire before the Contagious Diseases Acts'. *Environment and Planning D: Society and Space* 18, 3, 321-39.

Hughes, Donna. 2002. 'Foreign Government Complicity in Human Trafficking: A Review of the State Department's 2002 Trafficking in Persons Report'.

Testimony at the House Committee on Foreign Relations, 19 June.

—— 2006. 'Chancellor Missing Her Chance'. *National Review Online,* 1 May.

Humphreys, Bob. 1997. 'The Poor, the Very Poor and the Poorest: Responses to Destitution after Industrialisation'. *Recent Findings of Research in Economic & Social History,* 24. http://www.ehs.org.uk/pdfs/ Humphreys%2024a.pdf

Hymes, Dell, ed. 1969. *Reinventing Anthropology.* New York: Random House.

IHRLG (International Human Rights Law Group). 2002. *Annotated Guide to the UN Trafficking Protocol.* Washington, DC.

Instituto de Salud Carlos III. 1999. *Letras,* 2. Newsletter of Red Europea Prevención del SIDA entre la población subsahariana. Madrid.

International Migration. 2006. 44, 4. IOM.

Irigaray, Luce. 1977. *This Sex Which Is Not One.* Ithaca NY: Cornell University Press.

Ironmonger, Duncan. 1996. 'Counting Outputs, Capital Inputs and Caring Labor: Estimating Gross Household Product'. *Feminist Economics,* 2, 3, 37-64.

Irwin, Mary Ann. 1996. '"White Slavery" as Metaphor: Anatomy of a Moral Panic'. *Ex Post Facto: The History Journal,* 5. http://www.walnet.org/csis/papers/irwin-wslavery.html

IUSW (International Union of Sex Workers). 2000. *Respect! Bulletin of the International Union of Sex Workers,* No. 1. London.

Izquierda Unida Navarra. 1999. 'Proposición de Ley en el Congreso de Diputados de reconocimiento de los derechos sociales de las personas que ejercen profesionalmente la actividad de alterne'. Pamplona: Parliament of Navarra.

Jaget, Claude. 1975. *Une vie de putain.* Lyon: Les Presses d'aujourdh'hui.

Janssen, Marie-Louise. 2005. 'Images of Femininity: Reality and Imagination of Latin American Sexworkers in the European Sex Industry'. Unpublished PhD thesis, University of Amsterdam, Department of Political Science.

Jeffreys, Sheila. 1997. *The Idea of Prostitution.* Melbourne AU: Spinifex.

Jiménez, R. and Vallejo, R. 1999. *Estudio sobre la prostitución femenina en la comunidad de Castilla y León.* Valladolid: Junta de Castilla y León.

Johnson, Diane. 1999. 'Trafficking of Women into the European Union'. *New England International and Comparative Law Journal,* 5, 230-50.

Josephine Butler Collection. 'Illegal Detention of a Woman at the Royal Albert Hospital'. London: Women's Library.

Juliano, Dolores. 1993. *Educación intercultural: escuela y minorías étnicas.* Madrid: Eudema.

Kalayaan. 'Justice for Overseas Domestic Workers'. Available at http://ourworld.compuserve.com/homepages/kalayaan/home.htm

Kangaspunta, Kristina. 2003. 'Mapping the Inhuman Trade'. Paper presented at Expert Meeting on the World Crime and Justice Report, Turin, June.

Kanner, Barbara. 1972. 'The Women of England in a Century of Social Change, 1815–1914: A Select Bibliography'. In *Suffer and Be Still: Women in the Victorian Age,* 173-232, M. Vicinus, ed., Bloomington: Indiana University Press.

Kapur, Ratna. 2002. 'The Tragedy of Victimization Rhetoric: Resurrecting the "Native" Subject in International/Post-Colonial Feminist Legal Politics'. *Harvard Human Rights Journal*, Spring, 1-37.

—— 2005. 'Travel Plans: Border Crossings and the Rights of Transnational Migrants'. *Harvard Human Rights Journal*, 18, 107-19.

Karras, Ruth Mazo. 1996. *Common Women: Prostitution and Sexuality in Medieval England*. Oxford: Oxford University Press.

Kastner, Kristin. 2006. 'Cuerpo, corporeidad y migración: Nigerianas a ambos lados del Estrecho'. Paper presented at APDHA conference, Granada, Spain, May.

Kellner, Peter. 1999. 'We are Richer than You Think'. *New Statesman*, 19 February, 21-2.

Kelly, Liz and Regan, Linda. 2000. 'Trafficking in Women'. *Network Newsletter*, 20. British Council.

——, Burton, Sheila and Regan, Linda. 1996. 'Beyond Victim or Survivor: Sexual Violence, Identity and Feminist Theory and Practice'. In *Sexualizing the Social*, L. Adkins and V. Merchant, eds., 77-101. London: Macmillan.

Kelsky, Karen. 1994. 'Intimate Ideologies: Transnational Theory and Japan's "Yellow Cabs"'. *Public Culture*, 6, 465-78.

Kempadoo, Kamala. 1995. 'Prostitution, Marginality and Empowerment: Caribbean Women in the Sex Trade'. *Beyond Law*, 4, 14, 69-84.

——, ed. 1999. *Sun, Sex and Gold: Tourism and Sex Work in the Caribbean*. Lanham MD: Rowman & Littlefield.

—— and Doezema, Jo, eds., 1998. *Global Sex Workers: Rights, Resistance, and Redefinition*. New York: Routledge.

Kennedy, Iyamu and Nicotri, Pino. 1999. *Lucciole nere. Le prostitute nigeriane si raccontano*. Milan: Kaos.

Kincaid, Jamaica. 1990. *Lucy*. New York: Farrar, Straus & Giroux.

King, Russell and Wood, Nancy, eds. 2001. *Media and Migration: Constructions of Mobility and Difference*. London: Routledge.

—— and Zontini, Elisabetta. 2000. 'The Role of Gender in the South European Immigration Model'. *Papers*, 60, 35-52.

Kofman, Eleonore. 1999. 'Female "Birds of Passage" a Decade Later: Gender and Immigration in the European Union'. *International Migration Review*, 33, 2, 269-99.

Kong, Travis. 2006. 'What It Feels Like for a Whore: The Body Politics of Women Performing Erotic Labour in Hong Kong'. *Gender, Work and Organization*, 13, 5, 409-34.

Kracauer, Siegfried. 1937. *Offenbach and the Paris of His Time*. London: Constable.

Kristeva, Julia. 1991. *Strangers to Ourselves*. New York: Columbia University Press.

Krom, Frank (Director). 1993. *Me duele el alma*. Cesar Messemaker/Lumen Film (Production).

Kuate-Defo, Barthelemy. 2004. 'Young People's Relationships with Sugar Daddies and Sugar Mummies: What Do We Know and What Do We Need to Know?' *African Journal of Reproductive Health,* 8, 2, 13-37.

Kulick, Don. 1998. *Travesti: Sex, Gender and Culture among Brazilian Transgendered Prostitutes.* Chicago: University of Chicago Press.

Kymlicka, Will. 1995. *Multicultural Citizenship.* Oxford: Clarendon Press

Landes, Joan. 1988. *Women and the Public Sphere in the Age of the French Revolution.* Ithaca NY: Cornell University Press.

Laskowski, Silke Ruth. 2002. 'The New German Prostitution Act – An Important Step to a More Rational View of Prostitution as an Ordinary Profession in Accordance with European Community Law'. *International Journal of Comparative Labour Law and Industrial Relations,* 18, 4, 479-91.

Latour, Bruno and Woolgar, Steve. 1979. *Laboratory Life: The Construction of Scientific Facts.* Los Angeles: Sage.

Law, Lisa. 1997. 'Dancing on the Bar: Sex, Money and the Uneasy Politics of Third Space'. In *Geographies of Resistance,* S. Pile and M. Keith, eds., 107-23. London: Routledge.

Lazaridis, Gabriella. 2001. 'Trafficking and Prostitution: The Growing Exploitation of Migrant Women in Greece'. *European Journal of Women's Studies,* 8, 1, 67-102.

Leach, William. 1980. *True Love and Perfect Union.* London: Routledge.

Leidholdt, Dorchen and Raymond, Janice. 1990. *The Sexual Liberals and the Attack on Feminism.* New York: Pergamon Press.

Lenz, Ramona. 2003. 'Freedom of Choice or Force of Circumstance? Eastern European Sex-workers in the Republic of Cyprus'. Transnational Research Group Working Paper Series WP 4, Johann Wolfgang Goethe-University, Frankfurt am Main.

Leonini, Luisa, ed. 1999. *Sesso in acquisto: Una ricerca sui clienti della prostituzione.* Milan: Edizioni Unicopli.

Lerner, Gerda. 1986. *The Creation of Patriarchy.* Oxford: Oxford University Press.

Lever, Janet and Dolnick, Deanne. 2000. 'Clients and Call Girls: Seeking Sex and Intimacy'. In *Sex for Sale,* R. Weitzer, ed., 85-99. New York: Routledge.

Levine, Philippa. 1990. *Feminist Lives in Victorian England: Private Roles and Public Commitment.* Oxford: Blackwell.

Levitas, Ruth. 1998. *The Inclusive Society? Social Exclusion and New Labour.* London: Macmillan.

Likiniano. 2003. *Tráfico y prostitución: Experiencias de mujeres africanas.* Bilbao: Likiniano Elkartea.

Lim, Lin Lean, ed. 1998. *The Sex Sector: The Economic and Social Bases of Prostitution in Southeast Asia.* Geneva: International Labour Organisation.

—— and Oishi, Nana. 1996. 'International Labor Migration of Asian Women: Distinctive Characteristics and Policy Concerns'. *Asian and Pacific Migration*

Journal, 5, 1, 85-116.

Llácer, Alicia et al. 1999. 'Mujeres que ejercen la prostitución en la calle: prevalencia autoinformada y conductas de riesgo para la infección por VIH'. Madrid: Centro Nacional de Epidemiología, Instituto de Salud Carlos III and Médicos del Mundo.

Logan, William. 1843. *An Exposure from Personal Observation of Female Prostitution in London, Leeds and Rochdale, and Especially in the City of Glasgow; with Remarks on the Cause, Extent, Results and Remedy of the Evil.* Glasgow.

Lombroso, Caesar and Ferrero, William. 1895. *The Female Offender.* London: Fisher Unwin.

Lopes, Ana. 2006. *Trabalhadores do sexo, Uni-vos!* Lisbon: Don Quixote.

Lowman, John. 1985. 'Child Saving, Legal Panaceas, and the Individualization of Family Problems'. *Canadian Journal of Family Law*, 4, 4, 508-14.

Lu, Melody Chia-Wen. 2005. 'Commercially Arranged Marriage Migration: Case Studies of Cross-border Marriages in Taiwan'. *Indian Journal of Gender Studies*, 12, 2-3, 275-303.

Luddy, Maria. 1997. '"Abandoned Women and Bad Characters": Prostitution in Nineteenth-century Ireland'. *Women's History Review*, 6, 4, 485-503.

Lutz, Helma, Phoenix, Ann and Yuval-Davis, Nira. 1995. *Crossfires: Nationalism, Racism and Gender in Europe.* London: Pluto Press.

Lyngbye, Paul. 2000. *Mænd der betaler kvinder – om brug af prostitution.* Copenhagen: Roskilde Universitetsforlag.

MacCannell, D. 1973. 'Staged Authenticity: The Arrangement of Social Space in Tourist Settings'. *American Journal of Sociology*, 79, 589-603.

McClintock, Anne. 1995. *Imperial Leather: Race, Gender and Sexuality in the Colonial Contest.* New York: Routledge.

McHugh, Paul. 1980. *Prostitution and Victorian Social Reform.* London: Croom Helm.

McIntosh, Mary. 1978. 'Who Needs Prostitutes? The Ideology of Male Sexual Needs'. In *Women, Sexuality and Social Control*, C. Smart and B. Smart, eds., 53-64. London: Routledge & Kegan Paul.

MacKinnon, Catherine. 1990. 'Liberalism and the Death of Feminism'. In *The Sexual Liberals and the Attack on Feminism*, D. Leidholdt and J. Raymond, eds., 3-13. New York: Pergamon Press.

McLeod, Eileen. 1982. *Women Working: Prostitution Now.* London: Croom Helm.

McNay, Lois. 2000. *Gender and Agency: Reconfiguring the Subject in Feminist and Social Theory.* Cambridge: Polity.

Mahler, Sarah and Pessar, Patricia. 2006. 'Gender Matters: Ethnographers Bring Gender from the Periphery toward the Core of Migration Studies'. *IMR*, 40, 1, 27–63.

Mahood, Linda. 1990. *The Magdalenes: Prostitution in the Nineteenth Century.* London: Routledge.

Mai, Nicola. 2001. 'Transforming Traditions: A Critical Analysis of the Trafficking and Exploitation of Young Albanian Girls in Italy'. In *Mediterranean Passage: Migration and New Cultural Encounters in Southern Europe*, R. King, ed., 258-78. Liverpool: Liverpool University Press.

Mandeville, Bernard. 1724. *A Modest Defence of Public Stews: Or, An Essay Upon Whoring, As It Is Now Practis'd in these Kingdoms.* London.

Mani, Lata. 1990. 'Multiple Mediations: Feminist Scholarship in the Age of Multinational Reception'. *Feminist Review*, 35, 24-41.

Marcus, George. 1995. 'Ethnography in/of the World System: the Emergence of Multi-sited Ethnography'. *Annual Review of Anthropology*, 24, 95-117.

Mardomingo, Carmen. 1999. 'Prevalencia de infección por VIH y factores de riesgo asociados entre los trabajadores del sexo de cuatro áreas españolas'. Master's thesis, Centro Universitario de Salud Pública, Madrid.

Marie, Claude Valentin. 1994. 'The European Union Confronted with Population Movements: Reasons of State and the Rights of the Individuals'. Paper, 11th IOM seminar on Migration, 26–28 October.

Marrodán, M. et al. 1991. *Mujeres del Tercer Mundo en España: Modelo Migratorio y Caracterización Sociodemográfica.* Madrid: Fundación CIPIE.

Marx, Karl. [1857] 1986. 'Economic Manuscripts of 1857-58'. In K. Marx and F. Engels, *Collected Works*, New York: International Publishers.

Massey, Doreen. 1994. *Space, Place and Gender.* Cambridge UK: Polity Press.

Massey, Douglas et al. 1993. 'Theories of International Migration: A Review and Appraisal'. *Population and Development Review*, 19, 3, 431-66.

Matthews, Lyn. 1990. 'Female Prostitutes in Liverpool'. In *AIDS, Drugs, and Prostitution*, M. Plant, ed, 76-87. London: Routledge.

May, Meredith. 2006. 'San Francisco is a Major Center for International Crime Networks that Smuggle and Enslave'. *San Francisco Chronicle*, 6 October.

Mayhew, Henry. [1851] 1968. *London Labour and the London Poor.* Vol IV. 'Those That Will Not Work, comprising Prostitutes, Thieves, Swindlers and Beggars'. New York: Dover.

Médicos del Mundo. 1998. *Recursos sociales y sanitarios para la atención a las personas que ejercen la prostitución.* Madrid: MM and Ayuntamiento de Madrid. [Abbreviated version in English *Social Health Resources.*]

Mendelsohn, Isaac. 1949. *Slavery in the Ancient Near East.* New York: Oxford University Press.

Mendoza, Cristóbal. 2001. 'Cultural Dimensions of African Immigrants in Iberian Labour Markets'. In *Mediterranean Passage: Migration and New Cultural Encounters in Southern Europe*, R. King, ed. 41-57. Liverpool: Liverpool University Press.

Meulenbelt, Anja. 2002. Letter to *Feminista!* editors replying to Andrea Dworkin, August 25. http://www.anjameulenbelt.com/websiteanja/english.htm

Migration Policy Institute. 2006. http://www.migrationinformation.org/Data Tools/Washington DC.

Mingione, Enzo. 1985. 'Social Reproduction of the Surplus Labour Force: The Case of Southern Italy'. In *Beyond Employment: Household, Gender and Subsistence*, N. Redclift and E. Mingione, eds., 14-54. Oxford: Basil Blackwell.

Ministerio de Sanidad y Consumo. 2000. *¿Qué es el VIH / SIDA?* Leaflet produced by Secretaría del Plan Nacional sobre el SIDA and six other entities. Madrid.

Miriam, Kathy. 2005. 'Stopping the Traffic in Women: Power, Agency and Abolition in Feminist Debates over Sex-Trafficking'. *Journal of Social Philosophy*, 36, 1, 1-17.

Mitchell, Timothy. 1989. 'The World as Exhibition'. *Comparative Studies in Society and History*, 31, 2, 217-36.

Moch, Leslie Page. 1992. *Moving Europeans: Migration in Western Europe since 1650*. Bloomington: Indiana University Press.

Mohanty, Chandra. 1991. 'Under Western Eyes: Feminist Scholarship and Colonial Discourses'. In *Third World Women and the Politics of Feminism*, C. Mohanty, A. Russo and L. Torres, 51-80. Bloomington: Indiana University Press.

Monteros, Silvina. 2003. 'Las condiciones laborales y de vida de las mujeres inmigrantes en los trabajos sexuales'. Unpublished research report. Madrid: ESCODE.

Montgomery, Heather. 1998. 'Children, Prostitution, and Identity: a Case Study from a Tourist Resort in Thailand'. In *Global Sex Workers: Rights, Resistance, and Redefinition*, K. Kempadoo and J. Doezema, eds., 139-50. New York: Routledge.

Morokvasic, Mirjana. 1984. 'Birds of Passage are Also Women'. *International Migration Research*, 18, 4, 886-907.

—— 1991. 'Fortress Europe and Migrant Women'. *Feminist Review*, 39, 69.

Mort, Frank. 1987. *Dangerous Sexualities*. London: Routledge.

Mouvement du Nid. 1993. 'Slavery and Prostitution'. Special edition of *Prostitution and Society*. Clichy Cedex: Mouvement du Nid.

Mukherjee, Bharati. 1988. *Jasmine*. New York: Fawcett Crest.

Mukherjee, K. 1989. *Flesh Trade – A Report*. Uttar Pradesh: Gram Niyojan Kendra.

Mullings, B. 1999. 'Insider or Outsider, Both or Neither: Some Dilemmas of Interviewing in a Cross-cultural Setting'. *Geoforum* 30, 4, 337-50.

Mulvey, Laura. 1975. 'Visual Pleasure and Narrative Cinema'. *Screen*, Autumn, 6-18.

Mumm, Susan. 1996. '"Not Worse Than Other Girls": The Convent-based Rehabilitation of Fallen Women in Victorian Britain'. *Journal of Social History*, 29.

Munt, Ian. 1994. 'The "Other" Postmodern Tourism: Culture, Travel and the New Middle Classes'. *Theory, Culture & Society*, 11, 101-23.

Murphy, Alexandra and Venkatesh, Sudhir. 2006. 'Vice Careers: The Changing Contours of Sex Work in New York City'. *Qualitative Sociology*, 29, 2, 129-54.

Murray, Alison. 1991. *No Money, No Honey: A Study of Street Traders and Prostitutes in Jakarta*. Oxford: Oxford University Press.

Nader, Laura. 1969. 'Up the Anthropologist – Perspectives Gained from Studying Up'. In *Reinventing Anthropology*, D. Hymes, ed., 284-311. New York: Random House.

Nagle, Jill, ed. 1997. *Whores and Other Feminists*. New York: Routledge.

Nash, Mary. 1989. 'Control social y trayectoria histórica de la mujer en España'. In *Historia ideológica del control social (España-Argentina siglos XIX-XX*, R. Bergalli and E. M. Mari, eds., 151-73. Barcelona: Publicaciones Universitarias.

Nead, Lynda. 1988. *Myths of Sexuality: Representations of Women in Victorian Britain*. Oxford: Basil Blackwell.

Negre i Rigol, Pere. 1988. *La prostitución popular: Relatos de vida*. Barcelona: Fundació Caixa.

Nelson, Adie and Robinson, Barrie. 1994. *Gigolos and Madames Bountiful: Illusions of Gender, Power, and Intimacy*. Buffalo: Toronto University Press.

Neske, Matthias. 2006. 'Human Smuggling to and through Germany'. *International Migration*, 44, 4, 121-63.

Nuñez Roldán, Francisco. 1995. *Mujeres públicas: historia de la prostitución en España*. Madrid: Temas de Hoy.

Ocio Costa del Sol. 2004. Benalmádena: R. A. Publicidad.

O'Connell Davidson, Julia. 2001. 'The Sex Exploiter'. Paper for International Congress on Sexual Exploitation of Children/ECPAT, Yokohama.

—— and Anderson, Bridget. 2003. 'Is Trafficking in Human Beings Demand Driven?' Geneva: IOM Migration Research Series.

—— and Brace, Laura. 1996. 'Desperate Debtors and Counterfeit Love: The Hobbesian World of the Sex Tourist'. Leicester: Leicester University Discussion Papers in Sociology No. S96/3.

—— and Sanchez Taylor, Jacqueline. 1999. 'Fantasy Islands: Exploring the Demand for Sex Tourism'. In *Sun, Sex and Gold*, K. Kempadoo, ed., 37-54. Lanham MD: Rowman & Littlefield.

Oliveira, Alexandra. 2004. *As Vendedoras de ilusões: Estudo sobre prostituição e striptease*. Lisbon: Notícias.

Ong, Aihwa and Peletz, Michael. 1995. 'Introduction'. In *Bewitching Women, Pious Men*, A. Ong and M. Peletz, eds., 1-18. Berkeley: University of California Press.

O'Reilly, Karen. 2000. 'Trading Intimacy for Liberty: British Women on the Costa del Sol'. In *Gender and Migration in Southern Europe: Women on the Move*, F. Anthias and G. Lazaridis, eds., 227-49. New York: Berg.

O'Rourke, Dennis (director). 1991. *The Good Woman of Bangkok*. O'Rourke/Australian Film Commission (Production).

Osborne, Raquel. 1991. 'Del estigma a la solidaridad feminista y social'. In *Prostitución: Mesa Redonda*. Madrid: Forum de Política Feminista.

Oso, Laura. 1998. *La migración hacia España de mujeres jefas de hogar*. Madrid: Instituto de la Mujer.

—— 2000. 'Estrategias migratorias y de movilidad social de las mujeres ecuatorianas y colombianas en situación irregular: servicio doméstico y prostitución'. In *Mujeres inmigrantes en la irregularidad: pobreza, marginación laboral y prostitución*, A. Izquierdo, ed. Madrid: Instituto de la Mujer, unpublished report.

—— 2003. 'Estrategias migratorias de las mujeres ecuatorianas y colombianas en situación irregular'. *Mugak*, 23: 25-37.

—— and Machín, Sonia. 1993. 'Choque de culturas: El caso de los inmigrantes dominicanos en la CAM'. *Sociedad y Utopía*, 1, 193-99.

Otis, Leah Lydia. 1985. *Prostitution in Medieval Society*. Chicago: University of Chicago Press.

Parent-Duchâtelet, Alexandre-Jean-Baptiste. 1836. *De la prostitution dans la ville de Paris*. Paris: Baillière.

Parker, Richard and Aggleton, Peter, eds. 1999. *Culture, Society and Sexuality: A Reader*. London: UCL Press.

Parreñas, Rhacel Salazar. 2001. *Servants of Globalization: Women, Migration and Domestic Work*. Stanford: Stanford University Press.

Pastore, Ferruccio, Monzini, Paola and Sciortino, Giuseppe. 2006. 'Schengen's Soft Underbelly? Irregular Migration and Human Smuggling across Land and Sea Borders to Italy'. *International Migration*, 44, 4, 95-119.

Pateman, Carol. 1983. 'Defending Prostitution: Charges against Ericsson'. *Ethics*, 93, April, 561-5.

—— 1988. *The Sexual Contract*. Stanford CA: Stanford University Press.

Patton, Cindy. 1994. *Last Served? Gendering the HIV Pandemic*. London: Taylor and Francis.

Pearson, Michael. 1972. *The Age of Consent. Victorian Prostitution and Its Enemies*. Plymouth: David & Charles Newton Abbot.

Pedraza, Silvia. 1991. 'Women and Migration: The Social Consequences of Gender'. *Annual Review of Sociology*, 17, 303-25.

Peiss, Kathy. 1983. '"Charity Girls" and City Pleasures: Historical Notes on Working-class Sexuality, 1880–1920'. In *Powers of Desire: The Politics of Sexuality*, A. Snitow et al, 74-87. New York: Monthly Review Press.

Perkel, Marc. *How to Use Escort Services: A Men's Guide*. http://sex.perkel.com/escort/

Perkins, Roberta. 1999. 'How Much Are You, Love? The Customer in the Australian Sex Industry'. *Social Alternatives* 18, 3.

Perrot, Michelle, ed. 1990. *A History of Private Life, Vol. IV: From the Fires of Revolution to the Great War*. Cambridge MA: Belknap Press.

Perry, Mary Elizabeth. 1985. 'Deviant Insiders: Legalized Prostitutes and a Consciousness of Women in Early Modern Seville'. *Comparative Studies in Society and History*, 27, 1, 138-58.

Pessar, Patricia and Mahler, Sarah. 2003. 'Transnational Migration: Bringing Gender In'. *International Migration Review* 37, 3, 812-46.

Pheterson, Gail, ed. 1989. *A Vindication of the Rights of Whores*. Seattle: Seal Press.

—— 1996. *The Prostitution Prism*. Amsterdam: Amsterdam University.

Phillip, Joan. 1999. 'Tourist-oriented Prostitution in Barbados: The Case of the Beach Boy and the White Female Tourist'. In *Sun, Sex, and Gold*, K. Kempadoo, ed., 183-200. Lanham MD: Rowman & Littlefield.

Phizacklea, Annie. 1997. 'Sex, Marriage and Maids'. Paper presented at conference on Migration in Southern Europe, Santorini, Greece, September.

Phoenix, Jo. 1999. *Making Sense of Prostitution*. London: Macmillan.

Pickup, Francine. 1998. 'Deconstructing Trafficking in Women: the Example of Russia'. *Journal of International Studies*, 27, 4, 995-1021.

Piper, Nicola. 2003. 'Bridging Gender, Migration and Governance: Theoretical Possibilities in the Asian Context'. *Asia Pacific Migration Journal*, 12, 1-2, 21-48.

Piscitelli, Adriana. 2004. 'Entre a Praia de Iracema e a União Européia: Turismo Sexual Internacional e migracão feminina'. In *Sexualidades e Saberes, Convenções e Fronteiras*, A. Piscitelli, M Gregori and S. Carrara, eds. Rio de Janeiro: Editora Garamond.

Platt, Anthony M. 1969. *The Child-Savers: The Invention of Delinquency*. Chicago: University of Chicago Press.

Plummer, Ken. 1982. 'Symbolic Interactionism and Sexual Conduct: an Emergent Perspective'. In *Human Sexual Relations: A Reader in Human Sexuality*, M. Brake, ed., 223-41. Harmondsworth: Penguin.

Polanía, Fanny and Claasen, Sandra. 1998. 'Tráfico de mujeres en Colombia: Diagnóstico, análisis y propuestas'. Bogotá: Fundación Esperanza.

Pons, Ignasi. 1999. 'El enmascaramiento pseudocientífico del moralismo en el debate actual sobre prostitución'. *Historiar*, 2, July, 92-9.

Poovey, Mary. 1988. *Uneven Developments: The Ideological Work of Gender in Mid-Victorian England*. Chicago: University of Chicago Press.

—— 1995. *Making a Social Body: British Cultural Formation 1830–1864*. Chicago: University of Chicago Press.

Portes, Alejandro, Guarnizo, Luis and Landolt, Patricia. 1999. 'The study of Transnationalism: Pitfalls and Promise of an Emergent Research Field'. *Ethnic and Racial Studies*, 22, 2, 217-37.

Pratt, Mary Louise. 1992. *Imperial Eyes: Travel Writing and Transculturation*. London: Routledge.

Prochaska, F. K. 1980. *Women and Philanthropy in Nineteenth-century England*. Oxford: Clarendon Press.

Proyecto Esperanza. 2001. *Tráfico de Mujeres en España, julio-septiembre 2001, Dossier de prensa*. Madrid.

—— 2002a. *Memoria 2002. Red hispano-lusa de casas de acogida contra el tráfico de mujeres con fines de explotación sexual*. Madrid.

—— 2002b. *Evaluación y conclusiones del III Encuentro Internacional sobre Tráfico de Mujeres con Fines de Explotación Sexual, octubre 2002*. Madrid.

Proyecto Libertad. 1994. 'Nuevas voces en el valle'. Harlingen TX.

Pruitt, Deborah and LaFont, Suzanne. 1995. 'For Love and Money: Romance Tourism in Jamaica'. *Annals of Tourism Research*, 22, 2, 422-40.

Psimmenos, Iordanis. 2000. 'The Making of Periphractic Spaces: The Case of Albanian Undocumented Female Migrants in the Sex Industry of Athens'. In *Gender and Migration in Southern Europe: Women on the Move*, F. Anthias and G. Lazaridis, eds. New York: Berg.

Punternet. http://www.punternet.com/

Pupavac, Vanessa. 2002. 'Pathologizing Populations and Colonizing Minds: International Psychosocial Programs in Kosovo'. *Alternatives*, 27, 4, 489-511.

Pyle, Jean and Ward, Kathryn. 2003. 'Recasting Our Understanding of Gender and Work during Global Restructuring'. *International Sociology*, 18, 3, 461-89.

Rapp, Rayna, Ross, Ellen and Bridenthal, Renate. 1983. 'Examining Family History'. In *Sex and Class in Women's History*, J.L. Newton et al, eds., 232-58. London: Routledge & Kegan Paul.

Ratliff, Eric. 1999. 'Women as "Sex Workers", Men as "Boyfriends": Shifting Identities in Philippine Go-go Bars'. *Anthropology & Medicine*, 6, 1, 79-101.

—— 2003. 'The Price of Passion: Performances of Consumption and Desire in the Philippine Go-Go Bar'. PhD thesis, University of Texas at Austin.

—— 2004. 'Stages in Life: Narrative Practices and Identities of Filipina Go-go Dancers'. *Asia Pacific Journal of Anthropology*, 5, 1, 35-48.

Restif de la Bretonne, Nicolas. 1769. *Le Pornographe, ou Idées d'un honnête homme sur un projet de règlement pour les prostituées propre a prevenir les malheurs qu'occasionne le publicisme des femmes*. Paris: SECLE-Régine Deforges.

Reynolds, Tracey. 2002. 'Re-thinking a Black Feminist Standpoint'. *Ethnic and Racial Studies*. 25, 44, 591-606.

Ribeiro, Manuela and Sacramento, Octavio. 2005. 'Violence against Prostitutes: Findings of Research in the Spanish-Portuguese Frontier Region'. *European Journal of Women's Studies*, 12, 1, 61-81.

Richards, Janet. 1980. *The Sceptical Feminist*. London: Routledge.

Richards, Jeffrey. 1992. *Sex, Dissidence and Damnation*. London: Routledge.

Richards, Kathy. 2004. 'The Trafficking of Migrant Workers: What Are the Links between Labour Trafficking and Corruption?' *International Migration*, 42, 5, 147-66.

Riopedre, Pepe. 2004. *Mara y sus amigas: Investigación sobre la prostitución en Galicia*. Lugo: Manuscritos.

Rivas Niña, Myrna. 1992. 'Entre la realidad y el sueño: el caso de la inmigración de la mujer dominicana en España'. *Cuadernos Africa / América Latina*, 9. Madrid: SODEPAZ.

—— 1997. 'El análisis de los 'problemas sociales' y el desarrollo de políticas públicas desde una perspectiva psico-sociológica: la inmigración en la Comunidad Autónoma de Madrid entre 1989 y 1994'. PhD thesis: Universidad Complutense de Madrid.

Robbins, Bruce. 1994. 'Upward Mobility in the Postcolonial Era: Kincaid, Mukherjee, and the Cosmopolitain Au Pair'. *Modernism/Modernity*, 1, 2, 133-51.

Roberts, Helene E. 1972. 'Marriage, Redundancy or Sin: The Painter's View of Women in the First Twenty-Five Years of Victoria's Reign'. In *Suffer and Be Still: Women in the Victorian Age*, M. Vicinus, ed. 45-76. Bloomington: Indiana University Press.

Roberts, Nickie. 1986. *The Front Line*. London: Grafton Books.

—— 1992. *Whores in History: Prostitution in Western Society*. London: HarperCollins.

Robinson, Kathryn. 1996. 'Of Mail-Order Brides and "Boys' Own" Tales: Representations of Asian-Australian Marriages'. *Feminist Review*, 52, 2, 53-68.

Rodríguez, Néstor. 1996. 'The Battle for the Border: Notes on Autonomous Migration, Transnational Communities, and the State'. *Social Justice*, 23, 3, 21-37.

Rodríguez, Pilar and Lahbabi, Fatima. 2002. 'Intervención social con mujeres migrantes. El caso de las mujeres marroquíes que trabajan en la industria del sexo en Almería'. *Portularia*, 2, 213-30.

—— 2004. *Migrantes y Trabajadoras del sexo*. León: Del Blanco Editores.

Rose, Nikolas and Miller, Peter. 1992. 'Political Power beyond the State: Problematics of Government'. *British Journal of Sociology*, 43, 2, 173-205.

Rosenberg, Carroll Smith. 1971. 'Beauty, the Beast and the Militant Woman: A Case Study in Sex Roles and Social Stress in Jacksonian America'. *American Quarterly*, 23, 4, 562-84.

Rossiaud, Jacques. 1988. *Medieval Prostitution*. Oxford: Basil Blackwell.

Rubin, Gayle. 1984. 'Thinking Sex: Notes for a Radical Theory of the Politics of Sexuality'. In *Pleasure and Danger: Exploring Female Sexuality*, C. Vance, ed., 267-319. Boston: Routledge.

Rudolph, Hedwig. 1996. 'The New *Gastarbeiter* System in Germany'. *New Community* 22, 2, 287-300.

Ruggiero, Vincenzo. 1997. 'Trafficking in Human Beings: Slaves in Contemporary Europe'. *International Journal of the Sociology of Law*, 25, 3, 231-44.

Ruíz, Martha Cecilia. 2001. 'Personalizing Migration: Stories, Narratives and Identities of Ecuadorian Women in Amsterdam'. Master's Thesis, University of Amsterdam.

Ryan, Mary P. 1983. 'The Power of Women's Networks'. In *Sex and Class in Women's History*, J. L. Newton, M. P. Ryan and J. R. Walkowitz, eds., 167-86. London: Routledge & Kegan Paul.

—— 1990. *Women in Public: Between Banners and Ballots, 1825–1880*. Baltimore: Johns Hopkins University Press.

Salt, John. 2000. 'Trafficking and Human Smuggling: A European Perspective'. *International Migration*, 38, 3, 31-56.

Sánchez Hernández, M. 1994. 'La inmigración femenina en España'. In *La inmigración*, Colectivo Ioé, ed. Madrid: Editorial Popular.

Sanders, Teela. 2004. 'Controllable Laughter: Managing Sex Work Through Humour'. *Sociology*, 38, 2, 273-91.

—— 2005. *Sex Work: A Risky Business*. Cullompton: Willan.

Sanger, William. 1858. *History of Prostitution: Its Extent, Causes and Effects Throughout the World*. New York.

Sarmiento, Domingo Faustino. [1849] 1993. *Viajes por Europa, Africa i América 1845–1847*. Madrid: Colección Archivos.

Sassen, Saskia. 1996. *Out of Control? Sovereignty in an Age of Globalization*. New York: Columbia University Press.

—— 1998. *Globalization and Its Discontents*. New York: New Press.

—— 1999. *Guests and Aliens*. New York: New Press.

Sassen-Koob, Saskia. 1984. 'From Household to Workplace: Theories and Survey Research on Migrant Women in the Labor Market'. *International Migration Review*, xviii, 4, 1144-67.

Sayad, Abdelmalek. 2004. *The Suffering of the Immigrant*. Cambridge: Polity Press.

Schaeffer-Graebiel, Felicity. 2004. 'Cyberbrides and Global Imaginaries: Mexican Women's Turn from the National to the Foreign'. *Space & Culture*, 7, 1, 33-48.

Schreiner, Olive. [1885] 1988. 'To the Editor'. *Daily News*, 28 December. Reprinted in *Olive Schreiner's Letters, Vol. I*, R. Rive, ed., 70-1. Oxford: Oxford University Press.

Scott, Joan. 1987. 'L'Ouvriere, Mot impie, sordide: women workers in the discourse of French political economy, 1840-1860'. In *The Historical Meanings of Work*, P. Joyce, ed., 119-42. Cambridge: Cambridge University Press.

—— and Tilly, Louise A. 1975. 'Women's Work and the Family in Nineteenth-Century Europe'. *Comparative Studies in Social History*, 17, 36-64.

Seabrook, Jeremy. 1996. *Travels in the Skin Trade*. London: Pluto Press.

Sedgwick, Eve Kosofsky. 1990. *Epistemology of the Closet*. Berkeley: University of California Press.

Self, Helen. 2003. *Prostitution, Women and Misuse of the Law: The Fallen Daughters of Eve*. London: Frank Cass.

Sequeiros Tizón, José Luís, ed. 1996. *A prostitución no sur de Galicia*. Vigo: Xunta de Galicia.

Sexualities. 2007. Special edition, *The Cultural Study of Commercial Sex*, L. Agustín, ed., volume 10.

Shrage, Laurie. 1994. *Moral Dilemmas of Feminism*. New York: Routledge.

Sigma Dos. 2001–2. 'Concepciones y necesidades de salud de mujeres y transexuales que ejercen la prostitución en lugares abiertos de la Comunidad de Madrid'. Madrid: Consejería de Sanidad.

Signorelli, Assunta and Treppete, Mariangela. 2001. *Services in the Window: A Manual for Interventions in the World of Migrant Prostitution.* Trieste: Asterios Editore.

Silva, Elizabeth and Smart, Carol, eds. 1999. *The New Family?* London: SAGE Publications.

Simmel, George. 1978. *The Philosophy of Money.* London: Routledge & Kegan Paul.

Simon, Jules. 1861. *L'Ouvrière.* Paris: Hachette.

—— 1869. *La Famille.* Paris: Hachette.

Simpson, Antony. 2006. 'The Ordeal of St. Sepulchre's: A Campaign against Organized Prostitution in Early 19th-century London and the Emergence of Lower Middle-class Consciousness'. *Social and Legal Studies,* 15, 3, 363-87.

Singer, Linda. 1993. *Erotic Welfare: Sexual Theory and Politics in the Age of Epidemic.* New York: Routledge.

Singleton, Ann and Barbesino, Paolo. 1999. 'The Production and Reproduction of Knowledge on International Migration in Europe: The Social Embeddedness of Social Knowledge'. In *Into the Margins: Migration and Exclusion in Southern Europe,* F. Anthias and G. Lazaridis, eds., 13-33. Aldershot UK: Ashgate.

Skrobanek, Siriporn. 2000. 'Sexual Exploitation in the Prostitution Context'. Paper presented at Foro Mundial de las Mujeres: International Meeting on Biology and the Sociology of Violence, Valencia, Spain.

——, Boonpakdee, Nataya and Jantateero, Chutima. 1997. *The Traffic in Women: Human Realities of the International Sex Trade.* London: Zed Books.

Sleightholme, Carolyn and Sinha, Indrani. 1996. *Guilty without Trial: Women in the Sex Trade in Calcutta.* New Brunswick, NJ: Rutgers University Press.

Smart, Carol and Smart, Barry. 1978. 'Women and Social Control: An Introduction'. In *Women, Sexuality and Social Control,* C. Smart and B. Smart, eds., 1-7. London: Routledge & Kegan Paul.

Smith, Dorothy. 1974. 'Women's Perspective as a Radical Critique of Sociology'. *Sociological Inquiry,* 44, 1, 7-13.

Smith, Michael and Guarnizo, Luis, eds. 1998. *Transnationalism from Below.* New Brunswick NJ: Transaction.

Snitow, Ann, Stansell, Christine and Thompson, Sharon, eds. 1983. *Powers of Desire: The Politics of Sexuality.* New York: Monthly Review Press.

Sobo, Elisa. 1995. *Choosing Unsafe Sex.* Philadelphia: University of Pennsylvania Press.

Solana, José Luis. 2005. 'Mujer inmigrante y prostitución: Falencias y realidades'. In *Mujeres en el camino. El fenómeno de la migración femenina en España,* F. Checa Olmos, ed., 221-57. Barcelona: Icaria.

SOLIDAR. *Building Respect! Migrant Domestic Workers in Europe.* http://www.solidar.org/DocList.asp?SectionID=9&tod=205016

Sørensen, Ninna Nyberg. 2004. 'The Development Dimension of Migrant Transfers'. DIIS Working Paper 2004-16, Copenhaguen.

Sorrentino, Constance. 1990. 'The Changing Family in International Perspective'.

Monthly Labor Review, March, 41-58.

Spivak, Gayatri Chakravorty. 1988. 'Can the Subaltern Speak?' In *Marxism and the Interpretation of Culture,* C. Nelson and L. Grossberg, eds., 271-315. Champaign: University of Illinois Press.

Stalker, Peter. 2006. *Stalker's Guide to International Migration.* http://pstalker.com/migration/mgstats1.htm

Stallybrass, Peter and White, Allon. 1986. *The Politics and Poetics of Transgression.* Ithaca NY: Cornell University Press.

Stansell, Christine. 1982. 'Women, Children, and the Uses of the Streets: Class and Gender Conflicts in New York City, 1850–1860'. *Feminist Studies,* 8, 2, 309-35.

Stein, Martha. 1974. *Lovers, Friends, Slaves ...The Nine Male Sexual Types: Their Psycho-Sexual Transactions with Call-Girls.* New York: Berkley.

Stoler, Ann Laura. 1995. *Race and the Education of Desire: Foucault's* History of Sexuality *and the Colonial Order of Things.* Durham: Duke University Press.

—— and Cooper, Frederic. 1997. 'Between Metropole and Colony'. In *Tensions of Empire. Colonial Cultures in a Bourgeois World,* F. Cooper and A.L. Stoler, eds., 1-56. Berkeley: University of California Press.

Stone, Lawrence. 1977. *The Family, Sex and Marriage in England 1500–1800.* London: Weidenfeld and Nicolson.

Stoneking, Mark. 1998. 'Women on the Move'. *Nature Genetics,* 20, 219-20.

Stone-Mediatore, Shari. 2000. 'Chandra Mohanty and the Revaluing of "Experience"'. In *Decentering the Center*, U. Narayan and S. Harding, eds., 110-27. Bloomington: Indiana University Press.

Sullivan, Barbara. 1995. 'Rethinking Prostitution'. In *Transitions: New Australian Feminisms,* B. Caine and R. Pringle, eds., 184-97. New York: St Martin's Press.

Summers, Anne. 1975. *Damned Whores and God's Police.* Victoria AU: Penguin.

—— 1979. 'A Home from Home – Women's Philanthropic Work in the Nineteenth Century'. In *Fit Work for Women,* S. Burman, ed., 33-63. London: Croom Helm.

Tabet, Paola. 1989. 'I'm the Meat, I'm the Knife: Sexual Service, Migration and Repression in Some African Societies'. In *A Vindication of the Rights of Whores,* G. Pheterson, ed., 204-26. Seattle: Seal Press.

Tadiar, Neferti Xina M. 1998. 'Prostituted Filipinas and the Crisis of Philippine Culture'. *Milennium,* 27, 4, 927-54.

Tait, William. 1840. *Magdalenism: an Inquiry into the Extent, Causes, and Consequences of Prostitution in Edinburgh.* Edinburgh: P. Rickard.

Tampep. 1994. Tampep Manual. Amsterdam: Mr A de Graaf Stichting.

—— 1999. *Health, Migration and Sex Work: The Experience of Tampep.* Amsterdam: Mr A de Graaf Stichting.

—— 2001. Tampep Charter 2001. Position Paper on Migration and Sex Work.

—— n/d. Peer Education Manual. Amsterdam: Mr A de Graaf Stichting.

ten Brummelhuis, Han and Herdt, Gilbert. 1995. *Culture and Sexual Risk: Anthropological Perspectives on AIDS*. Amsterdam: Gordon and Breach Publishers.

Thomas, Rachel. 2006. 'Spotlight on Meena Seshu, SANGRAM: Sex Worker Rights in Rural India'. *Sexual Health and Rights Program (SHARP) Newsletter*, Spring. http://www.soros.org/initiatives/health/focus/sharp/articles publications/articles/seshu20060726

Tilly, Chris and Tilly, Charles. 1998. *Work under Capitalism*. Boulder CO: Westview Press.

Tolentino, Roland B. 1996. 'Bodies, Letters, Catalogs: Filipinas in Transnational Space'. *Social Text*, 14, 3, 49-76.

Tornos, A. et al. 1997. *Los peruanos que vienen*. Madrid: Universidad Pontificia Comillas.

Tristán, Flora. [1840] 1980. *London Journal: A Survey of London Life in the 1830s*. London: George Prior.

Tronto, Joan. 1987. 'Beyond Gender Difference to a Theory of Care'. *Signs: Journal of Women in Culture and Society*, 12, 4, 644-63.

Truong, Thanh-Dam. 1990. *Sex, Money and Morality: Prostitution and Tourism in Southeast Asia*. London: Zed Books.

—— 1996. 'Gender, International Migration and Social Reproduction: Implications for Theory, Policy, Research and Networking'. *Asian and Pacific Migration Journal*, 5, 1, 27-52.

Ueno, Chizuko. 2003. 'Self-determination on Sexuality? Commercialization of Sex among Teenage Girls in Japan'. *Inter-Asia Cultural Studies*, 4, 2, 317-24.

Unal, Bayram. 2005. 'Transient Valentines'. Presentation at ISA meeting 'From Emigration to Immigration', Cerisy, France, June.

UN Department of Economic and Social Affairs. 2005. *Women and International Migration*. New York: Division for the Advancement of Women.

UN Trends in Total Migrant Stock. 2005. www.un.org/esa/population/ publications/migration/UNMigrantStockDocumentation2005.pdf

Urcelai, Arantzazu. 2001. 'Evaluación del programa de prevención del VIH y otras ETS realizado por ONGS en el colectivo de personas que ejercen la prostitución'. Statistical analysis. Municipal AIDS-prevention programme.

Urry, John. 1990. *The Tourist Gaze: Leisure and Travel in Contemporary Societies*. London: Sage Publications.

Valcárcel, Amelia. 1997. *La política de las mujeres*. Madrid: Ediciones Cátedra.

Valiente, Celia. 1996. 'El feminismo institucional en España: El Instituto de la Mujer, 1983–1994'. *Revista Internacional de Sociología*, 3, 13, 163-204.

Valverde, Mariana. 1996. '"Despotism" and Ethical Liberal Governance'. *Economy and Society*, 25, 3, 357-72.

Vance, Carole S. 1984. *Pleasure and Danger: Exploring Female Sexuality*. London: Routledge & Kegan Paul.

Van Kerkwijk, Carla. 1995. 'The Dynamics of Condom Use in Thai Sex Work with

Farang Clients'. In *Culture and Sexual Risk: Anthropological Perspectives on AIDS*, H. ten Brummelhuis and G. Herdt, eds., 115-34. Amsterdam: Gordon and Breach.

Varela, Julia. 1995. 'La prostitución, el oficio más moderno'. *Archipiélago*, 21, 52-70.

—— and Álvarez-Uría, Fernando. 1989. *Sujetos frágiles: Ensayos de sociología de la desviación*. México: Fondo de Cultura Económica.

Vázquez García, Francisco. 1998. 'Los estudios históricos sobre la prostitución en la España contemporánea'. In *'Mal menor': Políticas y representaciones de la prostitución (siglos XVI-XIX)*, F. Vázquez, ed., 135-66. Cádiz: Universidad de Cádiz.

—— and Moreno Mengíbar, Andrés. 1998. *Poder y Prostitución en Sevilla (siglos XIV al XX)*. Seville: Universidad de Sevilla.

Velasco, Sara. 1999. *La prevención de la transmisión heterosexual del VIH/SIDA en las mujeres*. Madrid: Instituto de la Mujer/Plan Nacional sobre el Sida.

Vicinus, Martha, ed. 1977. *A Widening Sphere: Changing Roles of Victorian Women*. London: Methuen & Co.

—— 1985. *Independent Women: Work and Community for Single Women 1850–1920*. London: Virago.

Vogel, Katrin. 2006. 'Born *marico*, Made *travesti*: Venezuelan Sex Workers in Europe'. Paper presented at 'Reflection of Man', Institute of Ethnology, Charles University, Prague, 26–27 May.

Wagenaar, Hendrik. 2006. 'Democracy and Prostitution: Deliberating the Legalization of Brothels in the Netherlands'. *Administration & Society*, 38, 2, 198-235.

Walker, Dave and Ehrlich, Richard. 1992. *'Hello My Big Big Honey'*. Bangkok: Dragon Dance Publications.

Walkerdine, Valerie. 1997. *Daddy's Girl: Young Girls and Popular Culture*. Cambridge: Harvard University Press.

Walkowitz, Judith. 1977. 'The Making of an Outcast Group: Prostitutes and Working Women in Nineteenth-century Plymouth and Southampton'. In *A Widening Sphere: Changing Roles of Victorian Women*, M. Vicinus, ed., 72-3. London: Methuen & Co.

—— 1980. *Prostitution and Victorian Society*. London: Cambridge University Press.

—— 1994. *City of Dreadful Delight: Narratives of Sexual Danger in Late-Victorian London*. London: Virago.

Ware, Vron. 1992. *Beyond the Pale: White Women, Racism and History*. London: Verso.

Waring, Marilyn. 1988. *If Women Counted*. San Francisco: Harper & Row.

Weeks, Jeffrey. 1981. *Sex, Politics and Society: The Regulation of Sexuality since 1800*. London: Longman.

—— 1982. 'The Development of Sexual Theory and Sexual Politics'. In *Human Sexual Relations: A Reader in Human Sexuality*, M. Brake, ed., 293-309. Harmondsworth: Penguin.

—— 1995. 'Desire and Identities'. In *Conceiving Sexuality: Approaches to Sex Research in a Postmodern World,* R. Parker and J. Gagnon, eds., 33-50. New York: Routledge.

Weitzer, Ronald. 2005. 'Flawed Theory and Method in Studies of Prostitution'. *Violence against Women,* 11, 7, 934-49.

Werbner, Pnina. 2006. 'Vernacular Cosmopolitanism'. *Theory, Culture & Society,* 23, 2-3, 496-8.

Wijers, Marjan and Lap-Chew, Lin. 1996. *Trafficking in Women, Forced Labour and Slavery-like Practices in Marriage, Domestic Labour and Prostitution.* Utrecht: STV.

Willis, William. 1969. 'Skeletons in the Anthropological Closet'. In *Reinventing Anthropology,* D. Hymes, ed., 77-152. New York: Random House.

Wilson, Ara. 1988. 'American Catalogues of Asian Brides'. In *Anthropology for the Nineties,* J. Cole, ed., 114-25. New York: Free Press.

Wilson, Elizabeth. 1992. 'Feminist Fundamentalism: the Shifting Politics of Sex and Censorship'. In *Sex Exposed: Sexuality and the Pornography Debate,* L. Segal and M. McIntosh, eds., 15-28. London: Virago Press.

—— 1995. 'The Invisible *Flâneur*'. In *Postmodern Cities and Spaces,* 59-79, Sophie Watson and Katherine Gibson, eds., 59-79. Cambridge MA: Blackwell.

Wolf, Eric R. 1969. 'American Anthropologists and American Society'. In *Reinventing Anthropology,* D. Hymes, ed., 251-63. New York: Random House.

Wolff, Janet. 1985. 'The Invisible *Flâneuse:* Women and the Literature of Modernity'. *Theory Culture and Society,* 2, 3, 37-46.

—— 1993. 'On the Road Again: Metaphors of Travel in Cultural Criticism'. *Cultural Studies,* 7, 2, 224-39.

Womack, Mari. 1995. 'Studying Up and the Issue of Cultural Relativism'. *Insider Anthropology: NAPA Bulletin,* 16, 48-57.

World Sex Guide. http://www.worldsexguide.org/

Wouters, Cas. 1989. 'The Sociology of Emotions and Flight Attendants: Hochschild's *Managed Heart*'. *Theory, Culture & Society,* 6, 1, 95-123.

Yea, Sallie. 2004. 'Runaway Brides: Anxieties of Identity among Trafficked Filipina Entertainers in South Korea'. *Singapore Journal of Tropical Geography,* 25, 2, 180-97.

Zabaldi. 2000. *¡Abre la muralla! Semana de Solidaridad.* Elkartasunaren Etxea: Pamplona.

Zelizer, Viviana. 2000. 'The Purchase of Intimacy'. *Law and Social Inquiry,* 25, 817-48.

Zlotnik, Hania. 2003. 'The Global Dimensions of Female Migration'. Washington: Migration Policy Institute. http://www.migrationinformation.org/Feature/display.cfm?ID=109

PRIMARY SOURCES

Selection of NGO and government reports and research articles; policy and position papers; leaflets and educational/outreach material; commentaries made to governmental and NGO bodies; texts of proposed laws; listserve discussions by sex work organisations; conference materials. Gathered between 2000 and 2003 around Europe and analysed for this book.

ACSUR-Las Segovias. 2001. Derechos de las Ciudadanas Inmigrantes. Leaflet. Madrid.

ADAVAS (Asociación de Ayuda a Víctimas de Agresiones Sexuales). Leaflet. León.

—— Agresiones sexuales. Leaflet. León.

—— 2000. *Jornadas contra la Violencia Sexual*. Programme of conference. León.

AIDES Provence. Les préservatifs. Aujourd'hui, tout le monde dit oui. Condom pack. Avignon. Agence Francaise de Lutte Contre le SIDA.

Aids & Mobility. 1999. Annual Report. Woerden: NIGZ (Netherlands Institute for Health Promotion and Disease Prevention).

—— 2000. HIV/AIDS Care and Support for Migrants and Ethnic Minority Communities in Europe. Woerden.

—— 2001. East–West mobility in Europe: Overcoming barriers to HIV prevention for mobile and migrant sex workers: Seminar Report. Woerden.

—— 2002. *A & M News*, 3, April; 2, June 2001. Woerden.

AMDE (Asociación de Mujeres Dominicanas en España). 1993. *Tres mujeres dominicanas en Madrid: Sus historias contadas por ellas mismas*. Madrid: AMDE/ Comisiones Obreras.

—— 1993. *Cuadernos*. Madrid: Instituto de la Mujer.

Amnesty for Women. 2001a. Contra el Cierre de Amnesty for Women. Petition to municipal and national authorities against the withdrawal of funding. Hamburg.

—— 2001b. Commentary on proposed new German law on prostitution. Hamburg.

ANAFE. Program de Atención a Inmigrantes. Leaflet. Pamplona: Comisiones Obreras.

Andrade Taboada, Pablo and Casal Cacharrón, Marta. 2000. Unpublished paper on prostitution in Galicia using data from NGO project 'Marta'.

Andraize-COFES. 1992-99. Programa de Atención Socio-Sanitaria a mujeres que trabajan en la prostitución. Centro de Planificación Familiar y Educación Sexual, Servicio Navarro de Salud. Pamplona.

—— 1998. 'Consultas Realizadas' al programa al grupo de prostitutas.

Pamplona: Gobierno de Navarra, Consejero de Salud.

Andreieu-Sanz, Rosa and Vasquez Antón, Karmele. 1985. *Hacia una interpretación de la prostitución de mujeres.* Bilbao: Instituto de la Mujer.

ANELA (Asociación Nacional de Empresarios de Locales de Alterne). 2001. Book presenting new association of business owners. Valencia.

Anti-Slavery International. 1999. New ILO book calls on governments to recognise sex sector. London.

——— 2001. Guidelines for partners/consultants in conducting phase 2 of research on victim protection measures and trafficking.

——— (Pearson, Elaine) 2002. *Human Traffic, Human Rights: Redefining Victim Protection.* London.

APIS. 1998. Prevenzione HIV/AIDS nell'industria del sesso. Swiss network. Zurich.

APRAMP (Asociación para la Prevención, Reinserción y Atención de la Mujer Prostituta). Leaflets. Unidad móvil, Atención. Madrid.

Armistead Project. Safe in the City. For men under 25 working or socialising in Liverpool.

Asociación Española de Transexuales Transexualia. n/d-2002. Trabaja, Pero Segura: El VIH y las ITS. Leaflet describing feminisation process and AIDS prevention. Madrid.

Asociación Flora Tristán. 2001. Minutes of regional meeting debating 'prostitution' theory. León.

Asociación Pro Derechos Humanos de Andalucía. Leaflet.

——— /Federación Andalucía Acoge. 2002. Manifiesto por una Europa abierta y plural: 'Derechos Para Todos'. Cádiz.

Aspasie. 2000. Comments on sex work and the law in Switzerland. Geneva.

Associazione Lule (Svevo, Maria Paola). 1999. La tratta delle donne tra violazione dei diritti umani e schiavitù nei documenti internazionali ed europei. Milan.

Associazione On the Road. 1998. Terre Di Mezzo: esperienze ipotesi utopie nel Pianeta Prostituzione. Martinsicuro.

——— n/d. Unità di Strada. Information card in Italian, English, Albanian, Russian. Martinsicuro.

Barahona Gomariz, Maria José. 2001. *Tipología de la prostitución femenina en la Comunidad de Madrid.* Madrid: Dirección General de la Mujer.

Barandica, Amaia. 1998. 'Mujer inmigrada'. In *Informe anual sobre el racismo en el estado español,* 147-51. Barcelona: SOS Racismo.

Basis Projekt. Mit uns geht's besser. Sticker. Hamburg.

Cabiria. 2002. Femmes et Migrations: Les femmes venant d'Europe de l'Est. Lyon.

——— Action de santé communautaire avec les personnes prostituées. Postcard. Lyon.

Callboy Connection. 2001. Info Quickey, No. 1. Netzwerk männlicher Sexworker seit. Frankfurt.

Cáritas Diocesana de Pamplona. 1989. Estudio Preliminar Sobre las Características Socio-Sanitarias de la prostitución callejera en Pamplona. Pamplona.

—— 1997. Betania: Un Centro para la mujer fuertemente marginada. Pamplona.

Casas, María, Cordero, Tatiana and Foderingham, C. 1989. Here One Gives One's Life. Hague: Project Empowerment.

CATS. Sexo Seguro Safe Sex. Packet with condom and lubricant. Gijón.

Centro Reina Sofía para el Estudio de la Violencia. 2000. *Foro Mundial de las Mujeres: Reunión Internacional sobre Biología y Sociología de la Violencia*. Valencia.

1. Minority opinion document on prostitution.

2. 'Insisten mujeres del mundo en la urgencia de condenar la demanda masculina de sexo y luchar contra la explotación de mujeres y niñas'. Report by Mirta Rodríguez for CIMAC/CIPAF (México/Dominicana).

3. Programme.

CHANGE. 2002. Report on the Short Questionnaire on Trafficking. London.

COFES. Leaflet from Servicio Navarro de Salud. Pamplona.

COGAM (Colectivo de Lesbianas y Gays de Madrid). *Ponte sexy.* Card/ campaign.

Colectivo de Transexuales de Cataluña. 2002. Proposición no de ley. Draft. Barcelona.

Colomo, Concha, Cuadros, Alfonso and Mammar, Fadhila. 1998. *Salud y cooperación para el desarrollo*. Madrid: Médicos del Mundo.

Comas, Amparo. 1991. 'El adecentamiento del centro de Madrid y la prostitución'. In *Prostitución: Mesa Redonda*. Madrid: Forum de Política Feminista.

—— 1991. La Prostitución femenina en Madrid. Madrid: Dirección General de la Mujer.

Comisaría General de Policía Judicial. 1986. La prostitución en España. Madrid.

Comisión Anti-Agresiones y Coordinadora de Grupos de Mujeres de Barrios y Pueblos de Madrid. 1990. *Debates feministas*. Madrid.

Comisión de Derechos Humanos. 2000. Resoluciones sobre Mujeres. UNIFEM.

Comisión Española para la UNESCO. 2000. *Seminario sobre Prevención Educativa del SIDA en Paises en Desarrollo y en Subpoblaciones Marginales*. Programme. Madrid.

Comitato per i diritti civili delle prostitute. 1996. Progetto di informazione AIDS rivolto alle prostitute immigrate, Relazione finale. Leaflet. Pordenone.

—— 1999-2000. Booklet produced by project Agenda Legale: Guida Facile alla Legge Italiana. Pordenone.

—— 2000-2001. Leaflet on project Stella Polare: Percorsi di protezione sociale per favorire processi di autodeterminazione e sostenere coloro che chiedono di uscire da situazioni di schiavitù e sfruttamento sessuale. Leaflet. Pordenone.

—— 2001-2002. Leaflet on Project Fenarete: Professional training and support for the insertion and employment of peer educators within interventions aimed at persons who prostitute themselves. Pordenone.

—— 2001. Report on activities. Pordenone.

—— 2001. Commentary on sex workers' rights. Pordenone.

Condomerie Het Gulden Vlies. Card. Amsterdam.

Constitución de la congregación de las Adoratrices Esclavas del Santísimo Sacramento y de la Caridad. 1982.

Córdoba Vico, Mari Luz (La Hiedra). 1997. *Jornadas Sobre Prostitución.* 14–16 November. Córdoba.

—— 2000. 'La prostitución, factor que margina'. *Utopía*, 35.

Croix Rouge Luxembourgeoise. Dispensaire pour Sex-Workers. Leaflet in French, Flemish, Italian, English. Ministère de la Promotion Féminine. Luxembourg.

Cruz Roja Juventud. 1999. *Jornadas de Debate sobre Trabajo Sexual.* Programme of conference, 25–26 June. Gijón.

Daphne Programme, European Commission. 2001. Daphne-funded projects: illustrative cases. Brussels.

—— 2002. Europe Against Violence: Messages and Materials from Daphne. Brussels: European Commission.

Defensor del Pueblo Andaluz. 2002. La prostitución: Realidad y políticas de intervención pública en Andalucía. Report for parliament.

Del Amo, Julia. 2001. Prevención del VIH/SIDA en inmigrantes y minorías étnicas. Madrid: Plan Nacional sobre el SIDA.

De Rode Draad. 10 Jaar Hoeren in Beweging. Packet/nail files. Dutch, English, Spanish. Amsterdam.

Deutsche AIDS-Hilfe. 1994. Transmission du Virus HIV et Risque de SIDA. Booklet in English, French, Polish, Russian, Rumanian, Czech and Turkish. Berlin.

Díaz, Beatriz, ed. 1997. *Todo negro no igual – voces de emigrantes.* Barcelona: Virus.

—— ed. 1997. *La salud de los inmigrantes extranjeros en el barrio de San Francisco (Bilbao).* Bilbao.

Dirección General de la Mujer. Contra La Violencia. Campaign material. Madrid.

—— Educar en la igualdad y el respeto es prevenir la violencia. Campaña de prevención de malos tratos a mujeres. Materials. Madrid.

Dirección General de la Policía. 1986. La Prostitución en España. Madrid: Sección de Estudios e Informes.

Dirección General de la Policía de Córdoba. 1999. Informe de actuaciones. Córdoba.

Directorate of Human Rights. 1994. Final report of the Group of Specialists on action against traffic in women and forced prostitution. Strasbourg: Council of Europe.

Dutch Ministry of Social Affairs. 1997. Notraf: Results of the questionnaire on Trafficking in Women. Amsterdam: Mr A de Graaf Stichting.

ECOE (Equipo de Comunicación Educativa). 1998. Manifiesto de la iniciativa 'Papeles Para Todos'. Madrid.

ECP (English Collective of Prostitutes). Leaflet on positions. London.

—— 2002. Trafficking Used as an Excuse for Deportation. Demonstration announcement. London.

El Lloc de la Dona. Leaflet for project, Hermanas Oblatas, El Raval, Barcelona.

Emakunde (Instituto Vasco de la Mujer). 2001. La prostitución ejercida por mujeres en la CAE. Vitoria: Emakunde.

EMSI (Escuela de Mediadores Sociales para la Inmigración). Leaflet. Madrid.

ENMP (European Network Male Prostitution). 2001. Travel Guide. For sex workers. Amsterdam.

—— 2002. Newsletter. April. Amsterdam.

—— 2002. Report of the meeting-debate. 17 May. Madrid.

Escuela Andaluza de Salud Pública et al. 1995. *I Reunión Internacional en España Sobre Inmigración: Políticas Sociales y Salud.* Proceedings. Granada.

Espace P. Pour les personnes prostituées et leur entourage. Leaflet. Liège.

Europap. 2001. Survey of Training Needs. For network members. London.

—— 2002. Europap News, October, Issue 1. London.

—— Promoting the Health and Well Being of Sex Workers in Europe. Leaflet. London.

Europap and ENMP (European Network on Male Prostitution). 2002. *Sex Work and Health in a Changing Europe.*

1. Programme of conference, 18–20 January. Milton Keynes.

2. Organisers' report. 18–20 January. London.

Europap/Tampep 1998. *Hustling for Health: Developing Health Services for Sex Workers.* Brussels: European Commission.

Europap UK. 1999. Services for Sex Workers. London.

European Commission. 2001. Discussion paper, 'Short-term permit to stay granted to victims of trafficking or smuggling who cooperate in the fight against smugglers and traffickers'. Brussels: Justice and Home Affairs.

—— 2002. Council Framework Decision of 19 July on combating trafficking in human beings. Brussels.

EWL (European Women's Lobby). 2001. Towards a Common European Framework to Monitor Progress in Combating Violence Against Women. Observatory of the European Policy Action Centre on Violence Against Women. Brussels.

—— 2001. Comments from two ex-members, Marjan Wijers (Stichting Tegen Vrouwenhandel, Holland) and Rosa Logar (Wiener Interventionsstelle, Austria).

—— 2003. Remarks from Grainne Healy, Chair of EWL's Observatory on Violence against Women, at Seminar on Trafficking and Prostitution delivered on occasion of CSW meeting New York 11 March.

Federación de Asociaciones de Consumidores y Usuarios de Andalucía. Los inmigrantes y sus derechos como consumidores. Spain.

Fédérations des Centres de planning familial. La Pilule du lendemain. Booklet. Communauté Francaise de Belgique. Brussels.

Femmigration. Legal Agenda for Migrant Prostitutes and Trafficked Women on the Internet. Card for website.

Fernández, Blanca. 1991. Aproximación a la prostitución. Pamplona: IPES.

——— 1992. Estudio sobre prostitución en Navarra, aspectos médicos-sociológicos. Pamplona.

——— et al. [late 1980s]. Estudio aplicado de la sociovacuna en Navarra. Pamplona: Escuela Universitaria de Trabajo Social.

Fundación Esperanza. Leaflet of transnational project, Colombia–Holland. Bogotá–Amsterdam.

Fundación Triángulo. n/d. Yo trabajo sin riesgos. Booklet. Spanish, English. Plan Nacional sobre el SIDA. Spain.

Garaizábal, Cristina. 1991. 'La prostitución: un debate abierto'. In Prostitución: Mesa Redonda. Madrid: Forum de Política Feminista.

García, Andrea. 2000. 'Prostitución: un billón de pesetas al año en el Estado español'. Ardi Beltza. San Sebastián.

García Pérez, Inés. 'Inmigración Extracomunitaria en Navarra'.

Giraffa. 2000. Cabiria: Donne Unite Contro lo Sfruttamento Sessuale. Leaflet. Bari.

——— 2001. Donne e istituzioni contro lo sfruttamento sessuale. Bari.

Goded, Maya. 2001. Sexoservidoras (1995–2000). Exhibition notes. Madrid. Centro de Arte Reina Sofía.

Hetaira. Colectivo en Defensa de los Derechos de las Prostitutas. Leaflet. Madrid.

——— 1999. Memoria de actividades. Madrid.

——— Carta a los vecinos y vecinas del barrio. Madrid.

——— Cuido mi salud, uso condones. Cuido la ciudad, uso las papeleras. Madrid.

——— Guía de recursos dirigida a las mujeres que ejercen la prostitución. Booklet. Madrid.

Human Rights Watch. 2002. Briefing Paper on the European Commission Proposal for a Council Directive 'on the short-term residence permit issued to victims of action to facilitate illegal immigration or trafficking in human beings who cooperate with the competent authorities'. New York.

Hydra. 1996-2002. Leaflets, legal explanations, definitions, outreach material, position papers, health information, much in Spanish. Berlin.

——— Centro de reunión y orientación para prostitutas. Leaflet. Berlin.

Hydra and Highlights (Pro-Prostitutes Action Committee). 2001. Comments on German Draft of Parliamentary Bill sponsored by the Social Democrat-Green Party coalition on 'Setting Down of the Rights of Prostitutes'.

1. A better legal and social position for prostitutes in Germany.

2. Press release on occasion of passing of the law.

ILO (International Labour Organisation). 2002. Getting at the Roots: Stopping

Exploitation of Migrant Workers by Organized Crime, Symposium on UN Convention Against Transnational Organized Crime. Turin.

Instituto de Estudios Políticos Para América Latina y Africa-IEPALA. 1986. *Jornadas sobre Emigración, exilio y mujer.* Madrid.

Instituto de la Mujer de Andalucía. 2002. Programme, *Encuentro Internacional Sobre Tráfico de Mujeres y Explotación Sexual.* 23–24 September. Málaga.

Instituto de Migraciones y Servicios Sociales. 1998. Actitudes hacia los inmigrantes. Madrid.

Instituto de Salud Carlos III. 2000. *VI Taller Internacional de la Red Europea para la Prevención del VIH / SIDA entre las Comunidades Inmigrantes de África Subsahariana.* 10–12 January. Madrid.

Instituto Promoción Estudios Sociales (Fernández, Blanca and Vilches, Carlos et al). 1986. Prostitución en Navarra. Pamplona: IPES.

International Committee for Prostitutes' Rights. 1985. World Charter for Prostitutes' Rights. Amsterdam.

IOM (International Office for Migration). 1996. Trafficking in Women from the Dominican Republic for Sexual Exploitation: Migration Information Programme. Geneva: IOM.

—— 1996. Trafficking in Women for Sexual Exploitation to Italy: Migration Information Programme. Geneva: IOM.

—— 1998. Paper presented at the Regional Conference on Trafficking in Women organised by the United Nations Economic and Social Commission for Asia and the Pacific. Geneva: IOM.

Irene. 2000. Una Rete di Solidarieta contro la Tratta de Donne e Minori. Conference programme, poster campaign and press cuttings, Daphne project. Mantova.

—— 2001. Vademecum. L'Operatore di Polizia e la Tratta. Daphne project. Milan.

IUSW (International Union of Sex Workers). Sex Workers of the World Unite. Card announcing party. London.

KOK (Bundesweiter Koordinierungskreis) 2000. Federal Association against traffic in women and violence against women in the migration process. Leaflet. Potsdam.

Kvinnoforum. 1998. Trafficking in Women for the Purpose of Sexual Exploitation: Mapping the Situation and Existing Organisations Working in Belarus, Russia, the Baltic and the Nordic States. Stockholm.

—— 1999. Crossing Borders Against Trafficking in Women and Girls in the Baltic Sea Region. Research report. Stockholm.

—— 2001. Trafficking in Women and Children in Asia and Europe. Research report. Stockholm.

La Strada. 2002-2004. Prevention of Traffic in Women in Central and Eastern Europe. Utrecht.

Landa Aznarez, Mª Cruz et al. 1992. Estudio Sobre Prostitución en Navarra, Aspectos Médico-Sociológicos.

LICIT (Línea de Investigació: cooperació amb Immigrantes Treballadores Sexuals). 2002. *Derechos humanos y trabajo sexual. Encuentro internacional.* 7-14 July. Barcelona.

Linx Project. Confidential non-judgemental service to sex workers across Merseyside. Card. Liverpool.

—— Safety on the Street. Booklet. Liverpool.

——The Merseyside Prostitution Forum. Announcement of a meeting.

Lisistrata. 2002. SID–WID Newsletter, January. Society for International Development. Rome.

López de Munain et al. 2000. 'Seroprevalencia de VIH en pacientes de consultas de enfermedades de transmisión sexual, 1998–1999. Estudio anónimo no relacionado'. *Boletín Epidemiológico*, 8, 15, 157-68. Madrid: Instituto de Salud Carlos III.

Los chicos de alquiler no lloran. Card/advertisement, Editorial Berkana. Madrid.

Madonna. Beratung und Hilfe für Prostituierte. Bochum.
http://www.madonna-ev.de/

Maíz (Zentrum für Migrantinnen). 2002. Cupiditas 7: Information for Migrant Women Sex Workers. Linz.

Mak, Rudolf. 1991. 'Do prostitutes need more health education regarding sexually transmitted disseases and the HIV infection? Experience in a Belgian city'. *Social Science Medicine*, 33, 8, 963-66.

Malgesini, Graciela and Giménez, Carlos. 1997. *Guía de conceptos sobre migraciones, racismo e interculturalidad.* Madrid: La Cueva del Oso.

Martínez Veiga, Ubaldo. 2000. 'Evolución y clasificación del trabajo doméstico inmigrante'. *Ofrim/Suplementos*, 6, June.

Médicos del Mundo. 1997. 'Ángeles Rodríguez Arenas: Responsable de los programas de Cuarto Mundo'. *Noticias*, 29, 10–11 December. Madrid.

—— 1999. Informe de Exclusión. Madrid.

—— 2000. 'Médicos del Mundo CASSIM'. *Ofrim Boletín*, 31, 12-13.

—— 2000. Noticias de Médicos del Mundo, 57.

—— 2002. Análisis de la prostitución ejercida en la calle por mujeres extranjeras en la Comunidad de Madrid. Report from outreach team.

—— n/d Si eres extranjero ... asistencia sanitaria. Leaflet.

—— and Asociación Española de Transexuales Transexualia. Atención sociosanitaria a hombres y mujeres transexuales sin recursos. Leaflet. Madrid.

Médicos del Mundo Málaga. Prevención de SIDA y otras enfermedades de transmisión sexual. Leaflet.

Migrants against HIV/AIDS. 1997. French Report Recommends Mandatory HIV Testing for Pregnant Women. Geneva: MAHA.

Ministry of Social Affairs and Employment, Department for the Coordination of

Emancipation Policy, Ministerial Conference. 1997. The Hague Ministerial Declaration on European Guidelines for Effective Measures to Prevent and Combat Trafficking in Women for the Purpose of Sexual Exploitation.

Miura, Asunción. 1991. 'Abolicionismo, integración y propuestas sobre prostitución'. In *Prostitución: mesa redonda*. Madrid: Forum de Política Feminista.

—— 1999. 'Por las medidas de acción positiva'. Interview. *8 de marzo*, No. 34, magazine of the Dirección General de la Mujer.

—— 1999. 'Debate sobre la prostitución en Europa'. *8 de marzo*, No. 35, magazine of the Dirección General de la Mujer.

Movimento Italiano Transessuali. O mit para os trans. Leaflet. Bologna.

Mr A de Graaf Stichting. 1997. In Het Leven. Vier eeuwen prostitutie in Nederland. Leaflet for exhibition on history of prostitution in Holland. Apeldoorn.

—— Leaflet of Dutch Institute for Prostitution Issues. Amsterdam.

—— 'Zones of tolerance'. Amsterdam

MRI (Migrants Rights International). 2001. Migración, Refugiados y Xenofobia. Preparatory notes for World Conference. Spain.

Munk, Veronica. 2001. 'Repressive Laws and Hidden Women: Migrant Sex Workers in Germany'. *Research for Sex Work*, 4.

National Coalition of Anti-Deportation Campaigns. 2000. Immigration Laws Criminalise People. Birmingham.

Netverk North Against Prostitution and Violence. 2000. Leaflet. Tanu.

New Internationalist. 1994. 'Prostitution: Soliciting for Change'. No. 252, February.

Nielsen Netratings. 2001. *Ciberpaís*, 9, March, 13.

Nottingham Health Service. Sexual Health Services. Including POW, Prostitute Outreach Workers. Booklet. Nottingham.

NSWP (Network of Sex Work Projects). 1998. *Making Sex Work Safe: A Practical Guide for Programme Managers, Policy-Makers and Field Workers*. Rio de Janeiro.

Oficina del Alto Comisionado para los Derechos Humanos. 1992. Formas contemporáneas de la esclavitud. Leaflet. Geneva.

Open Society Institute. 2001. Commercial Sex Worker Harm Reduction Initiative Project Directory (Eastern Europe and former Soviet Union). New York.

Osborne, Raquel. 1998. 'Sexualidad, prostitución y patriarcado: ¿división entre mujeres o unidad de acción?' *Viento Sur*, 4, 86-91.

—— 'Comprensión de la prostitución desde el feminismo'. Comisión anti-agresiones y coordinadora de grupos de mujeres de barrios y pueblos del movimiento feminista de Madrid.

Papers. 2000. Special edition, 60: Female immigration in Southern Europe. Barcelona: Universitat Autónoma de Barcelona.

Parlamento de Navarra, Diario de Sesiones. 1999. Orden del Día: Toma en consideración, si procediese, de la proposición de Ley de reconocimiento de los derechos sociales de las personas que ejercen profesionalmente la actividad de alterne, presentada por el G.P. 'Izquierda Unida-Ezker Batua de Navarra'. Pamplona: IV Legislatura, Núm. 76, 15 April.

Payoke. 2001. Description of programming with prostitutes. Antwerp.

Pisano, Isabel. 2001. *Yo puta, hablan las prostitutas*. Barcelona: Plaza y Janés. Journalists' presentation of several sex worker stories.

Plan Nacional sobre el SIDA. 2000. *II Reunión Nacional del Grupo de Trabajo sobre Sida y Minorías étnicas/inmigrantes*. Programme. Madrid.

Plate-Forme Prévention SIDA. Permis de Séduire. Leaflet. Communauté Française de Belgique. Brussels.

Polanía, Fanny. 1997. 'Tráfico internacional de mujeres: Nuevas alternativas frente a un antiguo problema'. In *Ofrim/Suplementos*, December, 141-50. Madrid.

Portside, A Sexual Health Outreach Service. To avoid HIV/AIDS and other sexual infections always use condoms when having sex. Packet. Liverpool.

POW (Prostitute Outreach Workers Project). *Health and Sex*. Booklet. Nottingham.

PrensaMujer. 2001. Article on European Commission report on 'domestic slavery' in the EU. Madrid.

Presidenza del Consiglio dei Ministri. 2001. Se ti costringono a prostituirti ... Possiamo aiutarti. Numero verde project. Provincia di Lecce.

—— Progetto Libera: Un servizio di donne rivolto ad altre donne immigrate costrette all prostituzione. Provincia di Lecce.

ProFem. [nd]. Central European Consulting Centre for Women's Projects. Prague.

Pro Millora del Barri. 2001. Programme of conference on sex work, 15, 22, 29 November. Barcelona.

Pro Sentret. n/d. A National Resource Center on Prostitution. Leaflet. Oslo.

Prostitución en Madrid: un debate abierto. 1987. Programme for conference, 7–10 April. Madrid.

Prostitution Information Centre. 1997. *Who, What, Where, Why*. Amsterdam.

Rempe (Red Europea de Mujeres Periodistas). 2001. *Guía de Buenas Prácticas para periodistas y comunicadores: Prostitución y tráfico de mujeres con fines de explotación sexual en los medios de comunicación*. Madrid.

Research for Sex Work. 1998: 1; 1999: 2; 2000: 3; 2001: 4; 2002: 5; 2003: 6. Amsterdam: Vrije Universiteit.

Rodríguez, Ángeles. 2002. 'Prostitución en España, salud y políticas'. *Research for Sex Work*, 5, 8-10.

ROPP (Red Estatal de Organizaciones y Proyectos sobre Prostitución). 2001. Report on II meeting, 13–15 December. Gijón.

—— 2002. Leaflet stating aims, areas of work, list of members.

—— 2002. Report on III meeting, 24–25 May. Málaga.

Ruíz Olabuénaga et al. 1999. *Los inmigrantes irregulares en España: La vida por un sueño*. Bilbao: Universidad de Deusto.

SAD-Schorerstichting. Gay Sex: HIV & STD Risk or No Risk? Booklet, multiple languages. Consortium of sponsors. Amsterdam.

Salaun, Serge. 1999. 'El cuerpo del minero: Prostitución y sexualidad en La Unión'. *Historiar* 2, July, 35-51.

Sax, Marjan. 1987. 'The Pink Thread'. In *Sex Work: Writings by Women in the Sex Industry*, F. Delacoste and P. Alexander, eds., 301-04. San Francisco: Cleis Press.

Seminario Internacional sobre Prostitución. 2001. Madrid.

  1. Programme of conference, 21–23 June.

  2. Book of abstracts of presentations.

Seminario sobre Prevención Educativa del SIDA en Países en Desarrollo y en Subpoblaciones Marginales. 2000. Comisión Española para la UNESCO. Madrid. 16–18 November.

SHOC (Sexual Health Outreach). *Ugly Mugs*. Large photocopied sheets. London.

Simposio Internacional sobre prostitución y tráfico de mujeres con fines de explotación sexual. 2000. Madrid.

  1. Programme of conference, 26–28 June. Madrid: Dirección General de la Mujer, Consejería de Servicios Sociales.

  2. Dossier *Revista 8 de Marzo*, N.38. Reproduction/summaries of some presentations from the conference.

  3. *Declaración de Madrid*. Position paper from conference.

Stichting Man/Vrouw en Prostitutie. Leaflet on group for clients of prostitutes. Amsterdam.

—— *Tips for Clients*. Amsterdam.

Stichting SOA-Bestrijding. 1992. *Trabajo y Salud*. Picture story for sex workers produced in many European and Eastern European languages. Utrecht.

—— 1997. *Trabajar Seguro*. Picture novela for transsexual sex workers. Utrecht.

STV (Stichting Tegen Vrouwenhandel). Trafficking and Standard Minimum Rules. Draft. Utrecht.

—— 1996. Background Study on Basic Principles for a Code of Conduct within the Member States of the European Union to Prevent and Combat Traffic in Women. Utrecht.

—— 1997. La Strada Program: Prevention of Traffic in Women in Central and Eastern Europe (Poland, Czech Republic, Ukraine, Bulgaria, Belarus, Bosnia-Herzgovina, Moldova, Macedonia). Utrecht.

—— STV Can Help With ... Card. Utrecht.

Subsidios y Prestaciones. Las mujeres y nuestras familias reclamamos nuestros derechos. Leaflet of Red Las Mujeres Cuentan. Barcelona.

Tampep. 2001. Report on second meeting of regional commission of Southern Europe. Athens.

—— 2001. Cuestionario para ONGs. Spain.

Tamzali, Wassyla. 1997. 'La prostitución femenina en la Europa de hoy: cómo responder a esta cuestión'. Madrid: Dirección General de la Mujer.

Trabajo Sobre SIDA y Minorías Étnicas/Inmigrantes. 2001. Programme of meeting of work group, 13 December. Escuela Nacional de Sanidad. Madrid.

Transnational Training Seminar on Trafficking in Women. 1998. Proposal and schedule by Global Survival Network and Open Society Institute (Soros Foundation). Budapest.

Trousson, Patrick. 2001. Reply from head of Daphne Programme to Director of CATW regarding 'positions' on prostitution. Brussels.

UGT (Unión General de Trabajadores). 2000. *Informe sobre la prostitución.* Madrid.

UK Network of Sex Work Projects. 2002. Statement of aims. Telford.

UNAIDS. 2000. Men and AIDS – a gendered approach. Geneva.

Universida. 2000. ¡Me gustas más así! AIDS-prevention leaflet. Madrid.

—— 2001. Relax con vida, Relax sin SIDA. Programme description and materials. Madrid.

Urbez, L. 1979. 'Prostitución femenina'. *Razón y fe*, 978-979, 77-95.

USAID. 2002. Trafficking in Persons: The USAID Strategy for Response.

van der Helm, Thérèse y van Mens, Lucie. 1999. Mobility in Prostitution in the Netherlands: An Inventory done under the auspices of Europap-Tampep 1998–1999: A Report for the European Network for HIV/STD Prevention in Prostitution. Amsterdam: Europap.

Visser, Jan 1997. Prostitution in the Netherlands: The Dutch Law Proposal on Prostitution. Amsterdam: Mr A de Graaf.

—— 2001. Commentary on European Court case on non-European sex workers in Holland. Amsterdam: De Rode Draad.

Ward, Helen. 1999. 'Policies on sex work and health produced by the co-ordinating centre of the European network for HIV/STD prevention in prostitution, 1999'. London: Europap.

WHO (World Health Organisation) Programme on AIDS. 1993. Making Sex Work Safer: A Guide to HIV/AIDS Prevention Interventions. Draft by Priscilla Alexander. Geneva.

Wolffers, Ivan. 1998. 'Why this initiative is important'. *Research for Sex Work.* June. Amsterdam: Vrije Universiteit.

—— 2001. Proposal for funding of *Research for Sex Work* to Stichting Aids Fonds. Amsterdam.

Working Party on Women Migrants. 1978. *Migrant Women Speak.* London: Search.

World Council of Churches. 1991. 'Proclaiming Migrants' Rights: The New International Convention on the Protection of the Rights of All Migrant Workers and Members of Their Families'. In Churches' Committee for Migrants in Europe Briefing Papers No. 3, Geneva.

INDEX